What

The concept of organizational agility is maturing. A variety of researchers have begun to coalesce around the definition of agility and its characteristics. While there are still a few wrinkles, myths, and misconceptions to work out, a clearer picture is emerging. What is not clear is how to make the transformation from a traditional organization to an agile one. What's needed are more cases and examples of the processes of organizational redesign that demonstrate the challenges. In Syngineering, Richard Thayer, Monique Carnino, and Bill Zybach have provided us with the grounded, field-tested tools and descriptions that we need to help organizations become adaptable.

Chris Worley, Senior Research Scientist, University of Southern California Center for Effective Organizations, Research Professor of Management, Pepperdine University, co-author of *The Agility Factor, Built to Change*.

Whether you are leading, sponsoring, or participating in corporate change, Syngineering can help you understand the specifics of your organization's circumstances and determine the right approach to build in agility. The three case studies reveal the warts, sacred cows and reality that is rarely revealed, and they bring the book to life. They span a wide range: a family-centered retail business network that adapted the process to the culture and circumstances; a multi-national joint venture commodity producer whose leaders posed the greatest threat to the effort; and a business-to-business public sector IT provider whose leader departed before the finish line. The rich and concise discussion of their cases highlights how the approach works in the real world. Chocked full of practical tools with solid guidance throughout. From the common-sense idea of using the organizations' own language to the critical relationship between culture and design, as the 4 detailed approaches for change for each of 4 generic cultures found around the world, sets this book apart from others.

Naomi Stanford, organization design practitioner and best-selling author of six books including: *Organization Design: The Practitioner's Guide.*

Organization agility is achieved both through good design and through leaders who are able to work in new ways together. What I like about this book is that it focused as much on the design process as on the design deliverables. We have always found that involving members of the organization in structured design experiences helps them to practice and model their desired culture as they define the future state. Bill, Richard, and Monique have built on the classic foundations of organization design to show how to shape new organizations through the design methodology itself. Syngineering is a practical, clear guide that will be a valued resource for today's practitioner.

Amy Kates, skilled organization designer, Managing Partner at Kates Kesler, author of numerous books, including *Bridging Organization Design and Performance: Five Ways to Activate a Global Operation Model*

"Syngineering" is an easy to understand handbook for those who want to incorporate Agile thinking into organizational design. The authors synthesize many organizational design concepts providing the reader with a guide to what can be a very complex process. Recognizing that all organizational cultures are not alike, the authors show how to implement their ideas in directive, participative, flexible, and adaptive cultures. The reflective questions sprinkled throughout enhance the book and are food for thought. If you are thinking of starting an organization design process, this book is a much-needed roadmap for your journey.

Dick and Emily Axelrod, leading OD practitioners and co-authors, *Terms of Engagement: New Ways of Leading and Changing Organizations*.

Syngineering is one of the first books, if not the first, to integrate key developments in the fields of organization design and development, agile methodology, human dynamic principles of synergy, and change management into a practical case tested methodology. Key concepts followed with practical advice and methods will help a manager or design practitioner who wants to improve their organization's agility and responsiveness to change. As digital technology pushes customer driven Information processing to the operating model, this book shows the important contribution of organization design to create an agile operating model. The authors provide a practical guide for managers and practitioners to see how all the pieces fit together to create organizational agility.

Stu Winby, organization design, innovation, and strategy thought leader, former Executive Director of Strategy at HP, and founder, SPRING Network.

SYNGINEERING

Building Agility into
Any Organization

SYNGINEERING

Building Agility into Any Organization

Richard Thayer
Monique Carnino
Bill Zybach

A Do-It-Yourself Guide for Practitioners

CHANGEMAKERS BOOKS
www.changemakers-books.com

Winchester, UK
Washington, USA

JOHN HUNT PUBLISHING

First published by Changemakers Books, 2020
Changemakers Books is an imprint of John Hunt Publishing Ltd.
No. 3 East Street, Alresford, Hampshire SO24 9EE, UK
office@jhpbooks.com
www.johnhuntpublishing.com
www.changemakers-books.com

For distributor details and how to order additional copies visit
www.johnhuntpublishing.com/contact-details-jhp/jhp-how-to-order

ISBN: 978-1-78904-110-5 (paperback)
ISBN: 978-1-78904-110-1 (ebook)

Library of Congress Control Number: 2019941679

Graphics: Peter Gloege and Richard Thayer
Cover Image: Zurka Interactive LLC

UK: Printed and bound by CPI Group (UK) Ltd, Croydon, CR0 4YY
Printed in North America by CPI GPS partners

We operate a distinctive and ethical publishing philosophy in all areas of our business,
from our global network of authors to production and worldwide distribution.

Table of Contents

Agility is the ability to make timely, effective, and sustained organization changes. **Chris Worley**

I have been impressed with the urgency of doing. Knowing is not enough; we must apply. Being willing is not enough; we must do. **Leonardo da Vinci**

The key to strategy and strategic change is linking the possibility with who we really are culturally. **Ed Schein**

Preface

New World

Most efforts to transform organizations center on identifying the key few changes that best enable them to deliver on their strategy. To meet the new demands of today's world, the types of organizations and the complexity of their markets, as well as the methods and practices of change are critical factors. As the industrial age gave way to the computer age, the information age, and the emerging digital age, technologies have increased the complexity facing businesses and driven explosive volatility. Long ago Thomas Jefferson foresaw the implications: "As new discoveries are made, new truths discovered and manners and opinions change with the change of circumstances, institutions must advance also to keep pace with the times."

New Thinking

The increased volatility requires new thinking about business, informed by insights emerging from quantum physics, complexity theory, and neuroscience. Albert Einstein observed, "We cannot solve our problems with the same think-  ing we used when we created them." Last century's rigid rules and linear thinking must give way to more experimentation and deeper understanding; experts problem solving the right answers must give way to all employees asking the right questions, learning, and adapting meaningful and sustainable solutions. This is called 'design thinking' and it provides the responsiveness to handle today's increased volatility.

New Behaviors

New thinking leads to new ways of interacting and behaving. Charles Darwin noted, "In the long history of humankind and animalkind too, those who learned to collaborate and improvise most effectively have prevailed." Collaboration is required to bring together all those with the needed expertise so they can pool their knowledge to handle today's increased complexity.

New Approaches

Consulting approaches have shifted in response. Frederick Taylor's scientific management rules evolved into Edward Deming's process-focused continuous improvement projects, and then into Peter Senge's systems thinking in learning organizations. Now even this is inadequate to help

organizations foundering on the diverse realities of people, businesses, and industries in today's globalized world of information and data access. Approaches must move past discrete organizational engineering projects and interventions and into more continuous design, driven by maintaining awareness and adaptation. What is needed is agility, which Chris Worley characterized as: "the ability to make timely, effective, and sustained organization changes."

Syngineering

Syngineering represents this next wave of approaches needed to address the variety of organizations emerging today. It is a term we have coined for how people collaboratively use design thinking to build agility into the DNA of every organization. The enGINEERING aspect builds agile capabilities into the visible structural components and systems of the organization. The human dynamics SYNergy aspect actu-

ally incorporates agility into the design processes themselves. This book is anchored in these concepts and is designed to give you not only a working knowledge of Syngineering, but also some practical skills in how to apply it. Enjoy!

Acknowledgements

This book was made possible by our numerous global collaborators:

Jay Galbraith and Amy Kates helped us to see organizations as systems with components that control both the work and the culture. Dick and Emily Axelrod gave us their conference model of change and 'canoe approach' to effective meetings. Stu Winby and Jay Galbraith showed us how creativity and accountability can facilitate the design process using prototyping, design thinking, and rapid deployment.

Brian Robertson's Holacracy and Diana Larsen's leadership in the Agile Alliance have spread Agile with a capital 'A' around the world as a new form of operating model, not just an adaptation of the software development method. Noted author Naomi Stanford, in collaboration with Stu Wigham, brought continuous design and agility into the public sector. Chris Worley's research and teaching made us aware of what is emerging as agile organization design. Finally, Sally Parker and Argie Vasilakes, in comparing natural systems and organization design, inspired us to more overtly incorporate Gestalt principles.

We used these different perspectives to experiment with clients and practitioners in projects around the world, then used international conferences to solidify our thinking. We crowdsourced and iterated divergent inputs to develop the initial wire frame that became the book.

Our writing coach David Hazard saw the potential in our rough wire-frame and nurtured us through the initial stages of articulating and organizing our thoughts. His foresight and support were essential ingredients that helped move us towards the finished product.

We have thus co-created the book with our mentors, colleagues, and customers, as a practical example of agile working. The latest thinking is embedded in our integrated framework, customized by application to the real world of our clients. We think this new and unique offering respects time-honored principles without rigidly adhering to them, incorporates emerging thinking without obsessing over the latest shiny bling, and grounds itself in real-world case studies.

Abbreviations and Acronyms

We have tried to use simple business language with sparing use of acronyms and abbreviations, most often defined where they appear.

24/7 is used to describe continuous around-the-clock operations

3D is three dimensional, especially applied to multi-level feedback

A is for Authorize, one of the accountabilities in the RACI framework

Acct. is an abbreviation for accountabilities in some diagrams

ADKAR are the building-blocks in the Prosci change management approach: Awareness, Desire, Knowledge, Ability, & Reinforcement

BCE is Before the Common Era, a way of noting dates before year 0

BI as in Power BI Dashboard stands for Business Intelligence

C is for Consulted, one of the accountabilities in the RACI framework

CARE is the charity Cooperative for Assistance and Relief Everywhere

CC for most of the book is the Co-Configuration landscape

CC only in the Chapter 10 Wilderness case study is the Capability & Skill Development coordination council

CEO is the common abbreviation for Chief Executive Officer

Comms. is an abbreviation for communications

Conf. is an abbreviation for conference in some diagrams

COO is the common abbreviation for Chief Operating Officer

CS is an abbreviation for Customer Segmentation strategies

CTO is the common abbreviation for Chief Technical Officer

D → P denotes a Directive culture moving towards a Participative one

Direct. is an abbreviation for the Directive culture

DMV is Department of Motor Vehicles, a government agency

DNA is DeoxyriboNucleic Acid, the carrier of an organism's genetic code. It is a metaphor for embedding agility into a corporate culture.

ERP is Enterprise Resource Planning, integrated software tracking

Flex. is an abbreviation for the Flexible culture

FN is Wilderness's Financial coordination council, Chapter 10

GEICO was originally Government Employees Insurance Company. It is now an independent for-profit insurance company.

GR is Wilderness' Government Relations coordination council

H for High is often used in prioritizing as High, Medium, or Low

HR is an organization's Human Resource or personnel function

HS is Wilderness' Health & Safety coordination council, Chapter 10

I is for Informed, one of the accountabilities in the RACI framework

ING is the International Netherlands Group bank; an Adaptive culture

Intro. is abbreviation for prototyping introductions in some diagrams

iOps is integrated operations in the Chapter 10 Wilderness case

KPI's or Key Performance Indicators measure enterprise performance

KW is the Knowledge Work landscape

L for Low is often used in prioritizing as High, Medium, or Low

LEED is Leadership in Environmental and Energy Design

LNG is easily transported low-temperature phase Liquid Natural Gas

M for Medium is often used in prioritizing as High, Medium, or Low

MBA is an acronym for the Master's in Business Administration degree

MC is the Mass Customization landscape

MP is the Mass Production landscape

MRG is Middleburgh Regional Government in the Stratos case study, Chapter 8

NASA is the USA National Aeronautics and Space Administration

OE is an abbreviation for the Operational Excellence strategies

OKR is an abbreviation for objectives and key results

Org. is an abbreviation for organization in some sections and diagrams

P → A is a Participative culture moving towards an Adaptive one

Part. is an abbreviation for the Participative culture

PL is an abbreviation for the Product Leadership strategies

Prep. is short for Flexible prototyping preparation in some diagrams

Prop. is short for proposition as in the strategic value proposition

R is for Responsible, one of the accountabilities in the RACI framework

R&D is an organization's Research and Development function

RACI is an acronym that describes a standard way of describing a role's accountabilities: Responsible, Authorize, Consulted, and Informed

SIS is Stratos Information Solutions, the case study in Chapter 8

SP is Wilderness's Strategy & Planning coordination council, Chapter 10

SS as in Monte Carlo SS stands for Super Sport

T-Map or Transformation Map shows a strategic change roadmap

VP is Vice President, mostly used in the Wilderness case study

Wi-Fi is not an abbreviation but the name of a wireless technology

WLT is the Wilderness Leadership Team in the Chapter 10 case study

WPC is Wilderness Petroleum Company, the Chapter 10 case study

Introduction

The Shape of Today's Business World

Today's business needs and challenges are complex and ever changing. Customers are eager for new solutions, delivered at a fast clip. All of our institutions, from  global corporations to local businesses to non-profits, and government agencies, know that they must maintain a competitive edge or they'll lose ground. This requires agility, the ability to adapt quickly to changing conditions and demands in the market place. This book will help you achieve that agility, make you and your enterprise invaluable to your current clients, and help attract new ones.

Technology Solutions Can Help

Part of the answer is technology. Through the cloud, people can share data and resources almost anywhere in the world safely and securely. Tools like Kanban boards, Power BI dashboards, and Scrum burndown charts help to make work visible in real time so others can get involved early to solve problems and progress faster. 'Fail fast' and swarming can address issues in real time. However, this requires staff and leaders to trust each other more than in most organizations today, and failure must provide the basis to learn and move forward faster, not to punish.

Massive data sets from the internet of things and customer information capture, if analyzed quickly and easily, can facilitate informed decisions and responses that are more flexible. Organizations can re-strategize and test assumptions more quickly, more easily, with less risk, and often less cost than big bang approaches that attempt to solve all an organization's problems with large projects. For it to work, however, people must be able to make sense of and act on all this data.

With virtual systems, doctors can treat patients, and teachers can impart knowledge to audiences, anywhere in the world. This transforms the very nature of how work is done and who does what. This requires much tighter linkages than ever before. Imagine the complexity of open-heart surgery with patient and surgical equipment in a small Arctic village and the surgical team working virtually from distant medical centers. Minor communications glitches become life threatening.

The Promise of Agility

So, technology is not enough: institutions themselves must grow stronger and more agile. But what does this mean? The word 'agile' gained popularity in software development. Sequential project phases were replaced with simultaneous, incremental activities across  the involved work groups. Instead of planning towards a delivery date, agility broke the developmental process into iterative steps, allowing for flexibility, testing, and change throughout the project. Teams worked in sprints, typically two-week chunks of time. Frequent progress checks kept things on track and yielded a better final product. Agile methodology became a mindset or way of approaching a project, with capabilities to sense fluctuations in the environment, test possible responses, and implement timely changes.

Types of Agility

Agility shows up in three ways at the organizational level.

(1) Business or Strategic Agility are the capabilities that enable organizations to create strategic market disruptions or adapt to disruptions or innovations from others. The focus is on strategic outcomes like new-market-defining products, for example smartphones, or new transformative processes, for example 3D printing or robotic manufacturing.

(2) Enterprise or Organizational Agility are the capabilities that internal functions use to monitor continuously how they are performing in support of the enterprise's strategy and make adjustments. Integrated financial, human capital, and resource planning software is one com-

mon example, but this agility extends far beyond electronic systems and is rooted in the mindset of sensing and responding.

(3) Product or Service Agility is a capability focused on sensing how the organization's outputs, its products and services, are being used, how they are performing, and how well customer needs are being met.

Syngineering Delivers Agility's Promise

Syngineering works by enGINEERING into an organization's visible structures and systems agile capabilities using less visible but equally critical human dynamics SYNergies. Agility is not a software method, or type of culture, or leadership trait, or management task, but is instead the ability of an organization to sense and respond to changes in and around it. Syngineering not only builds these in but also uses agile practices in the process so they become embedded.

Syngineering Uses Collaborative Design Thinking

Less than one-third of today's workforce is fully engaged in their work, yet their lost expertise and creativity are the very things missing as com- panies work to optimize complex workflows. Syngineering engages and involves staff so that  change management is not bolted on; it is in the fabric of the work. It emphasizes forward-looking sustainable agile solutions, not traditional backward-facing diagnosis and problem solving. This provides the flexibility to deal with today's volatility.

Syngineering Addresses Corporate Culture

Culture is a ubiquitous yet poorly understood aspect of organizational life. Syngineering makes explicit the roles of business environment and strategy in shaping culture and provides tools to shift it to meet strategic needs. It tailors the approach to smoothly transition from an existing culture to a new one. Given how rapidly and critically culture is shifting, the importance of taking it into account in business cannot be overstated.

Syngineering Is Scalable

These Syngineering concepts have been successfully applied across a wide range of industries, company situations and sizes: the framework is scalable. Large companies like Microsoft in electronics, ING Bank in financial services, Kaiser Permanente in healthcare, Shell in energy, all benefit from the sort

of improvement practices that form the core of Syngineering. This is also true of medium-sized companies like Gore Industries and Spotify, and a myriad of smaller companies, even down to local and regional residential service providers. It is quite energizing to see a small business involving their employees and unleashing a stream of innovative and insightful ideas!

How the Book Is Laid Out

Part I describes Syngineering's eight fundamental concepts. Chapter 1 has the four synergies of Agility, Sense, Involve, and Resolve. Chapter 2 has the four engineering concepts of Landscape, Culture, Strategy, and Organization Design, which involves Mobilize, Frame, and Customize. The diagram shows how they relate.

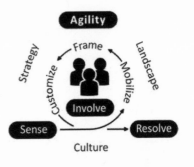

Part II has step-by-step approaches for applying the concepts in Part I to the four common corporate cultures introduced in Chapter 2: Directive, Participative, Flexible, and Adaptive. The diagram at right shows icons descriptive of each approach.

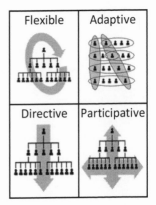

Part III contains case studies drawn from our own work as consultants, showing moves from hierarchical Directive cultures into each one of the other three cultures. Stratos shifted from a Directive government bureaucracy to a customer-focused Adaptive culture. Comfort brought together three separate Directive businesses to form a networked Flexible culture. Wilderness addressed the complexity in its landscape by moving from a Directive hierarchy to a more Participative culture.

In many ways, these case studies are the heart and soul of the book. Since they are not made-up simulations, they show how things play out under real-world circumstances. The behind-the-scenes wrangling for control at Wilderness, the journey to agility at Stratos, and the tentative explorations at Comfort, each humanize the methodology and show how it really works.

Part IV contains details amplifying the ten Syngineering deliverables, ideal for new practitioners. The detailed instructions and templates are especially helpful in Directive and Participative cultures but are also useful as a checklist for each of the four cultures.

Part I. Fundamental Concepts

Part I has two chapters. Chapter 1 describes Organizational Synergies, critical but under-utilized aspects of human dynamics: Agility, Sense, Involve, and Resolve. Chapter 2 covers Organization Engineering: Landscape, Culture, Strategy, and Agile Organization Design. While these concepts are not engineering in its strictest sense, they each involve analysis, so we use the label loosely but descriptively.

Chapter 1: Organizational Synergies

This chapter has four sections. The first defines Agility and how organizations can use its cycle of sense, mobilize, frame, customize, and resolve to build it in. The second section Sense covers the first stage of the agility cycle. It involves continuously analyzing data to identify tensions and decide when and how to take action. Most organizations today are ill equipped to do this. The third section outlines how and why to Involve people in ways that allow them to talk openly and honestly and develop the trust needed for genuine collaboration. The fourth section describes Resolve, the final stage of the agility cycle, and the integral roles of design thinking and agile leadership in it.

Organizational Agility

The Agility Cycle in Nature

Our early training exposed us to the Gestalt cycle of experience, which describes a pattern or configuration of components so unified as a whole that it cannot be described merely as a sum of its parts. The natural world is full of active organisms following this synergistic process, which produces nature's agility. Amoebas are the essence of this: they sense for threats or opportunities, mobilize the energy to act, frame possible ways to respond, customize the response to their current situation, and resolve the tension by moving towards

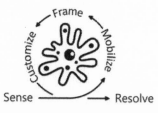

or away from the stimulus. All of this without conscious awareness.

People in the absence of overriding circumstances respond in much the same way, except they are sometimes aware of the stages. We are always Sensing our environment for the data we need to identify needs and assess issues. These may coalesce into images or descriptions. A person's nose receptors may begin sensing smells, their mouth begins producing saliva, and their stomach secretes digestive acids: "I'm hungry! I need to eat!"

If justified, we Mobilize the resources, decide to move forward, and lay plans to do so. "What's to snack? Or should I make plans for dinner? Let me check what's available." We then Frame and test possible solutions to the issues, choose one, and then formulate actions that will move us in that direction. "I'd like to eat out or have something delivered, but can't afford it. I'll cook. If I start now, I can eat by eight."

We Customize our chosen solution to the specific circumstances and take action. "There's pasta in the pantry and fresh vegetables in the refrigerator. I'll cook Italian." We implement the solutions, Resolve the tension, close things out, and return to Sensing in the new equilibrium. "That pasta dish and salad were delicious and just the right amount. I'm satisfied for now but may get a snack later tonight."

Agility in Organizations

Gestalt practitioners have also applied the agility cycle to organizations. The same five stages that we experience as individuals are present, but we add Involve, reflecting that this is no longer a single organism but a collection of people that must be engaged and involved.

Sense: Agile organizations sense their environment numerous ways. They gather information about their external landscape from customers, competitors, and industry sources. They assess their performance, evaluate how well they are realizing

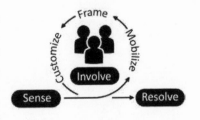

their strategy, and determine whether their current organizational configuration best supports these. As they identify tensions and issues, they determine whether, when, and how to move into action.

Mobilize: Here the leadership function, regardless of where it sits on the spectrum from hierarchical to shared, actually moves the organization to action. Leaders map out what needs to happen, commit resources to do it, refine the strategy, then diagnose what else needs to change along with criteria to be used. They may assign existing staff or work groups, or they may create new configurations to get it done.

Involve: The designated accountable staff draw on the experiences, insights, and expertise of a broad range of employees close to the work, not just a few experts or senior level managers. They design workshops, focus groups, online communication and feedback vehicles, and pilots or prototypes to involve enough employees to ensure all relevant information is available and considered.

Frame: The accountable staff then evaluate the core work and test possible high-level solutions to the issues typically revolving around the organization's operating model. They settle on a common picture and identify who needs to be involved in taking action in that direction.

Customize begins the actions to converge on the common picture across the entire enterprise. Each work group applies the high-level solutions and operating model to their specific circumstances. This often involves revising workflows, roles, accountabilities, working relationships, and supporting systems.

Resolve completes the cycle, ensures the tensions are addressed, and returns the organization to sensing. Design thinking, which seeks meaningful and sustainable solutions, is a key feature throughout the cycle but especially in this stage. Where there is continuous sensing, solutions need not be perfect, just good enough to address the immediate issues.

Mobilize, Frame, and Customize are the essence of agile organization design and will be covered in detail in Chapter 2. The three remaining concepts in Chapter 1 are Sense, Involve, and Resolve.

Reflection: Your Experiences with the Agility Cycle?

◇ *Think of an example of the agility cycle you have seen: an insect bite, an incident driving a car, and so on. Can you identify the stages of the cycle?*

◇ *Consider the latest organization improvement initiative that involved you. What sensing led to the effort? How was it mobilized? Was there framing, customizing, and resolving? If not, might they have helped?*

Continuous Sensing

This first stage gathers information on the organization, its performance, and its external landscape. This will be used to identify issues and determine whether to move into action. It is what most distinguishes agile organizations.

In fact, agility requires substantial focus on awareness, not just as a first step, but Continuous Sensing embedded in any change effort and beyond. While it often depends on massive amounts of data and analytics, it is not just an automatic, rote, or mechanical activity involving 'check-lists', but one that requires careful attention.

Sensing Process

Managing sensing is a primary accountability of the leadership function. Regardless of the organization's culture, those with leadership accountabilities are normally sensing. In agile organizations where everyone is responsible for sensing, leaders create procedures to systematize this. In doing so they exemplify the iterative nature of the agility cycle as a microcosm within each stage. They start by involving people. Many organizations have strategy and planning groups well positioned for sensing if they can shift from annual strategy cycles to just-in-time or continuous scanning.

Sensing requires more than this, however; it must involve staff from all key functions. Together they use multiple channels to scan from informal to advanced analytics to identify multiple perspectives on the strategic problems to be solved, the critical decisions to be made, the insights needed to clarify those decisions, the information that would produce the insights, and the data to collect, both external and internal to the organization. They then implement processes to do this.

Sensing the External Landscape

Information about the external environment or landscape around an organization typically falls into four broad categories: technology, markets, competitors, and regulatory.

Technology is making boundaries between industries more porous and providing opportunities for innovations that lead to dramatic shifts in market share: Uber, Barefoot Wine, Airbnb, eBanking. Each of these have captured significant market share by offering established goods or services in novel ways enabled by technology. Artificial intelligence and automation technology can improve efficiency, predictability and accountability while lowering risk, operating costs and lead times. How is technology changing the basis of competition in your industry? Which competitors benefit? Can technology help us enter new markets? What technologies are emerging that may soon become a factor? What maturing technologies are on the way out? What opportunities may result? What can you learn from industries outside your normal view?

Look at your customer and market trends. Who are your customers? Where do you recruit employees? How do these compare to the general population? Demographics? Diversity issues? Generational differences? How do your customers, the community and your competitors perceive you? How might this affect your current and future success? What is the overall economic situation in your target markets? Where is there shrinkage or growth? What are the opportunities and threats?

Who are your main and possibly future competitors? What drives their success? What hinders it? What do successful organizations in different industries teach you? Different ways of doing the same sort of work? Is this giving them an advantage? How do their staffing numbers compare to yours? What does it mean? What is their culture? How is it helping them? This may lead to some eye-opening if uncomfortable lessons. Can you identify potential partners with complementary competencies? Opportunities for outsourcing?

Operations in many industries are impacted by government regulatory oversight. This can involve not only constraints and requirements, but also opportunities for more effective compliance. Do you face health, safety, or environmental regulatory issues in your operations? How well are you addressing these? Are you or your industry associated with controversial public issues like sustainable development, or social justice, or data privacy, and so on?

Sensing How the Organization Is Doing

Sensing also involves finding out what's going on inside and across the organization as a whole. This often starts with metrics and outcomes. Are you meeting financial targets? If these results are adequate for now, are there future issues you anticipate? Is your strategy working? Adequate  overall financial performance may obscure shortfalls that could benefit from revisiting strategy and each of the strategic objectives.

In addition to these metrics you need to understand how well processes and systems support the organization's performance. How effective are the workflows? Are the required core capabilities and core assets present and effectively utilized? Are people organized into effective work groups? Are people, financial, and supervisory systems aligned with strategy and working?

The most intangible but perhaps most critical factors involve culture, leadership, and behaviors. How well do these support the strategy? Do specific aspects undermine it? What behaviors do you measure? For what sorts of things do you reward people? What are the organization's core values? Do they support the strategy? How well do people understand the strategy? In the absence of shared strategy, even well-intended individuals will do whatever makes sense to them, even if it doesn't to others. What values and behaviors do leaders demonstrate?

Assessing the Issues and Moving to Action

The information collected is used to assess issues warranting further attention. They typically fall into these categories: strategy, processes and systems, or culture and behaviors. Those in leadership roles review their severity to determine what, if any, action is needed. Part II provides roadmaps and details for a number of common circumstances.

Reflection: Your Experiences with Continuous Sensing?

◇ *How well does your organization sense? Do you gather the right information? Do you analyze it and use the results to take action?*

◇ *Have you been in or seen an organization that did sensing well? Was it built in or did employees manage the process informally?*

Involve through Group Process

Psychological Safety

Years ago, we encouraged clients to move beyond traditional 'change management' with its premise that just the right communication, words, or tools will somehow win over the mass of employee 'targets' to the changes they had little voice in creating. We offered the alternative of 'engagement,' with the premise that employees invested in shaping a new future will see the benefits, and even if they don't agree with the change, they may accept it more readily if they understand the necessity and how they fit in. Times have changed and engagement is no longer enough. It still implies that 'we' engage 'them' to get 'them' to do what 'we' want. Agility is the way we can move beyond that to involve people and to access their full capabilities.

This can only happen if people can reflect and talk openly and honestly. Research in industrial psychology and organization development reveals a concept known as psychological safety. This involves each individual's perception about whether they  can take interpersonal risks without being seen as ignorant, incompetent, negative, or disruptive. In groups it involves shared perceptions that the group will not embarrass, reject or punish any members for speaking up. It describes a climate characterized by interpersonal trust and mutual respect in which people are comfortable being themselves.

Interpersonal Relationships

All societies and groups recognize boundaries between what is public and private, what we talk about, what is socially acceptable, and what is over the line. In relationships between two or more they anticipate each other's behaviors using these accepted boundaries. These fall somewhere on a spectrum from total strangers to close family. Ed Schein has identified and described four levels of relationship that characterize the fundamental ways people relate in working together.

Level 0: Dependent: In level 0 relationships, one party has the upper hand and most of the power. Examples are parent-child, guard-prisoner, or supervisor-employee in 'sweat shops' where workers are trapped by legal, financial, or social strictures. Because of the power imbalance, the relationship depends on intentions. At worst it can be abusive, demeaning, cruel, and tyrannical, where those on the receiving end are considered nobodies without intrinsic rights.

Level 1: Transactional: Level 1 relationships center on the transactions between people who are strangers or know little of each other, except their roles. Every person has their roles to play, and they know how to do that. These relationships are  characterized by professional distance, rigid role definitions, and bureaucratic rule-defined behaviors. Customers and sales clerks have these relationships as do many hourly workers and their supervisors and managers. The terms 'bosses' and 'subordinates' capture the dynamics quite well.

Level 2: Personal: At this level, the individuals involved acknowledge each other as real people, total human beings with multiple facets and dimensions. They recognize their respective roles and fulfill them but in doing so have developed enough trust and openness to safely tell the truth in communicating. They recognize each other's individual strengths and shortfalls and work to  accommodate them. They treat each other as whole persons but without invading their individual boundaries or privacy. True teamwork requires this level.

Level 3: Belonging: This level involves emotional attachment: caring for another's well-being as a complete human, nurturing and supporting as appropriate, and challenging and probing when required. This can be the most effective level of all, and organizations that function at this level are exemplified by sports teams, which challenge each player to do their best in  the context of the entire team. They often feel like a purposeful family that is warm and inclusive and recognizes the strengths in their differentiated skills. This level is difficult to achieve fully. When done poorly it can be fraught with danger, especially for individuals who lack self-awareness regarding the boundaries between their own self-interests and those of others.

Group Process and Collaborative Working

For agile working, interpersonal relationships must be such that people can use 'group process' to integrate diverse viewpoints into robust solutions. Level 0 and 1 relationships cannot provide the needed psychological safety. Many change efforts don't succeed because they stay at level 1. The transactional hierarchy is a powerful creation that has long held sway in businesses and 70% of organizations still employ that style with its level 1 relationships, but that's not enough for agile: level 2 and 3 are required.

For this, leaders in these traditional organizations must role model agile behaviors. Change must be legitimized and start at the top. Otherwise employees won't feel safe and will remain at level 1. In strong level 1 'blame' cultures it may take a number of leadership examples before openness and trust show up and individual leaders cascade down into their work groups. To accelerate this, they can foster information flows, encourage decision-making at the right levels, and can model curiosity and ask lots of questions about the work and those doing it.

As things in their group open up, leaders must take care not to 'shoot the messenger' when the new honesty reveals bad news. They can speak of themselves as 'learners' and acknowledge their own fallibility. They can frame work projects as learning problems, not just as delivery problems. Rather than simply reporting news, announcements, and decisions from 'on high,' they can report what they have learned from senior executives and openly share their own interpretations and opinions. This sort of self-revelation from leaders can be quite helpful in exemplifying true collaboration.

Effective Teaming

This true collaboration can be facilitated through effective teams. Numerous recent studies document the move to collaborative teams and networks. Companies, conglomerates, as well as government agencies and schools now consider these as fundamental units of the organization. Software engineers in teams tend to innovate faster, see mistakes more quickly and find better solutions to problems. There is strong evidence that individuals in teams tend to achieve better results and report higher job satisfaction. But what is a team?

Most researchers agree that what most distinguishes work groups from teams is the interdependence of the tasks and activities of its members. Teams are highly interdependent: they plan work, solve problems, make decisions, and review progress in service of a specific project.

Decades of research have gone into understanding what motivates people to bring the best of themselves to their work together, create synergy from collective efforts, and manage the adaptive challenges teams face. Recent findings have confirmed many of the earlier conclusions but also furnish some eye-opening surprises. They identify these five key dynamics:

1. Psychological Safety: Effective teams get to know each other at relationship level 2 and share information about personal and work style preferences. Team members can talk about subtle issues in safe, constructive ways and define the desired team behaviors and norms.

2. Dependability: On effective teams, each member reliably completes quality work on time. Ineffective teams allow members to shirk responsibilities and take advantage of the ambiguity of shared goals. This is sometimes cited as a reason to avoid the use of teams, but the ambiguity can be minimized with proper procedures and systems.

3. Structure and Clarity: Effective teams define team and individual goals, roles and responsibilities, plans with deadlines and deliverables, linkages and interdependencies with other groups, and norms for working together. Individuals understand what is expected, the process for fulfilling them, and the consequences of performing or not.

4. Meaning and Purpose: Individual team members must find a sense of purpose in the work itself, the compensation, the outputs, or the interactions with satisfied customers. This meaning is highly personal and varies greatly from one individual to another: financial security, supporting family, helping the team succeed, or self-expression for each individual, for example. With enough safety, team members can talk freely about these and find ways for each one's needs to be addressed.

5. Impact: Team members need to see that the results of their work make a difference. They need to see how they are contributing to the team, the broader business groups, and the organization as a whole. Many teams create diagrams to show how they connect to customers.

A number of factors have surprisingly turned out to be less important: seniority or tenure of individuals, their individual performances, the extroversion of team members, the size of the team, the size of its workload, the location of teammates whether together or virtual, and even whether decision-making is consensus-driven.

Agility and Generations

The findings above are no surprise to anyone who has worked with teams. Technology has changed some of the tools of effective teaming but not the principles. However, people raised with such ever-present technology have some different worldviews. The broad generalizations below come from our observations of clients and colleagues.

Relationship to Technology: Younger employees cannot recall a world without internet connectivity and personal devices. Their handhelds and phones help them function more effectively and efficiently. They are as important as wallet, keys, or purse. Policies that restrict their use are intrusive and counter-productive. Feverish texting in business meetings may not be socializing but instead bringing in relevant and useful information to inform the discussion. Instant connectivity makes them impatient with paper procedures, snail mail, and poor web interfaces. Your customers probably share these feelings!

Relationship to Knowledge: Older workers often value experience, tenure, and expert knowledge gained by study and discipline. Younger ones are more accustomed to knowledge instantly available to anyone who can ask the right questions and evaluate the answers. This highlights how generations might learn from each other. Expert knowledge involves nuances not obvious in superficial web searches, so is best be harnessed by experts who see the nuances.

Relationships with People: Smaller families and adult attention lead many younger employees to expect more access to leadership and authority. They expect open, responsive, and inclusive leaders, real people who respond to e-mails but also have a life outside of work. They want a balanced life where late-night emergency consults are simply part of a flexible life schedule.

Reflection: How Do You Experience Involvement?

◇ *What level of relationships do you see in your work group?*

◇ *To what extent does your work group have the psychological safety needed for openness, honesty, and true collaboration?*

◇ *Does your organization use effective teaming and networking in its normal work and encourage effective collaboration?*

Resolve: Design Thinking and Leadership

The final stage in the agility cycle is Resolve, where the organization checks that the customized solutions resolve the initial issues, adjusts them if needed, then completes the cycle and resumes sensing. The key difference from traditional change efforts is design thinking, finding solutions to root causes not simply problem solving the presenting dilemmas. This requires a different style of leadership. Design thinking and agile leadership permeate the entire agility cycle but especially Resolve.

Linear Thinking

Traditional management is comfortable with the linear thinking required in solving tech- nical problems. These problems can be de-  scribed operationally and lend themselves to well-defined processes and procedures. They can often be efficiently solved by experts. The outcomes typically require changes in just one or a few places; often contained within a single business unit's or function's boundaries. They can often be implemented quickly by changing rules or work processes. Employees are generally receptive to the resulting changes as long as they understand them, and they make sense. Finally, these sorts of technical problems stay solved until something else changes.

Problem-solving is, in fact, essential for day-to-day operations. The trouble comes when its linearity is applied to more complex challenges. A great example of this was a large global client of ours losing significant numbers of mission-critical staff. Their HR function in response increased pay and developed a retention stock plan. Staff losses decreased but caused hard feelings among other staff. The retention program required substantial additional time to manage and was hard to dismantle once the crisis passed.

Design Thinking

A number of years later this same organization dealt with a similar challenge in a very different manner. A small ad hoc cross-functional team found working conditions and recognition much bigger drivers than pay. Temporary changes in employment terms were their 'good enough' solution. This stopped the staff exodus, was seen as fair, and was easily rescinded once the crisis passed.

This is design thinking. It recognizes that complex systems challenges are rarely rooted in a single well-defined problem. It starts by involving people who together have a comprehensive view of the system. They compile as much information as they can about the system. This information is used to discern patterns, sort out what are frequently multiple complexly interdependent problems, and identify the underlying systemic root causes. They then brainstorm creative solutions, select the most promising, and apply them to the root causes by involving those most impacted, often key customers.

One of our favorite observers of organization behavior, Chris Argyris, said, "Most people define learning too narrowly as mere 'problem-solving,' so they focus on identifying and correcting errors in the external environment. Solving problems is important. But if learning is to persist, managers and employees must also look inward. They need to reflect critically on their own behavior, identify the ways they often inadvertently contribute to the organization's problems, and then change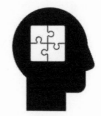

how they act." Argyris is describing an agile organization and its use of design thinking.

Agile Leadership

Inevitably, because of the systemic nature of the solutions, design thinking will create new challenges that will need to be addressed in concert. Because of this, traditional executives tend to shy away from such systemic changes unless they are absolutely required. However, when they finally take the plunge, and accept that any solution to a systemic challenge eventually creates new challenges, they

are freed up from having to control the process to find the 'right answer.' They see their role in a new light. What they once saw as problems stem from misalignments between the individual system components. By tackling the systemic challenges, they not only attend to finding sustainable solutions; they also free up resources formerly wasted on problem-solving firefighting and increase the capacity of the organization to respond to future challenges.

In any culture, introducing agility requires that those in legitimate authority sponsor and lead the changes. Whether their accountabilities flow from position, power, or their own initiative, they must exhibit the new thinking and new behaviors, enable design thinking, and ask the right questions instead of seeking expert answers. They must have the commitment and capability to see the effort through. Not everyone is capable of this. As ING Bank moved recently to a more agile customer focus, it is estimated that a third or more of the executives were not able to manage the new thinking and behaviors required.

We prefer not to talk about agile leaders, but what does this agile leadership look like? Its leaders not only champion the new behaviors, but also collaborate with other leaders to role model the behaviors and norms they want to foster. They must be clear on the organization's strategy and look for ways to encourage people to talk about subtle issues in safe, constructive ways.

It goes beyond this. For design thinking to become embedded requires a shift in focus. As people move towards developing customer-focused solutions and the associated entrepreneurial creativity and flexibility, leaders need to shift also. The 'true north' for agile leadership shifts from traditional 'management by objective' goals to objectives and key results (OKRs) centered on delivering products and services of value to the customer. Instead of day-to-day supervision and control, they must focus more on prioritizing and allocating resources and capabilities and ensuring that events are synchronized in support of the strategy. The essence of this leadership style was captured over 2500 years ago by Lao-Tzu; see the sidebar.

Reinforcing Agility

Extensive experience suggests that individuals can slowly change their behaviors, if the four conditions below are met.

Role Modeling: People look to those around them to gauge what is acceptable, especially those they look up to or aspire to become more like (role models). When role models 'walk the talk,' it exemplifies the norms.

Expectations: Everyone must understand the who, what, why, when, and how to use agile capabilities. It is not enough just to communicate this to them; people need to see examples, have a chance to safely mimic the behaviors they observe being modelled, practice with understanding, and then master these new agile behaviors.

Skills Needed: All staff should possess the skills needed to perform with agility. These may include some technical and managerial skills, but more likely will include many of the things highlighted in this chapter: continuous sensing and data analytics, collaboration and

> **On Leadership**
>
> The Bad Leader the People hate.
>
> The Harsh Leader the People fear, for one who does not trust cannot be trusted.
>
> The Good Leader the People obey and love.
>
> The Great Leader talks little. The People barely know he exists. He goes to them, he learns from them, and he loves them. He takes what they know and he builds on what they have. When his work is done, and his aim fulfilled, the People say: "We did it ourselves." *Lao-Tzu, Chinese philosopher, around the 6th century BCE*

teaming, design thinking, and agile leadership. Development programs may be needed if these skills are weak or absent.

Systems Reinforce: Formal policies and procedures, especially performance appraisal, compensation, and promotion, need to reinforce agile behaviors. Special attention should be paid to how people are treated after less-than-successful experiments. Are they rewarded for the lessons learned or punished for failure?

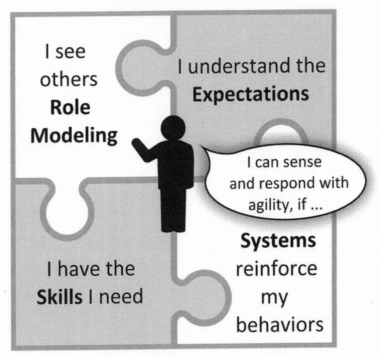

Reflection: Your Experiences with Design Thinking?

◇ *When facing large-scale complex issues, does your organization tend to use linear or design thinking?*

◇ *How successful has this been in resolving the issue so it doesn't recur?*

◇ *How many of the attributes of agile leadership do your leaders exhibit: design thinking, shared leadership, and collaborative working?*

Chapter 2: Organization Engineering

This chapter has four sections. The first describes Business Landscapes, the environments around an organization: industry, technology, markets, social conditions, and governments. The second section focuses on Corporate Culture, the distinctive 'look and feel' that emerges as decisions, actions, behaviors, and values combine to create an identity in its products, services, relationships, and operations. The third section provides an overview of Business Strategies: how organizations decide where to play and how to maximize value. The fourth section outlines Organization Design, where agile capabilities are actually built into the five components of the organization using ten deliverables. As we said before, these are not engineering in its strict sense; however, they each involve analysis, so we use the label loosely.

Business Landscapes

What Are Landscapes?

We call the environment around and within an organization and its industry its business land- scape. This includes those technologies rele-  vant to this industry, modes of production, and required knowledge and skills. It also includes the various products and their markets, the nature of competition and the associated strategies, and the impacts of national governments, regulatory regimes, multi-national considera- tions, and public perceptions.

The new world of business involves changes in two key dimensions: complexity and volatility. Complexity can be in markets, customers, the products, or the work required. The restaurant business, for example, is relatively simple compared to the complexity of the chemicals industry. Volatility is how quickly the technology, the products, their features, or markets change. Soft drink manufacturing and sales is relatively stable compared to the volatility of the clothing fashions.

These two dimensions naturally define four common landscapes as shown below. These are fundamental to the Syngineering framework. The descriptions are adapted and extended from the pioneering work of others.

Business Landscapes

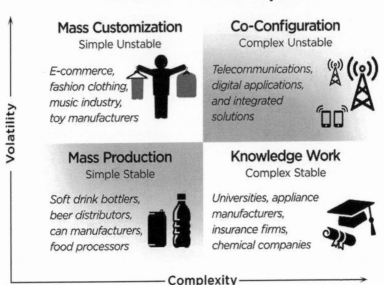

Mass Customization
Simple Unstable

E-commerce, fashion clothing, music industry, toy manufacturers

Co-Configuration
Complex Unstable

Telecommunications, digital applications, and integrated solutions

Mass Production
Simple Stable

Soft drink bottlers, beer distributors, can manufacturers, food processors

Knowledge Work
Complex Stable

Universities, appliance manufacturers, insurance firms, chemical companies

Volatility → (vertical axis)
Complexity → (horizontal axis)

The Mass Production Landscape

Environments are 'simple' when there are a small number of similar environmental factors and 'stable' when these factors remain the same or change slowly over time. This is the domain of soft drink bottlers, beer distributors, container manufacturers, and food processors. Soft drink bottlers meet consistent demand by  adding flavoring to water; what could be simpler? The challenge is in doing it cheaply and effectively and getting it to the masses. Success depends on mass production, churning out massive amounts of product that fit customer demands as cheaply as possible, so we call this the Mass Production landscape.

The Knowledge Work Landscape

Here the environment is 'complex' with numerous dissimilar factors, and stable. Success comes from expert processes that are continually tweaked and improved to increase quality and cut costs. This is Knowledge Work: creating, processing, and enhanc-  ing knowledge. This is the realm of colleges and universities like Harvard and Cambridge, appliance suppliers like Samsung and Maytag, insurance companies like Northwestern Mutual, the Hartford, and Progressive, and chemical firms like Shell and Dow.

The Mass Customization Landscape

Here the environment is 'simple' and 'unstable'; that is, the factors change frequently in erratic ways; they are not predictable. This is the domain of e-commerce, fashion clothing, music industry, and toy manufacturers. The key is Mass Customization, tai-  loring basic simple products to suit massive groups of customers. Here's where we find companies as diverse as Mattel and Expedia.

The Co-Configuration Landscape

Here the external environment is both 'complex' and 'unstable.' It involves building and sustaining integrated systems that can sense/scan, respond, and adapt to the individual experience of the customer. This is the domain of digital applications, telecom- munications, and integrated solutions. When a firm does this kind of work, it builds ongoing relationships where products evolve and emerge in each customer-product pair. Google and Apple sit in this landscape. We call this the Co-Configuration landscape.

Landscape Examples

The four landscapes are a simplification: volatility and complexity are each a continuum. The table on the next page shows some nuances. The industries within each landscape give some idea of the range it covers.

	Volatile			
Mass Customization			**Co-Configuration**	
Fashion Apparel	Online Pay Services	Consumer Electronics	IT Services and Solutions	
Nightclub Entertainment	Online Travel and Booking	Medical and Healthcare	Media and Telecommunications	
Mass Production			**Knowledge Work**	
Fast Food Retail Sales	Real Estate Sales	Airline Transportation	Drugs and Pharmaceuticals	
Grocery Sales and Distribution	Container Manufacturing	Mining and Extraction	Colleges and Universities	

Stable

Simple ⟵-----------------------⟶ Complex

One of the most simple and stable of the industries in Mass Production is the grocery industry. Supply and demand are relatively stable, and the industry is as simple as moving food products from suppliers to retail customers. Container manufacturing (e.g. plastic bottles, metal cans) is also stable, but manufacturing introduces more complexity. Fast food is simple like groceries, but changing consumer tastes introduce volatility. Technology has transformed the real estate industry. The technology required for online searches and virtual showing adds to the complexity of the industry.

In Knowledge Work one of the more stable industries is higher education (i.e. colleges and universities) which sits in a relatively stable environment: numbers and interests of students changes slowly over time. The complexity comes from the breadth of human knowledge across the various academic disciplines. While automobile industry designs are tweaked constantly, the underlying supply and demand is relatively stable. Making a car is more complex than manufacturing a bottle but less complex than teaching. Medical and healthcare is equally as complex as higher education. In fact, much medical research is done within higher education. The added volatility comes from technology, such as gene splicing. De-

regulation has introduced some volatility into the airline industry. The complexity of flight and navigation systems justifies placing it in this quadrant.

In Mass Customization, volatility can involve changes in customer tastes and demands, as in the fashion industry. Manufacturing clothes is relatively simple, often with a combination of machine and hand sewing. Running a nightclub is as simple as providing drinks and live entertainment,  but volatility comes from changing musical tastes and popularity. Online payment services have both volatility and complexity from the technology needed for secure service. The travel industry is relatively simple and not as volatile as an online payment service such as Bitcoin where an idea allows you to establish a business, but technology advances can wipe it out overnight.

In Co-Configuration, massive amounts of networked data and continually updated algorithms place IT services and solutions in the highest levels of complexity and volatility. A single innovation can disrupt a business and industry. The knowledge needed to come up with new medications makes pharmaceuticals quite complex. The pace of innovation is somewhat less volatile than IT. Consumer electronics are equally as volatile as IT since they too can disrupt industries. However, they are a bit less complex, involving specific products and not networked solutions. Telecommunications and media are similarly complex but not quite as volatile.

Reflection: What's Your Business Landscape?

◇ *Where is your industry and its products and services on the complexity axis? What drives this? Is it knowledge? Technology? Customers?*

◇ *Where would you place it on the volatility axis? What gives rise to this volatility? Technology? Customer tastes? Something else?*

◇ *Which landscape and which corner does this imply? Compare with the table. Does it make sense? Where is your landscape trending?*

Corporate Culture

What Is Corporate Culture?

Patterns in everyday actions and behaviors and the interactions of work groups combine to produce a distinctive 'look and feel' in every organization. Grocery stores feel different from mining operations. Car dealerships have a different aura than doctors' offices! This look-and-feel stems from how decisions are made, how power is distributed, what gets rewarded, who gets hired, how work is done, and the relationships between different parts of the organization and its customers. The sum total of this look-and-feel we call 'corporate culture.'

Many before us have observed that specific landscapes tend to favor specific cultures. Each culture has characteristics, which either help or hinder their survival in each landscape. The diagram below summarizes the discussions to follow.

Corporate Cultures

Flexible
Follow Principles

- *Flexible, Responsive*
- *Decentralized Decisions*
- *Sensing and Responding*
- *Entrepreneurial Creativity*

Adaptive
Adapt Principles

- *Principles not Standards*
- *Local Autonomy / Decisions*
- *Expertise distributed*
- *Coordination by principles*

Directive
Follow Orders

- *Unskilled labor*
- *Standard Processes*
- *Predictable Supply / Demand*
- *Decisions / Control Clear*

Participative
Follow Rules

- *Standard Processes*
- *Variance Control*
- *Broad Input into Decisions*
- *Expert Specialist Thinking*

Flexibility (vertical axis) — Empowerment (horizontal axis)

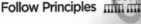

In general, cultures with more flexibility can respond more quickly to changing conditions and are the best fit in landscapes with increased volatility. Those that cascade authority, decision-making, or empowerment downwards tend to do better in landscapes with increased complexity. For these reasons, when we categorize cultures, we find it useful to change axes: flexibility becomes a useful proxy for volatility and empowerment for complexity. We have applied what we believe are neutral labels to each grouping of cultures.

Directive Cultures

The Mass Production landscape involves simple work done by unspecialized labor. Its stability and simplicity favor predictable demand and supply, work done within standard processes, central control, and strategic planning. Work is typically done through project management with two equally important aspects: (1) careful planning and rigorous processes and (2) active management to track progress and adapt plans and processes as needed. Since authority and knowledge are centralized, a key theme in this culture is 'following directions.' Our neutral label is the Directive culture.

Mass Production Landscape	Directive Culture
◇ Simple work steps	◇ Unskilled labor
◇ Repetitive tasks	◇ Standard processes
◇ Stable environment	◇ Careful planning
◇ Predictable demand	◇ Hierarchical control

These cultures are most efficiently controlled by a hierarchical pyramid from top management on down. Vertical reporting is designed as the primary coordination mechanism with clearly specified individual responsibilities at all levels. Linking across the hierarchy tends to be for advice only. Management, financial, and human re- source systems focus on control. Decisions go up the pyramid for approval to the right authority level and usually down for execution. The icon for this type of organization is a small classic organization reporting chart superimposed on a large vertical arrow to represent the tops-down nature of authority and control in this culture.

Directive is a tested and effective culture. It is typical of many companies and government agencies; it's estimated that 70%
of organizations globally are Directive. We placed fast-
food in the Mass Production landscape and as expected, McDonald's, Five Guys, and Chipotle all have
Directive cultures.

Each of our three case studies started with Directive cultures as well
described in the first few introductory pages of Chapters 8, 9, and 10.

Participative Cultures

The increasing complexity in the Knowledge Work landscape demands
specialized expert thinking, broad-based input, and more coordination
across the workflows. Work is typically done by groups or teams
instead of individuals through what's often called group process. Its
two key aspects are: groups with diverse perspectives and ideas can
solve problems that separate individuals could not, and groups tend to
take more ownership in shared outcomes than those imposed from
above. The standard directive processes can work here if they include
additional variance control and staff with specialized expertise. Since
knowledge and authority are shared, a key theme in this culture is
intelligently 'following rules' to arrive at shared solutions. Shared leadership is one of the agile capabilities this introduces. Since this culture
depends on functional specialist participation, we call it the Participative culture.

Knowledge Work Landscape	Participative Culture
◇ Multi-dimensional work	◇ Expert specialists
◇ Interdependent tasks	◇ Collaborative work
◇ Complex environment	◇ Matrix management
◇ Consistent demand	◇ Shared decisions

The stability still supports a vertical control structure and most employees report to a functional or process manager
whose authority flows vertically for overall performance and career. However, most also report day-
to-day to a project or product manager whose authority flows horizontally across the functional de-

partments. The relative strength of the horizontal increases with complexity. Decision-making is consultative and often delegated down to those with specialized expertise or knowledge. The icon for this is a small classic organization reporting chart with two large superimposed two-way arrows. The vertical one represents the same hierarchical flow of authority and control found in the Directive culture, but here it is accompanied by a horizontal arrow across work groups representing information flows, shared decision-making and collaboration.

This shows up in about 20% of organizations worldwide. We mentioned universities in the Knowledge Work landscape, and they typically have a Participative culture, with department experts sharing almost complete control over the work in their sphere. Mineral extraction and petroleum production companies fit into this landscape and most have some semblance of the Participative culture. Toyota has exemplified this culture for years. They have developed an employee-centered culture of adaptation, which is reinforced by leadership.

In the case study in Chapter 10, Wilderness Petroleum moved into a Participative culture, and features many of the attributes of that culture.

Flexible Cultures

The increasing volatility in the Mass Customization landscape requires entrepreneurial creativity and flexibility to respond in real time to changing conditions. This necessitates decentralized decision making to deal with the accelerated response times and works best when mindsets shift to design thinking as described in Chapter 1. These entities often convene groups of knowledge workers who use design thinking and prototyping to design and make decisions about new products or ways of working. Since knowledge and authority are decentralized, a key theme in this culture is 'following principles' in responding in real time. We call this culture Flexible culture and it incorporates many of the agile capabilities and practices we discussed in Chapter 1. The table below indicate that many of these are dictated by the landscape.

Mass Customization Landscape	Flexible Culture
◇ Simple sets of work	◇ Multi-tasking workers
◇ Tailored tasks	◇ Flexible mindsets
◇ Volatile environment	◇ Enabling leadership
◇ Unpredictable demand	◇ Consultative decisions

Flexible cultures currently form about 5% of organizations worldwide, but the dramatic growth in volatile e-commerce makes this the fastest-growing culture. Alegent Healthcare has moved to a Flexible culture and in fact has embedded design thinking and prototyping in their decision-making processes. Online travel giant Expedia's culture is truly Flexible: shared accountabilities and authorities start on an employee's first day on the job. Gore-Tex also illustrates this culture.

It's hard to distinguish truly Flexible organizations from Directive start-ups that exhibit these characteristics. Start-ups with few employees and simple activities often develop this culture. Time will tell if they can preserve this Flexible culture as they transition from a start-up, as is happening now with Indochino.

In the Comfort Home case study, three Directive organizations came together and morphed into a networked Flexible culture. Their journey is described in Chapter 9 and features many Flexible practices.

Adaptive Cultures

In the Co-Configuration landscape, the added volatility plus complexity require nimble access to multiple skill sets with local autonomy but organization-wide coordination; the whole needs to be resilient and adaptable to rapidly changing circumstances. Permeable boundaries allow access to the multiple 'brains' around or even outside the organization. Work often incorporates many agile capabilities of sense and respond. As individuals sense and articulate tensions in their immediate environment, they have built in means to have them addressed by those who are accountable for each particular topic, for example in regularly scheduled strategy, governance, task, or daily stand-up meetings. Since knowledge and authority are completely distributed in this way, a key theme in this culture is for individuals and groups to 'adapt principles' as they sense and respond to tensions. We call this the Adaptive culture.

Co-Configuration Landscape	Adaptive Culture
◇ Complex work sets	◇ Multi-skilled labor
◇ Interdependent tasks	◇ Linked networks
◇ Volatile environment	◇ Clear accountabilities
◇ Unpredictable demand	◇ Distributed decisions

The resulting organizations morph as market conditions change. There are often networked formal and informal structures or circles. Boundaries are fluid and porous: 'outside parties,' even competitors, can partner and collaborate in fulfilling specific assignments. Decision-making is diffused to those doing the work. Work is managed by clear 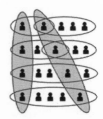 and transparent accountabilities. Continuous experimentation is encouraged. There is strong group accountability for outcomes to the customer. The icon for this type of organization moves away from fixed groups and reporting and instead shows individuals connected by task networks based on their mutual accountabilities coordinated by linking networks.

Although still less than 5% of organizations worldwide fit here today, that will almost certainly change as volatility drives industries out of the Knowledge Work landscape and up into Co-Configuration. We think Dell is a good example. Even after 20 years, it retains the informality and energy of a start-up company. Their flat organization fosters speedy decisions without the burden of superfluous hierarchy. The direct 'build-to-order' business model brings technology-rich products to market at lower cost by eliminating retailers and reducing inventory.

The Stratos case study in Chapter 8 is an excellent example of how an Adaptive culture can intentionally emerge. We also worked with a French manufacturing firm as they retooled their traditional business model into an Adaptive culture that increased productivity and customer satisfaction with reduced staff during a long downturn. Spotify is another great example. More recently the Dutch banking group ING have shifted from a traditional Directive organization to an 'agile' Adaptive model. For ING, agility is about flexibility and the ability to rapidly adapt and steer itself in a new direction: minimizing handovers and bureaucracy, and empowering people. Multidisciplinary teams, or squads of marketing, product, commercial, user-experience, data analysis, and IT specialists, focus on solving the client's needs, united by a common definition of success.

The Transportation Metaphor

Physical terrains and vehicles help visualize landscapes and cultures.

The Mass Production landscape compares to a simple flat physical landscape where the need is to transport people from point A to a single stable unchanging destination B. The vehicle corresponding to the Directive culture might be a train. It's well-suited to traversing flat landscapes from A to B but falters if multiple destinations or varied terrain are involved.

Traveling the Knowledge Work landscape can be thought of as moving from point A to a single stable unchanging destination B but with varied and complex terrain in between, perhaps mountains or oceans. An airliner from one airport to another might be the chosen vehicle, corresponding to the Participative culture. Large jet airliners do great at A to B but can't easily divert to other destinations, especially those without airports.

The physical analogue to the Mass Customization landscape is a flat terrain involving multiple constantly changing destinations. The Directive trains and tracks won't work here, nor would the Participative airplanes with their required airports. A better choice to represent the Flexible culture is some type of bus, able to shift destinations with the twirl of a steering wheel.

A physical terrain that might represent the Co-Configuration landscape would be complex and varied, perhaps with mountains or oceans, with passengers who need to travel to multiple and ever-changing destinations in this landscape. The analogue to the Adaptive culture might be a helicopter, with its ability to quickly adapt flight plans and reach almost any destination imaginable.

Which Culture Is Better?

As business has become more complex and volatile, some of our colleagues have concluded that only Adaptive is truly agile, so must be the 'best.' We prefer a more nuanced view. Each landscape favors a specific culture. For businesses in Co-Configuration, Adaptive may indeed be best, but trying to implement an Adaptive culture in another landscape may divert valuable resources and handicap the enterprise.

We have seen clients who struggled with their Directive culture finally realize that their landscape actually requires strong central controls. What's hampering their performance is not the centralization but the highly political ego-driven functional silos, which maintain separate uncoordinated and unaligned activities. As stop-gap solutions they often layer on bureaucratic gate-keeping procedures, which do little but defer action. This culture can benefit greatly from delegated decision making, collaboration, and other agile capabilities but as we will see in Part III, they must look different than they do in the Adaptive culture.

Reflection: What's Your Corporate Culture?

◇ *Where does your organization sit on the flexibility axis? Evidence?*

◇ *Where does it sit on the empowerment axis? Evidence?*

◇ *What are the implications for culture? Reread the characteristics of that culture. How well does it match with your organization? Surprised?*

◇ *How well does this culture fit with the landscape you identified in the previous section? How might this impact your change efforts?*

Business Strategy

What Is Strategy?

An organization's strategy is a description of how it intends to succeed in its marketplace: the products and services it provides, the customers who buy them, how they're distributed, and the resulting value proposition that gives distinctive advantage over competitors. It provides criteria to prioritize and allocate resources, guide decisions on where to play, and how to win to maximize long-term value.

When current and widely understood it provides the critical 'true North' to decide among options for any changes. When the landscape shifts, the strategy must change and with it the other components of the organization that sustain it. This is why it is important to explicitly articulate and update strategy when undertaking changes. The strategy should lead, not lag behind the changes.

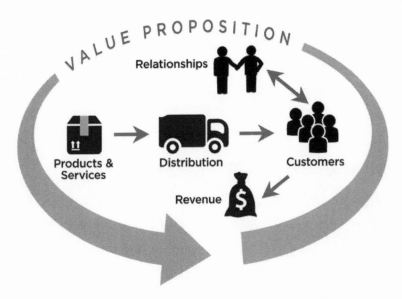

Strategy starts with the products and services as in the diagram above. These are anchored in the core purpose of the organization and draw on its unique capabilities: assets, people competencies, or knowledge technologies. Next is who will buy these products and services, the customers. These can be specific organizations, markets, or market segments. Distribution is how you get the product to its intended users. This can be through sales directly to consumers, or strategic partnerships, or retail distributors. Increasingly important considerations are brick-and-mortar vs. virtual, and issues around inventory storage. The result will be a revenue stream that funds the enterprise and provides returns on investment. The overall value proposition is why customers choose you instead of your competition.

Core Strategies

There are as many strategies as there are organizations, but they tend to concentrate into a few core types defined by two dimensions.

Market scope defines how broad a segment of the total population you target. Medication for rare diseases has a narrow market scope. Inexpensive cell phones target a broad market scope.

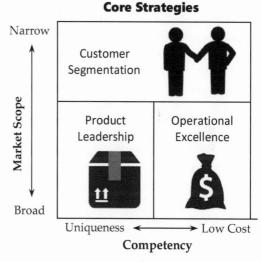

Competency describes the skills you need to give your competitive advantage. Expenses or costs lower than your competitors allow you to outcompete on price or profit margin. Uniqueness in product or service allows you to offer things no competitor can. Your product or service may be of higher quality, have more usefulness, be lower cost, or be supported by something else that your competitors can't replicate. It may involve strategic relationships that enable you to broker better deals than competitors. Your value proposition should offer targeted solutions that satisfy your customers' needs.

Operational Excellence Strategies: Cost leadership or operational excellence are financially driven strategies that seek to produce standard products, often commodities, at lower cost than the competition. The resulting cost margin translates directly into profits. Organizations that successfully pursue this strategy emphasize optimizing efficiency and minimizing costs. There are myriads of ways to do this: cost-advantaged assets, values and reward systems, which emphasize efficiency, and work processes and technologies, which improve efficiency and drive down costs.

McDonald's, GEICO, and Dell exhibit some or all of these characteristics. This strategy is not limited to for-profit enterprises. A number of international relief organizations market themselves as having low administrative costs. The value proposition for their donors is in maximizing the on-the-ground impact of their contributions.

Product Leadership Strategies: Product leadership or differentiation strategies offer products and/or services that customers prefer to those of your competitors. This preference justifies higher prices that translate into profits. Organizations that succeed with these strategies focus on developing and maintaining these products or services.
Some tend to value and reward effectively innovating, researching, and developing the distinctive products and bringing them to market.

Apple with its iPhones is a good example of this strategy. Others may focus on product quality and reputation. Harvard University is a not-for-profit that perennially perches atop university product leadership rankings. Tesla is another good example where people pay a premium for their electric cars.

Customer Segmentation Strategies: Customer or market segmentation spans a number of related strategies focused on specific markets or even individual customers, where it may be called customer intimacy. Deep understanding of these markets or customers enables satisfying their needs in ways competitors cannot. The emphasis is on providing exactly what each unique customer or market segment demands. Core values and reward systems center on delighting the customer. There are often specific customer-facing groups that each tailor products and solutions for specific markets or customers.

Whiting-Turner construction, headquartered in Baltimore, is perhaps less well-known than other companies we have mentioned, but they have a strong tradition of satisfied customers and repeat business. Wolfgang Puck Catering is arguably pursuing celebrity product leadership, but their success seems equally attributable to painstaking planning and tailoring each event around the client's vision.

Strategy in Today's New World

Strategies can no longer be purely one of these core strategies, if indeed that was ever true. Companies pursuing operational excellence must still pay attention to product features and market segments. Product leaders likewise must control costs. Pursuing a particular core strategy therefore suggests that the other two core strategies must be present at some threshold level. The lowest-cost product must still have a minimum threshold of features. Specialty medications must still be effective and reasonably priced. Product leaders must price their offerings at a reasonable premium above that of others.

The increased volatility in today's new world has led many to the concept of emergent strategy, a pattern of action that develops over time in an organization as intentions collide with and accommodate changing realities. The emphasis is on sensing and responding to emerging information and trends. It's less important to craft a particular winning strategy and more important to notice what's actually working and invest in that. There are numerous examples where success emerged through observing this gap between intention and reality and positioning the company on the reality. Nyquil built a brand on what had been a shortfall: it puts people to sleep! Viagra was originally a high blood pressure medication. We think that what others call emergent strategy is simply building in agility. The Mobilize stage incorporates adjusting strategy in real time.

Strategic priorities are also changing. Increasing emphasis on sustainable development has led to the concept of a triple bottom line: people, planet, and profit. The people component measures social returns for not only the employees, but also the community: fair trade, fair pay, fair supply chain procedures, and a purpose focusing on a more just world. Planet reflects a focus on sustainable and environmentally benign practices: organic farming, leadership in energy and environmental design (LEED) buildings, and minimal or positive long-term impacts.

Profits in many cases have benefitted as well. The above practices have shifted from being more expensive in a world focused on quarterly stockholder value to becoming the standard. What's called 'impact investing,' practiced by large retirement funds driven by their values-conscious shareholders, has resulted in billions of dollars of added value for companies that can demonstrate their focus on long-term sustainability: Whole Foods, Thrive Market, The Container Store, Seventh Generation, and Unilever.

Triple Bottom Line

Landscape Influences Strategy: Both Shape Culture

Effective strategies start from a deep understanding of industry environment or landscape and differentiate the enterprise from its competitors. Does each landscape favor a particular core strategy? Our conclusion from the examples below is that while landscape is a critical ingredient that must be considered in formulating strategy, any of the core strategies can succeed in each of the landscapes.

Mass Production: We put fast-food in this landscape. Several chains including McDonald's have succeeded with operational excellence. Five Guys is building market share by offering better burgers to position themselves as product leaders. Chipotle has rocketed to prominence with what is essentially a single product tailored to each customer's satisfaction and targeting an increasingly health-focused clientele.

Knowledge Work: We placed higher education here. Harvard anchors product leadership in this landscape. Specialty institutions like Juilliard compete on customer segmentation. Many state-funded systems offer affordable cost leadership alternatives.

Mass Customization: We placed clothing fashions in this landscape. While Ralph Lauren is known for product leadership and the Men's Warehouse for cost leadership, this industry is being transformed by online outfits like Indochino offering exactly what each customer wants and guaranteeing satisfaction.

Co-Configuration: We put consumer electronics in this landscape. Apple has long thrived with its laptops and iPhones in product leadership. In pursuing operational excellence Dell dramatically shortened the distribution process with the ability of each customer to build their own machine online. If you have heard of Razer, you know how their cutting-edge gaming laptops thrive in that market segment.

Numerous observations like these have convinced us that each landscape favors corporate cultures with some common characteristics. We have also observed that each generic strategy can compete in each of the four landscapes. But each strategy also requires certain cultural characteristics. The characteristics required by landscape somehow combine  with those required by strategy to produce the resulting culture.

To visualize this, let's return to our vehicle metaphor. The chosen vehicle depends on the landscape: train, airplane, bus, or helicopter. Strategy then is how you outfit that vehicle to beat the competition. Is your airliner Jet Blue? No frills, no snacks, extra fees for luggage, a bare bones economy enterprise? Operational excellence: United Airlines! Or perhaps Virgin Atlantic for first class all the way: unlimited amenities, five-star chefs, luxury fully reclining seats or beds with courtesy curtains? Product leadership! Or perhaps your airliner is outfitted for a specific clientele, maybe Qatar Airways for business folk: unlimited Wi-Fi, conference call facilities, lie-flat beds, onboard printers, and the like? Customer Focus! The vehicles in each landscape can be either economy, first class, or business class. Landscape dictates the type of vehicle. Strategy dictates the details needed for the desired application.

Corporate culture works the same way. Landscape dictates many features of the culture and describes the external world an enterprise competes in. The chosen strategy will be one that offers success in this landscape. It dictates what internal capabilities are required and these internal capabilities or competencies in turn fold into the culture on top of the landscape requirements.

Let's see how the core strategies shape the Participative cultures that emerge in the Knowledge Work landscape:

Operational Excellence in this Knowledge Work landscape will use the standard processes and controls to minimize cost. Broad participation of experts will focus on driving out waste. Decision-making must accommodate the needed breadth of expertise. Examples are Toyota and United Airlines. Other examples can be found in the table at the end of this section. In these types of organization, you are likely to encounter methods such as Lean, Kaizen or Six Sigma.

Product Leadership will instead emphasize processes that foster, enable, and reward innovation around developing new and unique products. There will be a premium on getting people with radically different areas of expertise to collaborate in new and different ways to drive innovation. Here you are likely to see a focus on R&D and innovation: NASA and Harvard.

Customer Segmentation focuses on tailoring products and services to a specific segment of the market. The culture will focus on deep collaboration between those expert in customer relationships and their needs and those expert in the range of products and services to draw from. Here you are likely to find a multitude of customer or user experience activities. Some banks and financial institutions, automobile manufacturers, and Whiting-Turner mentioned earlier are examples.

The results are three different cultures, but we call each Participative: they each involve a broad swath of different experts to navigate the increased complexity needed in the Knowledge Work landscape.

Examples of Landscapes, Cultures, and Strategies

We have found it useful to test the relationships between strategy, landscape, and culture by looking at a broad range of examples. The ten categories in the table below cover the breadth of today's industries. We have picked two well-known companies in each and filled in the entries, often radically simplifying things. Our purpose is not to be comprehensive or authoritative, but to get you thinking!

Example Landscapes, Cultures, and Strategies			Strategy	Landscape	Culture
	Company	Offerings			
Consumer Products	Toyota	Automotive	OE	KW	Part.
	Zappos	Clothing	OE	MC	Flex.
Leisure & Travel	Expedia	Travel Svcs.	PL	MC	Flex.
	Southwest Air.	Air Travel	OE	KW	Part.
Finance & Insurance	GEICO	Insurance	OE	MP	Direct.
	Berksh. Hathaway	Investment	PL	MC	Flex.
Healthcare, Medical	Liberty Medical	Treatment	CS	KW	Part.
	United Healthcare	Insurance	OE	KW	Direct.
Food, Agriculture	McDonald's	Restaurants	OE	MP	Direct.
	Wolfgang Puck	Catering	CS	MC	Flex.
Information Technology	Google	Online Svcs.	PL	CC	P → A
	Dell	Electronics	OE	CC	P → A
Energy & Construction	BASF	Chemicals	PL	KW	Direct.
	Whiting Turner	Construction	CS	KW	Part.
Aviation, Defense	Boeing	Aircraft	CS	KW	D → P
	Teledyne	Electronics	PL	KW	D → P
Government & Agencies	NASA	Space Projs.	PL	KW	D → P
	State DMV	Licenses	OE	MP	Direct.
Non-Profit, Education	CARE	End Poverty	OE	KW	Direct.
	Harvard	Education	PL	KW	Part.

We've abbreviated landscape, culture, and strategy labels as follows:

MP stands for Mass Production, KW for Knowledge Work, MC for Mass Customization, and CC for Co-Configuration.

Direct. is Directive, Part. is Participative, Flex. is Flexible, D→P is Directive moving to Participative, and P→A is Participative moving to Adaptive.

OE is short for operational excellence, PL is short for product leadership, and CS is short for customer segmentation.

These are generic strategies, and of necessity quite generalized. Whiting-Turner, for example, must keep a tight rein on costs, but where they shine is long-term client relationships. GEICO, the automobile insurance company, must provide adequate claims processing, but their competitive edge is cost: "15 minutes will save you 15%."

You may not think about 'strategy' for non-profits and government agencies, but if you work in these organizations, you know it is critical to understand their strategic directions. The US National Aeronautics and Space Administration (NASA), for example, depends on popular political support for their program funding. Their competitors are other government projects, so NASA must position their activities so they are preferred by decision-makers over others. CARE, the international relief organization, has a reputation for a lean administrative footprint and how their donations are leveraged by government and foundation grants and gifts-in-kind. Their operations and donor communication approach are aligned around an operational excellence strategy.

You may chuckle at seeing 'operational excellence' and DMV on the same line? The state or province or national Departments of Motor Vehicles (DMV), tasked with managing vehicle and driver licensing, are not known for efficiency. However, the sheer volume of work suggests that a focus on cost is a viable strategy.

Reflection: What's Your Organization's Strategy?

◇ *What strategy is your company pursuing to compete in its landscape?*

◇ *How well is this working? Is the strategy being executed well?*

◇ *How robust is your strategy against where your landscape is trending?*

◇ *What considerations does your strategy place on your culture? Are there any conflicts with your current culture?*

Agile Organization Design

As indicated in the Preface, organization design involves identifying those few key changes that best enable organizations to deliver their strategy. Traditionally this is done by mobilizing a design project to frame a high-level design, which 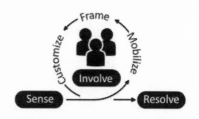 is then customized and implemented. In agile organizations, Mobilize, Frame, and Customize become the middle three stages of the agility cycle, used whenever Sense calls for it. They build in the agile capabilities: sensing, collaboration, shared accountable leadership, group process, and design thinking.

The Five Organization Components

To change an organization, you must tinker with the interdependent building blocks we call its components. Traditional problem-solving typically changes one component at a time. This may not help and can even hurt performance. To deliver on strategy requires that all components pull together and reinforce each other.

Leadership: Every organization, from the most Directive to the most Adaptive, has roles accountable for strategy, especially allocating people and other resources between competing priorities. Holding the keys to unlocking these resources is leadership in its broadest sense and includes how such authority is legitimized (whether from position,  power, or accountability), how decisions are made and shared, the required skills and capabilities, and the needed styles and behaviors.

Work: The activities and processes that create value and provide the organization's competitive advantage. It includes process flows, inputs and outputs, hand-offs, and requirements. Automation and expert systems have increasingly important roles in getting work done. Work may be voluminously documented or informally understood.

People: This component includes the skills and capabilities needed for the organization to get its work done. It starts with the core competencies that provide competitive advantage and translates these into the various roles, the account-abilities of each, and the number of people needed to fill each of these roles. Increasingly, routine roles are being systematized and automated.

Structure: More than just organization charts, this includes the formal reporting lines but also the relationships between different roles, the various locations where work is needed, and the co-ordination mechanisms needed to fit the other components.

Systems: Management systems operationalize the supervision of work outputs and delivery on accountabilities. Financial and reporting systems track the flow of money and the outcomes of business performance. HR systems ensure qualified people to perform the required roles, and they align and reward their efforts. The increasing complexity is being addressed by information technology systems, and their associated infrastructure, hardware and soft-ware applications, knowledge and expert systems, robotics and artificial intelligence.

The interdependence of these components is illustrated in the diagram on the next page, a slight adaptation of Jay Galbraith's well-known Star Model. Each component can be changed by design. Culture can't be, at least directly. It is a complex outcome of innumerable human interactions and dynamics, influenced by past history, the personalities of those in governance roles, the social fabric around the work locations, and then shaped by landscape and strategy as we discussed. Can it change? Some side with Peter Drucker in claiming that culture eats strategy for breakfast; that is, culture is inevitable and fixed and may well sabotage any changes in strategy.

While this is certainly true for organizations that have not worked at culture, it overlooks the reality that the above components are levers that can be changed to shape the culture in specific directions. A large part of this book focuses on just these sorts of designed changes. Where agile capabilities are built in, the resulting intentional culture can be a powerful factor in enabling delivery of the chosen strategy and sensing when and how it needs to change.

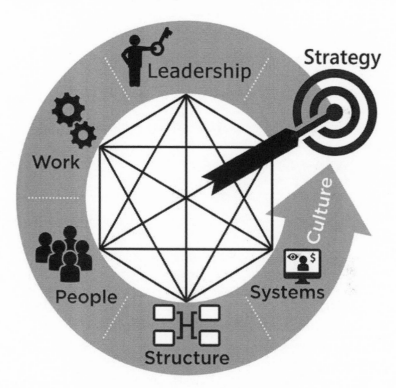

Organization Design Methods and Deliverables

There are a myriad of methods and frameworks to make systematic design changes in the above components. Many outline specific activities in a time-sequenced manner that get things started, develop high-level or macro-designs, then fill in and implement the resulting detailed designs. In our approaches we focus on the following ten deliverables:

Mobilize defines the effort, anchors it in strategy, and diagnoses the changes needed in the components.

◇ Deliverable 1: Charter defines the opportunity and its scope, identifies an approach that fits the culture, provides staff and resources, and outlines milestones and estimated timeframes.

◇ Deliverable 2: Strategy validates the organization's core business, assesses its landscape, and articulates how it will succeed: products and services, customers, distribution channels, and the resulting value proposition.

◇ Deliverable 3: Diagnosis gathers and synthesizes information about the organization's current state, identifies strengths and shortfalls, summarizes the key issues needing work, assesses the readiness for change, and agrees decision criteria.

Frame outlines the core work, any changes to the operating model, and how these changes will be deployed.

◇ Deliverable 4: Core Work identifies the key technologies and work activities that provide the organization's competitive advantage. This is the core of organization design: how work actually gets done, not reporting relationships.

◇Deliverable 5: Operating Model provides the high-level arrangement of components that delivers the strategy and desired future. It's the equivalent of a vehicle's chassis, motor, and drive train. It aligns the core work with the strategy and desired culture.

◇Deliverable 6: Deployment groups the key changes in the operating model and its components into initiatives and describes how they will be cascaded to the operating units so they can customize to their own situations and implement

Customize details how the work is done, the organization structure that best enables this, and the support systems required.

◇ Deliverable 7: Roles and Accountabilities specifies all needed technologies and processes and defines the critical tasks, activities, skills, job roles, and authorities needed to deliver them. These are consolidated into a complete picture of staffing skills and numbers.

◇ Deliverable 8: Structure groups the roles into first-level work groups and higher-level units, assigns reporting relationships, and describes coordinating mechanisms required to align activities across the enterprise.

◇ Deliverable 9: Support Systems define the details of the financial, management, IT, and HR systems needed to support the work. These are important mechanisms in aligning the administrative functions to reinforce the strategy and an intentional culture that sustains the agility necessary in the new operating model.

Resolve ensures that the customized solutions resolve the initial issues.

◇ Deliverable 10: Adjust involves all staff in learning their new accountabilities and starting up the new operating model. It resolves any remaining issues, draws lessons from the effort, and resumes sensing.

Reflection: What's Your Experience with Design?

◇ *Think about a recent organization change effort you were involved in. Did it involve all five of the components? Were any missing? Did this hurt the effort?*

◇ *Have you used each of the ten deliverables in your work, perhaps under different names? How did your application differ from what's here?*

Part II: Syngineering Framework

Part II welds the eight fundamental concepts in Chapters 1 and 2 into an integrated framework. We have used it across numerous industries and companies and offer it for you to use in your work. There are five chapters. Chapter 3 helps get you started Applying Syngineering and shows how to choose the right approach for your culture. Chapters 4, 5, 6, and 7 describe the approaches for building agile capabilities into Directive, Participative, Flexible, and Adaptive cultures. The cases in Part III adapt these approaches to move from one culture to another.

Chapter 3: Applying Syngineering

This chapter has four sections. The first provides guidance on how to Start with Sensing, especially in traditional hierarchies, and offers tools for assessing the organization's needs. The second section helps Fit the Approach to the Culture. The third section describes in detail how Change Management Is Built-In to each of the four Syngineering approaches. The fourth section emphasizes the importance of Developing Agile Capabilities in yourselves and those around you, your work groups, and the organization's networks to build in agility.

Start with Sensing

Learning Agility

Some 70% of organizations are still traditional
hierarchies, so in introducing agility, you are likely starting in a non-agile Directive culture. Sensing is the place to start. Hierarchies rarely foster the experimentation, testing, collaboration, and learning that characterizes agility, but Sensing is a logical, engaging, and non-threatening practice that builds on the strategic reviews that effective leaders have always conducted. It introduces the agile capability of

shared leadership to bring together multiple perspectives and systematizing the process to build a common view of reality. Using collective and collaborative tools in a safe psychological space provides Directive leaders new skills to address surface political dynamics. This section builds on the Chapter 1 section Continuous Sensing.

Engage the sponsors. Building in agility takes substantial leadership. No matter how issues surface, in a hierarchical culture it is almost always one or more senior executives that initiate action. These are the sponsors or champions. They have the authority to get things done and are most likely the people who involved you. You can help them learn agility, agree on their roles, and articulate their commitment. Review the Chapter 1 concepts of Agility, Sense, Involve, and Resolve. Work through the Chapter 2 concepts of Landscape, Culture, Strategy, and Agile Organization Design (Mobilize, Frame, and Customize). Provide a safe space for them to learn, challenge, practice, and support.

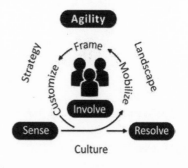

Enlist a coalition. Most change efforts ultimately involve most senior executives. Sensing can gain their trust with data-driven information compiled with strategic intent and delivered with non-confrontational candor. Support the sponsors in engaging their peers and managing upwards to get their efforts sanctioned. Keep them close to the effort, with frequent interactions that forge a close partnership. This is an iterative process that socializes the concept of shared leadership.

Gather Information

The next step is to work with executives to broaden involvement by identifying cross-functional groups with formal accountability for sensing. These groups incorporate the lessons from the Continuous Sensing section in Chapter 1 and start work. They should be encouraged to informally network with each other and the executives. They invite in experts who can see the entire industry, where it's been, where it is, and where it's headed. With them they develop a vision of how good things could be, desired solutions and/or outcomes.

These groups charged with sensing involve as many others as needed: functions, product lines, customers, and so on. Together they discern what information would be most useful. This has changed dramatically in recent years. The focus used to be on what data you have, what it tells you, and how to use it to make specific decisions. 'Advanced analytics' turns that around and works the other way. What strategic problems must be solved? What critical decisions must be made to do that? What insights would clarify those decisions? What information would produce those insights? What data would provide this information?

This starts with feelings and intuitions to develop hypotheses and alternatives. These are tested and winnowed down to a manageable set. The sensing staff then customize and implement processes that collect this data to surface tensions around customers and their relationships and identify pain points in the system.

Assess the Issues

Here agility fully shows up as executives meet with those doing the sensing and use design thinking to look beyond the data to the patterns beneath. This is highly iterative and follows this logic:

◇ Assess Performance: Organizations look to agile methodology because of current or anticipated performance shortfalls. Are these financial, or customer satisfaction, or internal process measures? These answers help decide whether to move forward and the scope of the effort.

◇ Assess Strategy: Senior leaders examine strategy in detail: products and services, customers and markets, distribution channels, revenue streams, and strategic objectives and targets. Are the performance shortfalls related to inadequacies in the strategy? If so, leadership needs to review and revise the strategy first.

◇ Assess Culture vs. Strategy Fit: If performance is inadequate yet strategy seems fine, the next stop is culture. Those involved often convene a wider sampling of employees for this. How is work done, how are decisions made, and how are activities coordinated? How do people behave? Does the culture support the strategy? The list below has some key features that support each strategy. Does the culture need to change?

Operational Excellence

○ Uses standard processes and controls to minimize cost.

○ Broad participation of experts focusing on driving out waste.

○ Decision-making accommodates the needed breadth of expertise.

○ Likely to institute activities such as Lean, Kaizen or Six Sigma.

Product Leadership

○ Emphasizes processes that develop new and unique products.

○ Fosters, enables, and rewards creativity and innovation

○ People with radically different skills collaborate in creative ways.

○ Heavy focus on research and development and innovation.

Customer Segmentation

○ Tailors products and services to a specific segment of the market.

○ Deep expertise in customer relationships and their needs

○ Customer-facing staff tightly linked to product/service providers.

○ Multitude of customer or user experience activities.

◇ Assess Culture vs. Landscape Fit: Have the executives and staff review the Corporate Culture section of Chapter 2. Where do they place the organization's culture? How is it trending over time? How well does it match the landscape? Has the landscape changed but the culture still reflects the needs of the previous landscape? If so, to what extent does this explain the performance shortfalls?

◇ Assess the Components: If the strategy is robust and the culture fits the strategy and landscape, then performance shortfalls must stem from one or more misalignments in the organization components. The details will be explored during Mobilize, but it is often helpful in Sense to walk through the components and fashion a high-level or macro-diagnostic of what significant issues need addressing.

Decide to Act

The accountable leaders now carefully consider whether the shortfalls in performance are severe enough to justify taking action. Do they need to revise strategy? Change the culture? Redesign the components?

Fit the Approach to the Culture

Syngineering builds in agility through the ten deliverables described in Chapter 2. The agile versions of each of the four common corporate cultures have a preferred operating style, which lead them to undertake these ten deliverables in quite different ways. This results in four approaches within the Syngineering framework, each of which can be further tailored based on the specifics of landscape and strategy. The approaches in Chapters 4, 5, 6, and 7 focus on building agile Directive, Participative, Flexible, and Adaptive cultures, respectively. The scenarios below are typical for the four approaches.

Building Agility into a Directive Culture

In this culture, senior executives typically start by initiating continuous sensing, then mobilizing a centrally managed project. The pivotal shift here is agreeing on a design team to look at the organization systemically to build in agility. The project follows the five stages and ten deliverables in a sequential but iterative order. They move from one deliverable to the next, developing recommendations on behalf of the hierarchy. The icon for this approach is a simple hierarchy with multiple employees symbolizing the increased involvement. Chapter 4 describes this approach. All three of the companies in our case studies in Chapters 8, 9, and 10 started with a Directive culture and undertook a traditional change project.

Building Agility into a Participative Culture

This culture starts with sensing, as with Directive, but leaders and staff must also learn about how agility reinforces group process, which is the predominant mechanism used in this approach. The central focus is the use of large staff conferences, as symbolized by the icon, to broaden involvement beyond the senior executives and leaders. This builds in agility through the five stages and ten  deliverables in a sequential but iterative order. Decision-making is explicit and shared as the conferences develop recommendations and demonstrate the power of group process to develop robust solutions. Chapter 5 describes this approach in detail.

Building Agility into a Flexible Culture

This approach departs from the linear sequence of deliverables and incorporates design thinking into prototyping workshops. The key focus is for executives early on to commit to implement workshop outcomes. The workshops convene a cross-section of staff who understand the work to prototype new ways of working. The icon symbolizes the diffusion of the prototype to staff who were not at the workshops. Chapter 6 describes this approach in detail.

Building Agility into an Adaptive Culture

There are few truly Adaptive cultures today and those few tend to have many if not all of the capabilities we associate with agility. It typically centers around self-managed, cross-functional, interlocking teams, frequently called circles or squads, symbolized in the icon. Each circle has transparent and rigorous accountabilities to their customers. Circles are networked together, with clear accountabilities for responding to changing conditions. Chapter 7 describes how change happens organically in this culture, but we provide it more as an end-member for changing from another culture, as discussed in the next paragraph.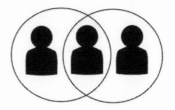

Roadmaps for the Four Approaches

Each approach has a generalized roadmap. These are described in detail in Chapters 4, 5, 6, and 7, but the table below compares them. Directive cultures address the ten deliverables explicitly in sequence, as numbered. Participative, Flexible, and Adaptive cultures do much the same work, but in different ways and sequences. The numbers in brackets indicate where there is a corresponding deliverable. Flexible and Adaptive cultures integrate the activities more holistically, as can be seen by the increased amount of white space in their roadmaps.

Directive	Participative	Flexible	Adaptive
Begin to Sense	**Begin to Sense**	**Begin to Sense**	**Begin to Sense**
◇ Learn Agility	◇ Learn Agility	◇ Learn Agility	◇ Learn Agility
◇ Information	◇ Information	◇ Information	◇ Information
◇ Assess Issues	◇ Assess Issues	◇ Assess Issues	◇ Assess Issues
◇ Decision to Act	◇ Decision to Act	◇ Decision to Act	◇ Decision to Act
Mobilize Phase	**Mobilize Confer.**	**Prepare**	**Take Action**
1. Charter, Plan, and Resource	I. Prepare and Introduce [1]	◇ List Actions [1]	◇ Resource [1]
2. Strategy	II. Strategy [2]	◇ Arrange [1]	◇ Plan [1]
3. Diagnosis	III. Diagnose [3]	◇ Socialize	◇ Strategy [2]
◇ Decide Culture	IV. Decide Culture & Approve	**Prototyping**	**Change Circle**
◇ Approve	V. Plan & Engage	I. Introductions	◇ Sense Gaps [3]
◇ Announce		II. Inspiration [3]	◇ Core Work [4]
Frame Phase	**Frame Conference**	III. Aspirations [2]	◇ Oper. Model [5]
4. Core Work	I. Prep & Intro	IV. Operating Mod. Prototype [4-5]	**Task Circles**
5. Oper. Model	II. Core Work [4]	V. List Actions [6]	[via linked circles]
6. Deploy Plan	III. Oper. Mod. [5]	**Operationalize**	◇ Roles [7] and Structure [8]
◇ Approve	IV. Deployment [6]	[in Business Units]	◇ Systems [9]
◇ Engage	V. Plan & Engage	◇ Roles/Acct. [7]	◇ Adjust [10]
Customize Phase	**Customize**	◇ Structure [8]	◇ Resume Sense
◇ Deploy Detail	◇ Deploy Detail	◇ Systems [9]	
7. Roles/Acct.	◇ Roles/Acct. [7]	**30-Day Iterations**	
8. Structure	◇ Structure [8]	◇ Adjust [10]	
9. Systems	◇ Systems [9]	◇ Resume Sense	
◇ Engage	◇ Conference		
◇ Approve	**Resolve**		
Resolve Phase	◇ Adjust [10]		
10. Adjust	◇ Conference		
◇ Resume Sense	◇ Resume Sense		

Changing Culture

When the culture does not fit the strategy or landscape, the culture needs to shift. The organization then faces a huge decision, perhaps the single most important one in Syngineering. The education process needs to extend past agility and focus also on the need for culture change, what the new culture will look like, and the approach that will best transition from the current culture to the new one. This must be an informed decision. If the choice is not yet clear, we suggest they follow the Directive approach, and defer culture change to the major decision point at the end of Mobilize.

When shifting culture, the organization needs to begin with the approach best suited to the current culture, most often Directive, and over time introduce and employ the practices of the new culture.

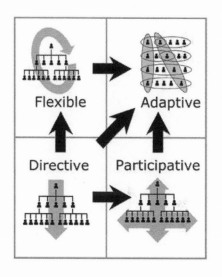

When moving to a Participative culture, the transition occurs early in the process and conferences are used in Mobilize to broaden involvement. The Wilderness case study in Chapter 10 illustrates this shift.

When moving to a Flexible culture, the transition also occurs early, and a prototyping workshop brings together the needed informed workers. The Comfort Home case study in Chapter 9 shows how three Directive organizations shifted to a networked Flexible network.

Moving to the Adaptive culture requires substantial behavior change and organization adjustments so the transition is often deferred until Customize, when the shape of the new organization is clear. The Stratos case study in Chapter 8 is an excellent example of how this shift occurs in an actual organization.

Change Management Is Built In

Change Management Models

As we were applying Syngineering in one of our projects, the client asked, "Where is change management?" Not satisfied with our answer that it is built in, they insisted on separate deliverables for charter and project, communications, change management, and engagement plans! In the end, we helped them develop a single comprehensive timeline and plan with separate columns for project team activities, formal leadership communications, leadership engagement with staff, and informal change management activities. This led us to include this section to articulate exactly how we built it in.

We have used a myriad of change management models in our practice. We have been inspired by three in particular. We used the principles behind Kotter's 8-step change model as a basis for our approaches. The powerful yet simple description of how people experience change in Bridges' Transitions Model fits nicely into the agile cultures we advocate. Prosci's ADKAR Model offers five building blocks essential for individuals to change and we find many of their tools and templates useful in applying Syngineering at a tactical level.

It is not our purpose here to detail or advocate for these three or any other models, but between them they encapsulate what we think are the important facets of good change management. The paragraphs that follow illustrate how these facets are integral to Syngineering.

John Kotter's 8-Step Change Model

For the Directive and Participative cultures these steps are integral to the deliverables or discrete entries in the roadmaps above. In Flexible and Adaptive cultures, they are organic to the way that prototyping and circle activities are conducted.

Step 1 is to establish a sense of urgency. This happens in our Sense stage, as it examines market and competitive realities to identify current or potential crises and opportunities, and captures results in Deliverable 1: Charter | Case for Change.

Step 2 is to create a guiding coalition, the leaders we call sponsors, those with the power to make the changes. We identify them in Deliverable 1: Charter | Resource and Involve and collaborate with them throughout the process.

Step 3 is to develop a compelling vision of an attainable future and realistic strategies for achieving that vision. This is the focus of Deliverable 2: Strategy, although it is done in very different ways in different cultures.

Step 4 is to communicate the change vision, with the guiding coalition role modeling desired behaviors. Directive cultures have their leaders announce and engage. Participative ones use leaders and conference participants and Flexible ones use leaders and workshop attendees. In Adaptive, the circles manage this.

Step 5 is to remove obstacles, systems, or structures that undermine the vision, and encourage experimentation. The heart of our approaches for each culture is the activities to design structures and systems. The heavy use of pilots and prototypes exemplifies this experimentation.

Step 6 is to generate short-term wins and recognize and reward those who produce them. This step is the focus of Directive and Participative engagement activities, especially the use of pilots and prototypes. In Flexible and Adaptive cultures, the prototypes generated will naturally gain visibility as changes diffuse across the organization.

Step 7 is to consolidate gains and produce more change by completing the systems and structure changes in Step 5 and initiating additional projects as needed. The activities in our Resolve stage drive this step.

Step 8 is to anchor the new culture through customer and productivity focused behaviors and leadership. This is the essence of building in agility with Syngineering.

William Bridges' Transitions Model

Transitions describe the psychological processes people go through in working through the Endings of the old, the messiness of the Neutral Zone, and the promise of the new Beginnings.

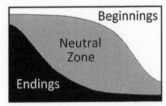

Endings: Here people process what they will keep, what they are leaving behind, and learn how to manage these losses. These include relationships, processes, locations, and team members. The Involve aspect of Syngineering provides psychological safety for employees to understand and test the changes.

Neutral Zone: This messy step is the time between the old reality and sense of identity and the new one. People are creating new processes and learning their new roles, but things are in flux and do not feel comfortable yet. It is the seedbed of the new beginnings. Psychological safety gives employees the space to shape their own situations.

New Beginnings: These new understandings, new values and new attitudes are marked by a release of energy in a new direction, the expression of a fresh identity. The Involve aspect of Syngineering provides psychological safety and effective team functioning for employees to accommodate.

Prosci's ADKAR Model

These five building blocks describe how individuals respond to change.

Awareness is the first step and involves providing answers to these key questions: What is the change? How does it align with the organization's vision? Why is it being made? What are the risks of not changing? How will the change affect us? What is in it for us? These questions form the basis of our Deliverable 1: Charter and each culture's initial statements.

Desire is people choosing to support and participate in the change. It depends on the nature of the change and individual situations but can be fostered through effective sponsorship, risk mitigation, involved employees, and incentives systems that support the change. These are built into Deliverable 1: Charter, Deliverable 3: Diagnosis, and Deliverable 9: Systems. The use of group process and shared leadership significantly increase Desire.

Knowledge provides information about processes, tools, behaviors, systems, job roles and techniques that employees must possess to implement the change in their area. Any gaps must be remedied with effective training programs, job aides to help learn new processes, coaching and mentoring as needed, and forums or networks to share problems and best practices. These are each integral to our Deliverable 10: Adjust.

Ability covers the skills, aptitudes, and resources needed to achieve the change. These can be mental (writing, verbal, science, or math skills) or physical (strength, size, manual dexterity, or eye-hand coordination). Resources needed include funds, tools, coaching, and access to subject matter experts. Syngineering provides the psychological safety for teams to realistically appraise and balance out members' skills and weaknesses. Deliverable 10: Adjust provides the opportunities to turn knowledge into skills.

Reinforcement comes from any event that strengthens and sustains the change. Deliverable 10: Adjust builds in accountability mechanisms that can be used for recognition, rewards, or celebrations. With shortfalls in performance made visible, the organization can take corrective action as needed.

Developing Agile Capabilities

Whether you are an internal or external consultant, a human resource professional, or a leader or manager, the purpose of Syngineering is not just about providing a change method for the immediate problem. It is also part of developing an agile organization with the capacity to sense-and-respond to changing conditions in the moment so it can adapt and change as needed. The use of collaborative teams and design thinking help you to role-model level 3 relationships in every facet of the effort.

This happens at multiple levels:

◇ Individuals must be aware of their own agility cycles and learn how to change and improve their own responsiveness.

◇ Interpersonal relationships must have the ability for people to use 'group process' to integrate diverse views into robust solutions.

◇ Groups across the enterprise must be connected in ways that foster information flows, encourage decision-making at the right levels, and exemplify true collaboration.

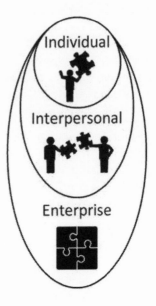

Developing Individuals: Yourself

Implicit in improving and building agility into your organization is that in the process you will grow as well. Have a clear idea of who you are now, and where you are in your own development. There are myriads of resources for assisting you with this. Learn as many change methods as you can. Attend workshops, read books on consulting, create networks of folks already doing this. Understand and know the difference in roles and skills between facilitator and content expert. Seek technical advice and wisdom from people knowledgeable about the organization's work. Get mentors who can provide emotional support and challenge you when you risk running aground.

Pay attention to your inborn preferences. Use your entire mental, emotional, spiritual, and physical 'self as instrument' to listen, discern, and intervene. Know which tools, techniques, and approaches you naturally favor. In which culture are you most comfortable? Least comfortable? Do not use methods based on your comfort or preferences if they do not work in this client's context. Serve your customer, not your comfort. To utilize Syngineering to the fullest, develop comfort in each of the four approaches.

Know when you need help. One of the
authors learned this the hard way. His
vintage Monte Carlo SS failed its emissions
inspection after passing for 15 years. As a
certified mechanic, he got the parts and the
day before the inspection due date he began
work. Sadly, the bolts were highly corroded.
For eight hours they refused to budge! A

desperate call to a practicing mechanic got the work done in two hours.
Syngineering requires similar clarity about when to solicit help.
Recognize the 'corroded bolts.' Bring in help: there may even be
unexpected benefits that come with experience. Afterwards, the Monte
Carlo's mileage jumped by seven miles per gallon: 30% improvement!

Be ready to adapt everything in the book. Our recommended activities
are general, to be adapted to your specific context. Some fit easily, but
some do not. Feel free to ignore these! Turn to your advisory network,
team, or sponsors for guidance. It is much better to ask for help than to
fail because you have not. The book is not an exhaustive encyclopedia
but a reference point, reminder checklist, and a learning guide.

Developing Interpersonal: Collaborative Work Groups

If you are in a safe organization where you can fail and receive support,
you can experiment with tools, sense when they are not working, and
adapt, all the while learning skills. If there is no room for safe
experimentation, you may instead choose to do this in your change
group, even if not a fully developed team as described in Chapter 1.

With this safety, a group of different people can look at things from a
broad range of different perspectives and pay particular attention to
what others may have ignored or missed. Rather than seeing any one
view as right or wrong, the group can
hold off any decision until they have a
variety of perspectives and have had
extensive review and reflection. If there
are anomalies, the group can continue
to be curious about them until they
make sense. This is the genius of agility.

Help these groups develop listening skills and to look beyond words, which only provide 30% of the meaning. Help them pay attention to body language, intonations, behaviors, what is actually said, how it is said, and what is not said! Help them ask the difficult questions. Whatever the responses, they will learn useful tidbits about individuals, the organization, and how things really work.

In enlisting these groups, it is important to recognize the spectrum of skills needed. Whether Directive project teams, Participative conference planning teams, Flexible prototyping workshops, or Adaptive circles, you need this diversity of thinking. Help the organization see this. There are numerous instruments available for helping individuals know their preferences, develop these preferences into skills, learn their less-developed functions, and learn to work together to blend and balance and leverage their preferences and skills in the spirit of true collaboration. Our only guidance would be to try one and not just read about it. The best way to learn is by 'doing' rather than 'knowing.'

Developing Networks across the Enterprise

Agile organizations extend the characteristics of teams to ad hoc groups and connect them together into networks. These can be recognized as part of the formal reporting structure, but as important are the three broad categories of informal networks:

◇ 'Advice' network's spokes and nodes are people and their mentors or advisors respected for their reliable and deep knowledge.

◇ 'Trust' networks link people who mutually trust each other to serve the greater good. They share their inner opinions and vulnerabilities, those they do not generally share for risk of judgment.

◇ 'Communications' networks link people to those individuals who always seem to know what is really going on. People look to these nodes to explain and rationalize official pronouncements.

Organizations that leverage these networks as a complement to the formal structure can emerge with new knowledge about why things happen the way they do, why they do what they do, why they feel the way they feel, and why they want what they want. The more the formal and informal structures work together, the easier for agile capabilities to emerge.

Reflection: Thoughts about Applying Syngineering

◇ *How well does your organization sense? Can it act as needed?*

◇ *Have you been involved delivering an agile organization? Were both organizational engineering and people synergies involved? How well did the effort resolve the initial problems? Was it agile one year later?*

◇ *Do you have a network of trusted advisors available to help? Who are they? How often do you call on them? How do they respond?*

Chapter 4: Agile Directive Approach

This chapter describes the Syngineering approach for building agility into Directive cultures. It has six sections. The first describes what the Agile Directive Culture looks like. The other five summarize how this culture uses project management to work through the stages of the agility cycle: Sense, Mobilize, Frame, Customize, and Resolve. Both Stratos in Chapter 8 and Wilderness in Chapter 10 used this approach until the decision point at the end of the Mobilize phase.

The Agile Directive Culture

The 'default' Directive culture that emerges from the Mass Production landscape has central control with delegated authority, simple work done to standard processes, unspecialized labor but a number of functional experts, work groups with formal vertical reporting in a hierarchical pyramid, and systems designed to facilitate control and reinforce individual performance.

What would it look like with agility? We talked recently about this with a national retailer. While intrigued by the possibilities, the idea of 'squads' or 'scrum teams' roaming hundreds of retail outlets sounded like pure chaos and a danger to their operational excellence strategy. We linked them up with those familiar with the Best Buy turnaround. Most people had assumed that all big-box retailers would fall under Amazon's steamroller, but Best Buy survived and thrived. How?

Senior executives began listening to rank-and-file employees. They learned about customer behaviors and preferences. They empowered teams in headquarters to experiment and pilot ideas. To combat 'showrooming,' where customers tested products in stores then bought cheaper online, they matched the online prices. They piloted a free in-home consultation program, then rolled it out nationwide. They merged online ordering with local store delivering, instantly creating 1,000+ mini warehouses. Along the way, the headquarters teams began to function much like agile scrum teams, and in-store employees began acting more like true teams. Numerous new ways of working, including 'results only work environment', helped.

Our client began to see what agility looks like and how it could work: sensing and listening to staff, customers, and suppliers, being aware of significant changes, and then quickly mobilizing teams to pilot key features before scaling up. We helped them recognize that they did not need 'product' agility, but rather 'enterprise' and 'strategic' agility.

Directive Sense Phase

In traditional Directive cultures, change efforts are typically initiated by senior executive sponsors sensing that something is not quite right with their organization's current or projected future performance. As they reach out for help in moving to agility, they work through the section Start with Sensing in Chapter 3. They often refer to these activities as 'pre-chartering' since it leads up to Deliverable 1: Charter.

This often starts with senior executive sponsors learning about Directive agility as discussed in the section above and the Directive approach from the Chapter 3 section Fit the Approach to the Culture. This is summarized by the roadmap, at right, with a centrally managed project developing the deliverables for executive review. As they ponder about Mobilize, they must realize they will not be able to put the 'genie back into the bottle' after chartering starts! The project will need to follow its course, with sensing providing critical information throughout.

Directive Roadmap

Begin to Sense
- ◇ Learn Directive Agility
- ◇ Gather Information
- ◇ Assess the Issues
- ◇ Decision to Act

Mobilize Phase
1. Charter/Plan/Resource
2. Revisit Strategy
3. Diagnosis & Criteria
- ◇ Decide on Culture
- ◇ Approve Project
- ◇ Announce Project

Frame Phase
4. Core Work
5. Operating Model
6. Deployment Plan
- ◇ Approve Oper. Model
- ◇ Engage Staff

Customize Phase
- ◇ Deployment Detail
7. Roles/Accountabilities
8. Structure
9. Support Systems
- ◇ Engage Staff
- ◇ Approve

Resolve Phase
10. Adjust
- ◇ Resume Sensing

Directive Mobilize Phase

Here the executives agree on a charter that defines the project, clarify and socialize the strategy, and diagnose the current state of the organization to focus the design priorities. Agility in this stage comes from using the conclusions from Sense to revisit strategy and diagnosis, and convening cross-functional groups, not just a few experts, to collaborate with decision-makers. A critical decision at the end of this stage is whether to move to a new culture if needed.

Deliverable 1: Project Charter

This is the place to capture, coordinate, and update important project information. As more people are involved, the charter is the touchstone that keeps everyone on the same page, most often maintained by a designated project manager. Part IV has details for each of these ingredients.

Charter Ingredients
◇ Scope
◇ Involvement
◇ Plan

Project Scope: This project manager typically works with the executive sponsors to turn the roadmap into a draft charter, starting with the first ingredient that goes into the charter, project scope, and its three elements, case for change, boundaries and givens, and goals and objectives. This iterative process is most often a case of informal conversations that continue throughout the project. Each executive will have their own perspectives on the effort and will hopefully be open to changing their views as additional information surfaces.

To broaden input into the scope, this culture increasingly turns to a new chartering tool that nicely models agility, Project Canvas. Here the project manager convenes representatives from across the affected parts of the organization to surface and validate the unique perspectives, drivers, and underlying intentions of each interested party or stake-holder. Together they paint a shared vision, much like a painter's can-vas, of the project's scope in its context within the larger system. They use this to revise the draft scope and develop shared ownership and understanding. Various software packages can facilitate this process and the visualization of the project 'at a glance' can be a powerful driver for collaboration.

Executives discuss the draft scope, often in a formal review. The case for change establishes the opportunity and urgency. If the boundaries and givens discussions surface non-negotiable issues or givens, especially around strategy or behavior, openly discussing these can enable sponsors and the project to work together with integrity. Sponsors should be clear on the intensity of their involvement. Desiring close involvement can be an early signal that the sponsors are serious about agility. It can also avoid huge formal decision-gate reviews at the end of each stage. The scope as reviewed will not yet be a complete charter. Resourcing will likely just be a list of suggestions, and the project plan little more than the roadmap with times and accountable parties listed. However, this is enough for the executives to understand what will be required so they can approve starting up the project.

Involvement: The first element in this ingredient, Syngineering approach, will initially be the Directive approach in this chapter. The project manager together with the sponsors handles the second element, resources and staffing. They establish who will steer the effort and name a project team, often simply called the 'design team.' In this culture, it is important to initiate this team officially. This can be as informal as a series of ad hoc virtual conversations with the sponsor and project manager or as formal as a several-day workshop. It can be an iterative process using smaller group discussions, but at some point, everyone needs to agree on the plans and how the team will function. Face-to-face sessions can help team members get to know each other and be an ideal laboratory to work on team dynamics.

The third element, engagement needs, is often the first agenda item of substance for the design team working together. This session can be a useful platform for introducing some of the effective teaming suggestions from Chapter 1 as they discuss how to use focus groups, informal discussion, or staff conferences to engage key stakeholders.

Plan the Project: This ingredient is often the second major agenda item for the design team. They develop the first element, risk analysis, and identify any mitigation needed. They then turn to the second element, the communications plan. Even the most hierarchical organizations need broad-based staff support to build in agility. They must hear formal announcements directly from sponsors to assure its legitimacy. These alone are not enough. Leaders need to engage staff directly and informal communications need to span all three levels: senior executives, middle managers and supervisors, and front-line employees, because each sees a different reality of the organization. A communication feedback loop needs to be set up involving staff, customers, and any other stakeholders.

Communications must reflect agile behaviors and values as people consciously and subconsciously notice all sorts of subtle cues. The design team needs to address it as a group because they are tied into informal information, advice and trust networks, which transmit the messages that people rely on above and beyond the formal communication. A communications person or team can help package key messages and interpret feedback for the design team and through informal meetings may have access to feedback not available to others on the design team.

The design team maps out a multi-pronged campaign in the third element, integrated plan. The Project Canvas approach mentioned above can be a good way to do this and identify natural streams or chunks of work that can be assigned to teams or individuals. These can then be the basis for detailed plans that include deadlines, dependencies, staffing and funding needs. Based on this, the design team should carefully review and revise the charter and seek leadership approval if needed for any substantive changes.

Deliverable 2: Strategy

This deliverable builds on concepts in Chapter 2 to review and possibly revise the strategy. It may be done by leadership, before, in parallel with, or together with the design team. Part IV has details of these ingredients.

Strategy Ingredients
◇ Core Business
◇ Landscape
◇ Revised Strategy

Core Business: The design team begins or continues collaboration with the groups the executives identified to sense in the 'pre-chartering.' Together they compile the four elements of the organization's core business: the purpose or reason it exists, its values, the existing critical capabilities or competencies, and its key assets. Since these are rarely reviewed on any sort of regular basis, this may be unfamiliar territory, and often highly enlightening for the design team.

Landscape: The design team and those handling sensing continue working and deepen the landscape scan from Sense. They use formal documents, informal focus groups, staff surveys, competitive analyses, and anything else available, including ideally customer input, to develop the four elements of landscape: technology trends, markets and customers, competitors, and regulatory and government. They use this information on business landscape and its trajectory as input to revising strategy and deciding on culture.

Revised Strategy: This explores the elements of products and services, customer value proposition, strategic goals and objectives, and how these shape organizational characteristics. This can be more difficult than it sounds as these are not always found in formal documents. The design team continues with the sensing, strategy, and planning groups to analyze documents, informal understandings, even in some cases inferences from patterns of decisions and actions.

If the 'pre-charter' assessment suggested that strategy was inadequate, this also includes revising it. The design team and the groups doing sensing take what they've learned and develop recommendations for executive review: Can executives articulate the core business and current strategy? Do they use it in decision making and resource allocation? Do they recognize the landscape? Do they agree with the strategy analysis and recommendations for revising? Where this is confidential, sessions may be limited to the project manager, and a few strategy experts. After executives decide on the recommendations, the design team and 'sensing groups can refine.

It is critical in this culture that senior executives now announce the validated strategy and engage staff in two-way communications. They may use e-mails, town halls, and/or cascaded workgroup meetings. The strategy will be exciting for some employees and threatening to others. Executives need to communicate everything that can be, while acknowledging what can't. This should use the feedback loops that have been set up to gather information and attend to rumors before they get out of control and damage morale and productivity. The design team will need to build up the capability and capacity of the leaders to support their staff and effectively address significant concerns, starting with their own!

Deliverable 3: Diagnosis

This diagnoses gaps between the current state and what will be needed for the revised strategy. It also establishes decision criteria for the design process. The design team manages this using some or all of the ingredients in the sidebar. Part IV has detailed descriptions.

Diagnose Ingredients
◇ Information
◇ Synthesis
◇ Change Readiness
◇ Decision Criteria

Information: The design team considers the size and traditions of the organization to design the process, the first element. They might convene focus groups of experts and representative staff, or use broad-based questionnaires, or interview selected leaders and individuals to gather information, or use themselves as a focus-group, or some combination. An especially agile way to do this is mini-conferences with 50 to 100 workers of varying levels of expertise, much like the Participative culture uses. This dramatically increases the amount of engagement, quantity and quality of information available, and receptiveness of staff to the resulting findings. The key to preserving the Directive culture is to involve the executives. While it may seem risky, it can reinforce agility's collaborative working even as it clarifies leadership thinking. The remaining seven elements gather the information on leadership, work, people, structure, and systems as well as awareness of strategy and culture.

Synthesis: The design team synthesizes this information into an honest, objective, and concrete assessment of what needs to change. They typically use these elements: issues, themes, levers, root causes, and priorities. A key focus needs to be assessing whether either strategy or landscape have changed enough to warrant changing culture. This should be done before revising the operating model and deployment plan in Frame since they depend heavily on the desired culture.

Change Readiness: The design team manages this, often with focus groups to explore the readiness of the organization to make the changes identified in diagnosis. They use the elements: change history, effort priority, and organizational factors. The focus groups can be the same as those in the diagnosis, but often benefits from broader representation.

Decision Criteria: Design criteria guide the entire project and enable key decisions. The design team either on their own or with a few additional experts work through the elements in Part IV: Component Requirements and Strategic Considerations. They finish the diagnosis deliverable by revisiting the project plan and making any changes required by the revised strategy and diagnosis.

Decide on Culture

This is a major decision point and the design team collaborates with the executive sponsors in a meeting or series of meetings. They review Deliverable 3: Diagnosis and update conclusions from Sense. If culture change is indicated, they review the approach in the appropriate chapter - 5, 6, or 7 - especially the learning and education required to function in that culture. Where executives are fully informed and ready to transition from the Directive approach to one of the other three, they typically move directly to the Sense stage in the relevant chapter.

Wilderness in Chapter 10 at this point concluded that they needed to shift to a more Participative culture and began planning a Mobilize conference. The leadership of Stratos in Chapter 8 agreed on the need for an Adaptive culture but chose to also hold a Mobilize conference as a way of broadening involvement and easing into Adaptive.

Approve Project

If the culture will remain Directive, the design team reviews with executives the updated project plan. Do they find the design team representative, functioning well, and credible? Is the updated plan reasonable, with adequate resources? Is engagement underway with two-way information flow? Are they ready to move forward? If not, should they just pull the plug if the project no longer makes sense? You will have substantial insights from the chartering, planning, and executive reviews to help them assess this. It is sometimes better for the project manager, the executives, and you to make this decision without the design team.

Announce Project

Once the decision is taken, formal communication needs to signal this. A combination of announcements, large town halls, and small group meetings cascaded downwards is ideal and should prominently feature the strategy, diagnosis, decision criteria, and updated plan, and solicit feedback and suggestions to gain perspectives and insights from those in the organization who will have to implement the changes. At this point the feedback loops established earlier will be important in surfacing rumors and concerns. They can be used to acknowledge the challenges ahead, focus on the opportunities, and test to see if the executives are committed.

Directive Frame Phase

Frame outlines the organization's core work, fashions an operating model around it, and maps out a deployment plan for broader involvement to Customize the solutions. You are staying with the Directive culture, so the design team continues to convene agile cross-functional groups to provide information for decision-makers.

Deliverable 4: Core Work

The first deliverable in configuring the organization is to identify the actual work required by that strategy. The design team works through the ingredients in the sidebar and their elements as detailed in Part IV. The design team keeps executives briefed during this deliverable, just not via formal review and approval.

Core Work Ingredients
◇ Key Technologies
◇ Value Chain
◇ Workflows

Key Technologies: New and disruptive technologies can completely transform the nature of an organization's business and work. Because of this the key technologies must precede any reviews of the work involved. The communications on strategy, diagnosis, and updated plans will trigger tremendous interest across the organization. The design team uses this to convene focus groups or mini-conferences of selected staff to explore the key tech-  nology elements: product and service innovations, operational, and customer focus technologies. While the strategy may mention or mandate specific technologies, this opens the opportunity for more diverse inputs.

Value Chain: This links the organization's strategic inputs through the various steps, which add value, to the finished products. The design team builds a high-level picture of the core work, using the elements of customer outputs,  advantage work, enabling work, and hand-offs and inputs from Part IV.

Workflows: Using the value chain as a guide, the design team enlist select work groups to map out more detailed descriptions of the workflows for the macro processes that have been identified. They use the Part IV elements: process descriptions, capabilities and functions, and flows between processes. Even when workflow is not an issue, this can help clarify the business for everyone. This needs enough detail to inform the operating model discussions, but no more. Deep process mapping, if needed, can wait for Customize.

Deliverable 5: Operating Model

Your operating model is a high-level description of how your organization is configured to achieve your strategy. The adoption of a new or revised operating model is perhaps the largest single change that this culture can make. For this reason, the senior executives must be fully engaged in its development. The

Oper. Mod. Ingredients
◇ Org. Components
◇ Structure Options
◇ Option Selection

design team manages the process and engages the executives using some or all of the ingredients in the sidebar and their elements as detailed in Part IV.

Organization Components: These summarize at high level how leadership, core work processes, people skills and numbers, and support systems combine to produce and deliver products and services. Here the design team compiles and reviews the components they have already developed from the Sense discussions and the first four deliverables.

Structure Options: There is no perfect structure; each has advantages and disadvantages, benefits and challenges. It is important to compare a number of different alternatives. This is typically done collaboratively by the executives and design team with selected others. They use the component descriptions from the previous paragraph to develop various realistic structure options. The elements here, as detailed in Part IV, keep each option close to the strategy. Each starts by grouping the advantage work, arranges the remaining work around this, and finishes with high-level coordination mechanisms.

Option Selection: With all this in mind, the design team and executives work through the two elements of this ingredient. They first prioritize the decision criteria, and then compare options and select or revise the operating model. This then needs to be almost immediately communicated to the wider organization. This reduces unnecessary anxiety and associated productivity dips. This needn't include much depth since the key details will be developed during Customize.

An innovative way to do all of this deliverable is to pull together the workers that have the needed knowledge and lead them through a prototyping workshop, described more fully in the Flexible approach in Chapter 6. The Directive culture can be honored by having executives review and approve the prototypes and the associated deployment plan. Substantial effort is saved by going with a prototype instead of exhaustively analyzing and selecting an operating model. Additional savings come as work groups begin implementation even as they fill in the details required in Customize. Ideally the executives and those who have been involved in prototyping engage staff together to highlight and legitimize the design thinking involved.

Deliverable 6: Deployment

The deployment plan defines how the operating units and functions will engage on and customize the operating model. The design team navigates the ingredients in the sidebar to outline these plans, as detailed in Part IV.

Deployment Ingredients
◇ Initiatives
◇ Change Impacts
◇ Deployment Method
◇ Accountabilities

Initiatives: The first element is a list of changes, everything that will change with the adoption of the new or revised operating model. They work through the five components and itemize what they come up with. The second element is to group these itemized changes into a few broad initiatives that will actually implement the changes. The groupings most often fall along functional, business unit, or product lines. The final element is to prioritize the initiatives. The Stratos and Wilderness case studies provide good examples of how to do this, and there are several more in Part IV.

Change Impacts: The design team next work with the appropriate function, business unit, and/or product line to convene focus groups, which compile information on their stakeholders and explore the resulting impacts from the changes. These should include substantial cross-functional representation for completeness in considering deployment approaches in the next step.

Deployment Method: The design team considers all this input as they select a procedure for deploying the operating model, identify the groups involved, and plan the engagement with local work units. As shown in the table in Part IV, Directive cultures traditionally cascade it down through business unit, functional, and/or product line leadership who commission local teams to provide content expertise in Customize.

A variation, if just a few groups are intensely affected, is to initiate focused cross-functional initiative workstreams. Another variation is to undertake small-scale pilots to help judge whether your design can be scaled up to the entire organization. Multiple pilots running at the same time can give opportunities to test a number of different designs. If the operating model has been developed as a prototype, deployment will most naturally look like the Flexible operationalizing in Chapter 6.

The design team informally stays in touch with executives and focus group attendees and may even reach out to customers or their representatives to sharpen their design. This is the essence of agility, allowing rapid feedback and modification.

Accountabilities: The design team works with business unit, functional, and product line leadership to codify deployment by identifying accountabilities. Which groups are involved in which initiatives? Who takes the lead? What are they expected to do?

Approve Operating Model

Executives have been closely involved in developing the operating model, so the need now is to formally review and approve moving ahead with Customize. Is the plan for deployment realistic? Does it cover the key changes needed? Are the priorities right? Is it consistent with the culture and does it take advantage of its strengths? Do the executives understand their roles in it? Have broad segments of staff been involved in providing input?

Engage Staff

Formal communication of these via announcements and town halls are a start, but engagement around deployment must be cascaded and owned all the way down the hierarchy. The Customization phase will deploy the operating model to all work groups, who customize and implement it. All staff who will be involved need to know what's changing and their role in it. The key is to solidify the new operating model as a high-level frame and the 'big rules' for the lines of business and the functional units to do their detailed design work against.

Directive Customize Phase

This begins concrete and systemic change. The focus shifts from executives and the design team working at high levels to the managers and staff of the operating units and functions defining the day-to-day roles and accountabilities, reporting structure, and supporting systems.

Detailed Deployment Plan

At this point the design team has typically completed its design work, and transitions into a coordination team. It may retain some members to ensure continuity and add members to fill missing needed skills. This team ensures that processes spanning multiple units are coordinated. Their first activity is to help operating units and functions use the high-level deployment plan to map out detailed plans.

Deliverable 7: Roles and Accountabilities

This deliverable hammers out the nitty-gritty details that translate the work required by the operating model into a staffing model. The ingredients in the sidebar are most often handled by business unit, functional, and/or product line teams using some or all of the elements in Part IV.

Role Ingredients
◇ Technology
◇ Process Details
◇ Roles Needed
◇ Skills & Numbers

Technology: Staff from the operating units and functions validate from Deliverable 4 the key technology requirements in their sphere of work. They then identify any supporting technologies needed to support other aspects of the work. Examples are enhanced IT security systems, enterprise-wide databases, and innovative technical systems not directly related to the core business. The staff working on this track the components affected by these supporting technologies: leadership, work, people, structure, and systems.

Process Details: The function and business unit staff then describe the business processes with these three elements: tasks and activities cover the work to be performed, required skills define what are needed to do the work, and flow details link these into integrated workflows. This shouldn't be overly complicated. Involving the people closest to the work will keep things fit for purpose and avoid exhaustive detail. In fact, the critical outcomes of this step are the key tasks, skills, interfaces, and hand-offs.

Roles Needed: The function and business unit staff work through the three elements. The first is to define roles by grouping together similar tasks that require the same capabilities. The second is to define their accountabilities, what needs to happen for a role to complete its tasks. These include responsibilities, key outputs, delegated authorities that facilitate shared leadership, collaborative behaviors, and important relationships. The third is to look for role efficiencies through the use of technology, outsourcing, or elimination of work no longer needed.

Skills and Numbers: The coordination team works with the operating units and functions on the three elements: a complete list of the full range of roles and the specific skills required, benchmarking to establish a basis for estimating numbers, and then final numbers.

Finally, the design team updates the communications plan and begins quickly getting the word out. In Directive cultures information vacuums get filled by gossip, rumor, and innuendo. It can be especially encouraging for people to hear that staff reductions will be handled via reassignment, retraining, and/or reasonable severance packages.

Deliverable 8: Structure

The Operating Model, Deliverable 5, defined the high level of reporting structure. Here you set operating unit and function internal structures and cross-functional coordination, using the ingredients in the sidebar, which have detailed elements in Part IV.

Structure Ingredients
◇ Unit Staffing
◇ Final Grouping
◇ Coordination

Unit Staffing: Using the list of all roles, accountabilities, and numbers, the functions and operating units staff their work units. The operating model provides a general scheme of organizing, and the number of levels in the organization. Units are generally well-defined for the core work units and support functions like HR and finance. The coordination team starts from these and works with the operating units and functions. This can be messy and iterative. The elements in this ingredient first define the mandate of each work unit, then populate the units with the roles from the prior deliverable, then determine the best size for each unit, and finally evaluate and test the resulting units.

Final Grouping: Operating units and functions now draft a picture of how each will structure themselves. These must fit seamlessly into the operating model. All key interfaces with internal and external stakeholders, especially customers, must be adequately addressed. The work units collected together at each level should fit easily into the unit accountabilities at the next highest level. Part IV offers two elements that help with this: Organization Map and Grouping Evaluation.

Coordination: The coordination team leads development of vehicles for sharing information and coordinating business activities across business units and functions. The three elements are: identify critical interfaces, define the type of coordination needed, and select a coordination solution. These solutions can reinforce collaborative behaviors and can serve to mitigate some of the negative consequences of the silos often built into this culture's reporting structure choices.

Deliverable 9: Support Systems

In parallel with the above deliverables, the functions are reworking the supporting systems, which can be critical in anchoring agility. These are often one or more of the identified initiatives, led by the appropriate function using cross-functional teams with

Systems Ingredients
◇ Management
◇ Financial
◇ HR and People

operating unit representatives. The coordination team helps the functions list the requirements for these systems from the work so far.

One alternative to design supporting systems is using prototyping workshops as described in the Flexible approach in Chapter 6. A less radical approach is to pilot key changes in a few work groups and then scale up once they are proven to work. Pilots are often welcome in business units frustrated with the status quo and thereby willing to try out and experiment with the new designs.

The coordination team and executives are closely involved in the pilots or prototypes, experimenting and taking corrective actions as indicated. Senior executives can further role-model agility by granting the functions and their design teams substantial latitude in scaling these experiments up to the entire enterprise. One common fail-safe feature is to have briefings in normal leadership meetings where implementation can be discussed and halted if necessary.

Management Systems: While in this culture these systems help the hierarchy control operations, numerous adjustments can facilitate agility. Strategic planning can be shifted from periodic reviews to continuous sensing and analysis. Reporting and reviews, which typically focus on quantitative aspects, can add entries that harvest and summarize staff and customer feedback.

Financial Systems: Electronic data systems and analytics can easily provide real-time monitoring and support the continuous sensing of the management systems.

HR Systems: The performance management system and its metrics and goals heavily influence behaviors. Employees are sensitive to how rewards are handed out and how to 'get ahead.' Modifications can be made to reward more listening, collaboration, and team behaviors. Training and leadership development programs can reinforce the same agile characteristics. While retaining their role as agents of the hierarchy, HR can become more aware of patterns in employee conversations and concerns.

Engage Staff

The Customize phase can involve substantial iteration, piloting, and experimenting. The higher the degree of authentic engagement across functions, operating units, and product lines, the more this phase can exponentially accelerate implementation of the new operating model. Communications and staff engagement continue, even as the effort shifts to Resolve, but mostly from within the operating units and functions and their work groups.

Approve

The deliverable outputs are reviewed and shaped by senior executives in partnership with functional and operating unit leaders and key staff, and the coordination team. This may be done in one big review at the end of Customize, but it exemplifies more agility for the senior leaders to stay in closer touch and give notional agreement as structure features are recommended. In any case, it is useful to ask: Have broad segments of staff been involved in the design work? Do these designs fit seamlessly and support the chosen strategy? Do emerging behaviors and ways of working show agility? Is there commitment to follow through and complete the change?

Directive Resolve Phase

Resolve completes implementation of the new operating model and smoothly transitions to the new organization and ways of working. Executives and coordination team focus on closing out the project and returning to agile scanning as soon as practical.

Deliverable 10: Adjust

The focus shifts from designing and testing to institutionalizing the results. Each of the initiatives and design efforts converge. Staff involvement broadens to literally everyone as they live the new design. The ingredients in the sidebar are typical. This deliverable often takes

Adjust Ingredients
◇ New Accountabilities
◇ New Operating Model
◇ Emerging Issues
◇ Effort Close

greater effort than earlier ones as the design changes are actually adopted. It's potentially the messiest, especially when there are significant changes in roles, accountabilities, and reporting lines.

New Accountabilities: In this ingredient everyone learns the new individual accountabilities and unit mandates and make sure they have the skills to deliver on them. This can be done as formal training sessions, but just as people work their current and new roles in parallel for some period. In this culture, the new leaders take lead roles but must be collaboratively supported by the current leaders.

New Operating Model: This is often switched on for all or part of the organization in three elements: planning, 'go live,' and follow-up. The symbolism in a Directive culture can be powerful with people leaving work one day as part of the 'old' operating model and then coming to work the next day in the 'new' one.

Emerging Issues: The transition to the new operating model will surface a myriad of issues needing correction. Work units and leaders practice agility as they bring up issues as they arise and either resolve them or assign them to the relevant decision-making authority. These issues may even question the effectiveness of the new operating model.

One of our clients surfaced issues so severe that they needed to revert to their old state while redesigning the components in question. We coached the sponsors to withhold criticism and praise the design effort. Failure in implementation can result from the very experimentation pushing the boundaries demanded by agility!

Effort Closure: Are employees and work groups living their new roles? Are channels for identifying and resolving emerging issues working effectively? Do behaviors and ways of working reflect the new agile culture? Are benefits from the new design starting to show up? Can you move from project mode to day-to-day operations? If so, the end of the effort is near. Executives have been closely involved but now need to review formally where things stand.

There are three elements. The first is to learn. How effective was the project? What can you do differently so the next one is even more agile?

The second element is to acknowledge and celebrate its success. This should reflect the organization's culture and not be overdone, but even office trinkets with a logo or mention of the effort can provide a lasting reminder of the new culture. At least some significant recognition for those highly involved, especially the critical early adopters that got others onboard, increases the likelihood that future efforts are embraced.

The third and final element of Effort Closure completes the cycle and actually moves the organization into the agile practice of continuous sensing. Once a Directive organization successfully implements agility, the 'new normal' is far from the old routine. Sensing is continuously surfacing new issues. Executives, business units, and functional leaders need to encourage all staff to use the hierarchy to flag them so they can be resolved before they escalate.

Reflection: Your Experience in Directive?

◇ *Have you worked on a change effort to introduce agility into a Directive culture? How did the approach differ from the one presented here?*

◇ *How well did that change effort succeed? Can you relate the outcome to any particulars in the approach?*

Chapter 5: Agile Participative Approach

This chapter describes how Syngineering can shift a non-agile Directive culture to Participative. There are six sections. The first describes the Agile Participative Culture. The other five summarize how this culture uses highly participative staff conferences to work through the stages of the agility cycle: Sense, Mobilize, Frame, Customize, and Resolve. The Wilderness case study in Chapter 10 started with a Directive approach then shifted to Participative in the final stretch of the Mobilize phase. Stratos in Chapter 8 used the Mobilize and Frame conferences in this approach.

The Agile Participative Culture

The 'default' Directive culture in Chapter 4 features central control, delegated authority, simple work, standard processes, unspecialized labor, functional experts, formal vertical reporting in a hierarchical pyramid, and systems which facilitate control and reinforce individual performance. Introducing agility involves sensing and listening to customers and staff, calling attention to significant changes, and then quickly mobilizing teams to pilot key features before scaling up.

The agile Participative culture moves towards more shared leadership, with consultative decisions. The added complexity requires that knowledge experts use group process to adapt complex standard processes involving specialized expertise, broad-based input, and collaborative teams with  formal vertical and horizontal coordination. Systems are focused on supervision, but also information sharing, and rewarding team behaviors. Sensing of significant changes leads to mobilization of response teams as with agile Directive, but these teams likely extend out to customers and/or suppliers and are often existing teams or networks.

This culture tends to approach change efforts using group process in staff conferences. Agile capabilities are built in through the deliverables worked and agreed in conference sessions. Engagement, involvement, and implementation are planned to flow naturally as conference participants return to their work groups. This is the culture chosen by Wilderness Petroleum in the Chapter 10 case study.

Participative Sense

Learning Participative Agility

As with the Directive approach in Chapter 4, this typically starts with senior executive sponsors learning about agility and how Syngineering builds it in. The sequence of deliverables, however, will center around staff conferences. Sponsorship and an executive coalition are as important as in Directive cultures, but with a twist. From the very first discussions, they need to understand the importance of beginning to experience shared leadership and group process. These are best built into regular meetings instead of having special training.

Gathering Information

As in Directive, this involves building a continuous sensing capability, but the added complexity in Participative suggests that those doing the sensing should not just be cross-functional but also involve diagonal slices of employees at multiple levels. Their perspectives can be dramatically different and what is murky at one level may be clear at another.

Assessing the Issues

These sensing groups need to be charged with coordinating the analyses and identification of issues and collaborating with the executive sponsors. The information flowing in, coupled with the executive sponsors learning about agility, group process, and shared leadership, all feed into a picture of what's needed.

Deciding to Act

The decision to move to action will be iterative as you introduce sensing to the organization. If it already looks like the culture needs to shift to Participative, then this is a major decision for the sponsors. Review the Participative roadmap and approach summary below and check that they are willing to invest the time, energy, and resources it will take to build agility into their organization.

The Participative approach emphasizes group process in large staff conferences with executives sponsoring, facilitating, participating, and sharing some decision-making. Between conferences, attendees and leaders engage staff through formal channels, organic informal networks, and 'walkthroughs' where they socialize results with people who did not attend and solicit additional feedback. There is typically one conference for each of the stages: Mobilize, Frame, Customize, and Resolve, often retitled to fit the language of the specific enterprise.

A dedicated team plans and synthesizes results. They will typically develop draft versions of the ten numbered deliverables and their ingredients and elements as detailed in Part IV, but the real work is done in the conferences, so we have indicated the deliverable numbers in brackets. If it is not yet clear which culture fits best, you might prefer to follow the Directive approach in Chapter 4 and wait for the major decision point at the end of Mobilize. At that point you will probably want to hold a Mobilize conference.

Participative Roadmap
Begin to Sense
◇ Participative Agility
◇ Gather Information
◇ Assess the Issues
◇ Decision to Act
Mobilize Conference
I. Prep & Introduce [1]
II. Revisit Strategy [2]
III. Diagnosis & Criteria [3]
IV. Culture & Approve
V. Plan and Engage
Frame Conference
I. Prep & Introduce
II. Core Work [4]
III. Operating Model [5]
IV. Deployment Plan [6]
V. Plan and Engage
Customize
◇ Deployment Details
◇ Roles & Accountab. [7]
◇ Structure [8]
◇ Support Systems [9]
◇ Customize Conference
Resolve
◇ Adjust Designs [10]
◇ Resolve Conference
◇ Resume sensing

Participative Mobilize Conference

The executive sponsors have now learned agility, have understood how it shows up in the Participative culture, have appreciated the effort and commitment the conference approach requires, and have agreed to move ahead with it.

Preparations and Session I: Introduction

Planning Team: The sponsors most often assign a central planning team to arrange, coordinate, and document these conferences and synthesize the outputs. They typically collaborate with the sponsors to plan the conferences, invite the right participants, and support the executives who facilitate. They need to be a representative cross-section, which mirrors the conference participants and the wider organization.

Charter: The executive sponsors often develop an informal version of this deliverable to convene and inform the planning team. As they learn the nuances of conferences, the planning team develops a project plan. This includes not only the roadmap of all conferences and their preparations, but typically involves the same sort of detailed project management used in Directive cultures. The work to be done is broken down into details and the effort required, duration, schedule, budget, detailed risks, preventative actions, and contingencies identified for each. They reach out to others, often with focus groups, to help shape and validate these plans.

The planning team often identify a separate team or sub-team to manage the documentation of conference results and distribution to conference participants for informal communications. This is the group that captures key messages and outcomes throughout the conferences and prepares material for participants to shape into communications. They provide clarity, consistency, and accuracy in what is shared. Increasingly organizations find it useful to post these proceedings online in real time and hold the equivalent of virtual feedback sessions even as the conference is in progress. With interactive chat sessions, instant rewards, and entertaining stories, significant portions of the workforce can be engaged. This might look much like the Flexible culture prototyping postings.

Conference Agenda: The critical deliverables from this conference will be the revised strategy and a broad-based diagnosis. They collaborate with the sponsors on how to approach these, the scope and boundaries of the discussions, and relevant materials. The planning team then design the sessions to use group process and foster design thinking and collaborative behaviors. They are ever mindful that how this first conference unfolds paves the way for the entire effort.

Conference Participants: The planning team identifies representatives from all significant functions and operating units. This includes those knowledgeable about strategic planning, regardless of current role. It also includes those  familiar with and expert in every aspect and facet of the organization's work and functioning, including but not limited to those in official leadership roles. It is important to select the formal and informal thought leaders and communications nodes: when they talk people listen. Those selected are informed, open-minded, inquisitive, and collaborative. Skeptics, but not cynics, are frequently included because of their important role in informal networks, and if the effort is authentic, they often become ardent promoters.

Participant Preparation: Participants receive draft documents, which may include confidential strategic information, agendas, participant lists, and logistics. They are asked to read and assimilate, discuss with others, and share their own articles and any information which might contribute to the success of the event, such as relevant trends and industry events. You are trying to get them into a collaborative, expansive 'conference state of mind.' These discussions are often framed as an informal organization diagnosis using the topics and questions in the section on Deliverable 3: Diagnosis in Part IV.

Executive Preparations: The executive sponsors balance three critical roles at this conference. (1) They own and facilitate each conference session with full knowledge and confidence in the process. The planning team rehearses them on their roles, responsibilities, and ways of operating together (2) They represent the authority and legitimacy of the organization in endorsing conference decisions when needed, but this is more of a final decision endorsement role than in Directive. They need to let go of controlling outcomes and instead trust that they can surface the wisdom across the organization. They still own the strategy as with  Directive, and may have sessions before the conference to review, but are ready to listen to critical information from conference participants that may change minds. (3) Finally, they speak their own truths as participants, but in ways that open up genuine inquiry and dialogue. The planning team works with the executives to clarify and build skills in all three roles.

Session I: Introduction

It is often the most senior and authoritative executive who gives this briefing. It clarifies why this change is needed, what's been done to date, and what can be expected. It outlines the conference methodology and what will happen in this first conference. It needs to be personal and from the heart to set the tone for the conference. It is often followed by an interactive introduction of participants, their capabilities or why they're here, and their needs or expectations. This can involve partici-  pants capturing their own experiences with or reactions to the executive briefing on paper or electronically. The creative energy unleashed in this type of exercise often makes for a good start.

Session II: Revise Strategy

This culture depends on group process, an assemblage of people with diverse perspectives together owning and solving problems which are intractable to individuals alone. Much of the conference is based on group process, starting with this session on strategy. The session draws heavily on the materials in Deliverable 2: Strategy in Part IV.

Core Business: Executives or strategic planning experts review the existing materials, give the groups instructions, and then facilitate the process. Numerous small groups are first asked to take a hard look at the core purpose, values, competencies, and assets. People rotate around until everyone has had a chance to review and comment on each one. Then groups are combined into larger groupings and the results reconciled. This continues until a consistent picture emerges.

Strategy Revision: This often starts with outside speakers objectively providing landscape scan data. These can be authors, researchers, suppliers, or even competitors, but the most informative are often customers describing personal needs and concerns. The group process discussions then evaluate and revise products and services, value proposition, business objectives, and organizational characteristics.

Strategy Decision: The session concludes with a formal executive endorsement of the results. This can take different forms depending on the maturity of the culture. The executives might adjourn for a special closed-door meeting. However, they can accelerate the entire process with their deliberations in a 'fishbowl' where conference participants can observe, comment, or even participate. In the most mature Participative  cultures, executives can even vest full authority in the conference to make decisions, still reserving the right to veto for extraordinary circumstances. Whatever choice they make, aligning their decision with the session outputs will signal that they are listening.

Session III: Diagnosis

This session and its pre-work draw on Deliverable 3: Diagnosis in Part IV. There are these four ingredients. (1) Information has been brought in by the participants themselves. (2) Synthesis comes as the conference uses group process to sort through  and make sense of this information, identifies overarching themes and issues, discovers the root causes, and builds the synthesis. (3) Change Readiness emerges as the participants bring in pre-work focused on the ability and readiness of the organization to deal with more change, discuss in small groups, and reach agreement. (4) Decision Criteria are agreed collaboratively with executives providing boundary conditions on givens and facilitating the reaching of consensus.

Session IV: Assess Culture and Approve

In this session various constellations of participant groupings review all of the sensing, charter, strategy, and diagnosis information relevant to the landscape and whether the current culture is the best fit. They then reach agreement as in earlier sessions, and executives endorse. If this confirms the need for a more Participative culture, all is well. If a more Flexible or Adaptive culture is indicated, the planning team and executives may want to consider incorporating some of the features of those approaches from the next two chapters.

Session V: Plan and Engagement

Revise Plans: The planning or communications team documents the conference discussions and decisions. In this session they review the charter and comprehensive project plan and any conference decisions, such as strategy revisions, that may affect subsequent activities. The executives facilitate a discussion to reach agreement on any recommended changes and responsible parties. They may ask small task forces to compile materials for the Frame conference, especially if strategy changes may impact technology and core work.

Key Messages: The time between conferences is as important as the conferences themselves in socializing the outcomes, harvesting critical information that may not have surfaced in the conference, and identifying key information to include in the next conference. The planning or separate communications team captures key messages and outcomes throughout the conference and prepare for participants to shape these into communications. They review this, and then executives facilitate a discussion to agree. This ensures clarity, consistency and accuracy in what is shared. Formal communications are based on these key messages and use a combination of newsletters, posters, e-mails, and websites.

Informal Engagement: Participants are asked to discuss how they will engage staff informally. This should be as natural and comfortable as possible, and the net effects across the organization should inspire hope, positive ideas, and encouragement. They should focus on sharing conference results, describing the process and sense of community, and  solicit ideas for ways to address the gaps identified in the diagnosis.

Plan Walkthroughs: Formal engagement is often done through what are called 'walkthrough' sessions, mini conferences run by executives and conference attendees for staff not able to attend the conference. They review conference outcomes and solicit additional feedback. Sometimes conference proceedings are posted online, and feedback solicited even as the conference is in progress. In this discussion they settle on which executives, conference attendees, and planning team members will run which events, what materials will work best, and what topics need the most discussion and additional feedback.

Coordination: The high levels of engagement and socialization of new ideas and different perspectives from all functions and levels of the organization are intended to help people form a comprehensive view of the organization and create a shared view of where, what, and how the organization will mobilize to align and accelerate the delivery of the strategy. Any barriers or issues likely to derail implementation tend to surface early. The executive sponsors, planning team, communications team, and many of the conference participants work together to synthesize relevant themes and key ideas that surface, and use them in planning the next conference.

Participative Frame Conference

This conference pulls together all the feedback surfaced between conferences with key knowledge workers to review and intelligently revise the operating model. The deliverables from this conference are most importantly the operating model supported by the core work, but also the deployment plan which describes how Customization will be addressed.

Preparations and Session I: Introductions

Participants: This conference needs to focus on the customers you identified in strategy and on the work needed to deliver products to them. Consider inviting key customers. Also ensure you have multiple representation from every aspect of the organization's work and functioning. There needs to be continuity across all conferences with perhaps a quarter to a third of the participants attending each one. These should be carefully chosen as the recognized content experts and/or respected thought leaders,

Materials: The planning team collaborates with the steering team on the scope, boundaries, and relevant materials. To prepare participants they are sent draft deliverables, the agenda, the participant list, and the conference logistics. They circulate as much of this as possible to all employees for discussion, understanding, and comment. This will trigger tremendous interest across the organization and result in substantial feedback.

Facilitation: The executive sponsors and planning team will both have learned much from the first conference. They compile observations on what worked well and where they need to improve. These guide them in agreeing what in their behaviors and the process needs to be refined in this next conference.

Session I: Introductions: This briefing comes across best if given by a senior executive closest to the core work, the Chief Operating Officer (COO), a technical functional executive, or the like. It is much shorter than the one in the Mobilize conference and summarizes where you are in the process and what will happen in this conference. It reiterates the importance of group process and shared leadership. This is often followed by short introductions of participants, with those who were at the first conference welcoming those who are new.

Session II: Core Work

This session uses draws heavily on Deliverable 4: Core Work in Part IV. There are three ingredients. (1) Key Technologies are identified by participants, starting with the strategy, which frequently mentions or mandates specific technologies. Industry experts are often brought in to stimulate conversations around novel ideas. (2) The Value Chain is then described, focusing on modifications required to reflect the new technologies. (3) Workflows, including the macro-processes and processes, are mapped to the extent needed to determine what impacts they have on other components: people, structure, and systems. Executives are often skeptical that this session can provide much illumination, but it is amazing how much can get done by groups of knowledge workers who are prepared, open-minded, and well-facilitated.

Session III: Operating Model

Executive facilitators lead participants through discussions around Deliverable 5: Operating Model in Part IV. The words in bold are its ingredients. Participants summarize the characteristics of the Organization Components identified in the previous deliverables, then use the small-to-large group process to develop Structure Options and finally work through Option Selection.

In addition to the high-level operating model, it helps in Customize if participants can establish and define all units and their high-level mandates at least down to the generic individual work group level. This should avoid exhaustive detail: labels like 'surveying team' or 'plant maintenance' suffice as the operating units and functions will be iterating in Customization.

It can speed things up to use the proto-typing technique of the Flexible culture. This might be only for session III, or the entire conference might be handled as a prototyping workshop, possibly even combined with the Mobilizing confer-

ence. This might cut several weeks or even months from the process. The Participative culture can still be honored by having executives participate and formally approve the prototype and deployment plan.

Since changing the operating model can have significant enterprise-wide resourcing issues, the session concludes with the executive's formal endorsement. If they used a closed-door meeting in the first conference, they may experiment here with a 'fishbowl.'

Session IV: Deployment Plan

The conference now turns its attention to deployment. Some organizations work through the materials in Deliverable 6: Deployment in Part IV. However, one of the strengths of conferences is the ability of the group process to work on multiple things in parallel. Small groups begin seated as the existing functions and business units and then rotate participants until they converge on an agreed set of initiatives, accountabilities for each initiative, and the deployment method. Two common methods:

Mini-Conferences: Executives and conference participants facilitate mini-conferences to handle Customization. Here representative and knowledgeable staff use group process. Ideally all staff can participate in or least provide input for these mini-conferences. They range in duration from a few hours to a few days and offer great laboratories to experiment and pilot novel solutions.

Dedicated Workstreams: Uses dedicated workstreams for each initiative. This is often the preferred choice for large cross-enterprise initiatives where mini-conferences may be unwieldy. Sometimes these methods are combined with a dedicated workstream planning mini-conferences and synthesizing results.

The choice of method has significant enterprise-wide resourcing issues, so the session concludes with the sponsor's formal endorsement.

Session V: Plan and Engage

This session is structured much like the first conference, but the context after the conference will be dramatically different. The individual functions and business units will begin immediately the deployment activities that will culminate in the Customization conference. The engagement plans must be seamlessly integrated into and support these activities. One effective way to do this is to use the walkthrough sessions for detailed function and business unit deployment planning.

These plans need to take advantage of participants' experiences in the conference. Any reluctance or resistance emerging during the conference will have been addressed by group process. How this happened can shape engagement. What were people thinking? What were their fears and concerns? Which were well-founded and ended up changing the consensus view? Openly sharing these stories enhances the participants' ability to listen to and constructively address concerns.

It's not common, but some Participative cultures kick off the initiatives at the end of the conference. Most key staff will be participants and any others can be alerted ahead of time. The initiative teams save time by meeting and planning based on the agreed deployment plan.

Participative Customize

Function and Business Unit Deployment Details

After the Frame conference, the functional and operating unit leaders follow the agreed deployment method to engage their staff and build detailed plans for Roles and Accountabilities (Deliverable 7), Structure (Deliverable 8), and Support Systems (Deliverable 9).

The planning team's work shifts from planning large conferences to supporting the ongoing Customization work and helping the executives coordinate. They focus especially on ensuring that the operating processes that span multiple units are coordinated. The two final conferences, Customize and Resolve, serve these purposes: support and coordinate. This 'new' coordination team may keep members for continuity or add new ones for missing skills.

Participative cultures can accelerate decision-making and exemplify shared leadership by delegating some decisions to subsets of leadership. We supported one change where the coordination team recommended three sponsor sub-teams, one each for financial, people, and technology issues. Each had the relevant functional leader, a business unit leader, and two coordination team members. They worked closely with initiatives in their area of focus and had full decision authority. When issues touched two or more of their areas, they met as a 12-person coordination team. The resulting efficiency was noticed and sped up implementation. Interestingly, none of the decisions were ever questioned in the larger executive meetings.

Roles and Accountabilities (Deliverable 7)

Operating units and functions each work through the three ingredients of this deliverable: technology, process details, roles needed, and staff skills and numbers needed to handle them. This deliverable builds in a key difference in the Participative culture from the Directive one: accountabilities flow not only vertically up the hierarchy but also horizontally across functions. Each employee may have distinctly different business and functional accountabilities answering to different supervisors. Participative supporting systems in Deliverable 9 will be developed in parallel and need to provide for this with separate reward and consequence systems. Executive sponsors and the coordination team arrange for benchmarking and rationalizing numbers across the enterprise.

Structure (Deliverable 8)

The operating units and functions work through the three ingredients of this deliverable as described in Part IV. (1) Unit Staffing is addressed using the unit mandates as identified in the operating model conference and Deliverable 7: Roles and Accountabilities. (2) Final Grouping is iteratively drafted from the mandates. (3) Coordination mechanisms are finally developed to fill needs not addressed by the reporting structure. The sponsors and coordination team monitor these operating unit and function internal structures and cross-functional coordination mechanisms for the next conference.

Systems and Support Functions (Deliverable 9)

Major system refinements in Participative cultures most often focus on improving collaboration in the face of the increasing business complexity. People and HR Systems can be reshaped to encourage group over individual accomplishment. Technology can support virtual teams. Management Systems can enable widespread access to data and information. Data analytics decipher how to interpret and utilize this mass of data. Financial Systems can detail every step of every process and provide the basis for informed decision-making.  These initiatives are most often handled by the owners of each system, typically finance, human resource, administration, reporting, and/or planning functions. They validate the requirements, prototype the systems, and then test the designs across the businesses.

An issue that sometimes arises, especially in larger organizations, is how to design systems when different parts of the organization require radically different cultures. A financial firm might have a strategic edge in deep and brilliant quantitative analyses, but these are used differently by various product lines. The trading arm takes bold positions in mixed portfolios of high-risk and high-reward investments. The pension management arm requires much more traditional and conservative positions. How to build incentives that reward both of these behaviors? The short answer is that you can't. Any one system will end up damaging one or more of the desired behaviors. The support systems must be 'ambidextrous,' carefully tailored to the specific cultures. This can be especially challenging when it is the support functions themselves that require a different culture. The finance culture often needs to be much more Directive than the rest of the organization.

Customize Conference

Preparation: This conference addresses issues that have arisen as the operating units and functions have developed roles and accountabilities, structure and coordination mechanisms, and supporting systems as part of Customize. The coordination team works with functional and business unit leaders to agree the agenda, determine on materials to be used, and decide the list of participants to be invited.

Participants should have similar profiles as those at earlier conferences, with every key role represented, especially those leading work groups or providing cross-unit coordination. The coordination team circulates as much information as they can to all employees for discussion and comment. There should be great interest and substantial feedback.

Executive sponsors and the coordination team continue their facilitation and documentation roles; they have learned much from the earlier conferences and should continue to improve behaviors and the process.

Session I: Introductions: This briefing comes across best from one of the function or operating unit leaders. It should be short and to the point. This leader speaks from the heart about the hard work that's been done and highlights the issues  to be resolved. They remind participants about group process and lead a short introduction of participants, encouraging participants from earlier conferences to welcome those who are new.

Sessions II, III, and IV: Roles, Structure, and Systems: These sessions have similar activities. Participants together review and identify the issues that have surfaced in Customize. This should include any pilots or prototypes and recommendations for how to cascade to the remaining work groups. Then in shifting groups they clarify and reconcile differences and thereby resolve the issues. Finally, the groups determine what impacts these changes will require in the other organization components and either resolve in real time or defer to the next session. Decision-making is ideally shared among participants with leaders providing strategic guidance.

Session V: Integration: Once all the separate issues have been addressed it's time to review the entire new organization. As designed, will it deliver on the strategy? This can be as simple as group discussions, but most reviews effectively involve simulations. These can use software but work best in a conference like this with work groups walking through step-by-step a number of the most common and/or important scenarios. How do you handle large scale or unusual orders? Customer service inquiries? Manufacturing downtime? These breakdowns are either resolved in the conference in real time or if not so easily handled, the conference decides how they will be and by whom. The presence of all the senior leaders ensures that these are adequately resourced.

Session VI: Revise Plans and Close: This session reviews and revises the deployment plans and plans engagement. The planning discussions normally start in natural work groups and have participants rotate around until all the plans support and reinforce each other. The engagement planning looks much like the earlier conferences, but in the context of the functions and business units immediately moving into implementation. Walkthroughs and informal engagement plans must be seamlessly integrated into and support these activities.

Participative Resolve

Resolve completes the cycle. Operating units and functions each ensure that their tensions are addressed. The Resolve Conference does the same at the enterprise level. The ingredients in Deliverable 10: Adjust in Part IV have details. The key with agility is that the solutions need not be perfect, just good enough to resolve the immediate issues so the organization can resume sensing and be in position to take action as new tensions arise.

Adjust (Deliverable 10)

Now the focus shifts from designing to testing the designs and institutionalizing them. All the initiatives converge as involvements broaden. It is critical that engagement and communication continue within the operating unit and functional work groups as they undertake the first two ingredients of Adjust:

New Accountabilities: The first is to ensure everyone has learned and understands the new individual and group accountabilities. The current leaders and any new leaders must collaborate on this. For minor changes, this may be on-the-job instruction, but for major ones it may be done as formal training sessions.

New Operating Model: Next is for all units to begin living the new operating model. This can be a carefully planned transition with a formal 'Go Live' event or a series of informal changeovers by individual work groups. Then begins the really intensive work of Implementation, managing the transition, engaging with key stakeholders, tracking progress, and identifying issues.

Resolve Conference

The executive sponsors and coordination teams consider: Are leaders firmly in their new roles and exemplifying the agile operating model? Are employees living in their new roles, behaving as desired, and raising emerging issues as needed? Are there adequate procedures for resolving these issues? Are you starting to see benefits from the new design? Are you ready to move from project mode to every-day operations? If so, this conference is called and addresses the remaining two ingredients of Adjust: Emerging Issues and Effort Closure.

The participants should represent every group in the organization, and in fact, ideally, everyone can attend, at least for the close-out and celebration. If this isn't feasible, then often there are often celebrations at every work location, patched in virtually to the main conference for at least some portion. To prepare participants for the conference, they are sent draft deliverables, the agenda, the participant list and the conference logistics. They are asked to assimilate the materials and be ready to resolve the issues identified.

Session I: Introductions: The same authoritative executive who began the Mobilize Conference gives this briefing to close the loop. It should be personal, from the heart, and reflect the successful completion of the effort. It is followed by a short introduction of participants and any remote locations connected in virtually.

Session II: Emerging Issues: Before the effort closes, it is important to either resolve any remaining key issues or arrange for them to be resolved. The executive sponsors facilitate participants as they review and validate these issues, resolve the ones they can in the conference, and assign accountabilities for the rest.

Session III: Lessons Learned: This captures learnings before memories fade. The lessons should suggest how the next improvement project could go better. Using group process, the participants consider: What went well and not so well? Are there any opportunities for further improvement? What lessons have we learned from this experience that can be used elsewhere or in future projects or initiatives? What actions might be assigned to which groups to incorporate these learnings?

Session IV: Celebration and Recognition: This is the second element of Effort Closure. It should reflect the actual accomplishments and not be overdone. If remote locations are connected in, it's important to have similar celebrations at each, and to arrange things to include as many employees as possible.

Session V: Close and Resumption of Sensing: Senior executives now formally end the effort and reiterate the new continuous sensing. They move into a 'new normal' of sensing and responding.

Reflection: Your Experience with Participative?

◇ *Have you worked on a change effort in a Participative culture? How was the approach similar to or different from the one presented here?*

◇ *Are there things that worked for you that are missing here?*

◇ *Was the investment in staff time to plan, participate in the conferences, and then engage those not in attendance afterwards worth the effort?*

◇ *How successful was that effort? How did the approach hurt or help?*

Chapter 6: Agile Flexible Approach

This chapter describes how Syngineering can shift a non-agile Directive culture to Flexible. There are six sections. The first describes the Agile Flexible Culture. The second summarizes how it navigates the Sense stage. The third details how it Prepares for prototyping, and the fourth outlines the Prototyping workshop. The final two describe how the prototype is Operationalized and adjusted in 30-Day Iterations.

The Agile Flexible Culture

The culture that thrives best in a Mass Customization landscape involves leadership roles substantially different from Directive and Participative. There is still a vertical hierarchy but the increased volatility and need to respond requires leaders less focused on command and control and more on enabling activities such as staffing and resourcing. Decision-making remains centrally led but is shared collaboratively across all levels. Knowledge workers own the work processes and iteratively respond to changes as needed. People are collaborative, multi-skilled with design thinking mindsets, and work on collaborative teams with lateral networks helping coordinate within the hierarchy. Systems are primarily for knowledge sharing, coordination, and transparency.

This culture tends to approach change using prototyping. A prototype is an early sample, model, or release of a product or service built to test a concept or process and be replicated if  successful. Companies use them to test new products, services, or processes, but here the scope is broader: employees who know the business get together and use design thinking to visualize what the business requires and build a prototype for the whole enterprise. This is then diffused to the rest of the organization.

Sponsors are closely involved, but not for command and control as in Directive or Participative. Their primary accountabilities are strategic context, performance, and allocating resources to fit these needs. They must be involved closely with the work to do this in real time without formal reviews. In change efforts they convene the prototyping sessions, select the organizational components to be prototyped, decide how these will be operationalized, and ensure resources are available. They must role model the inquiry and openness of design thinking.

Flexible Sense

Learning Flexible Agility

As with the Directive approach in Chapter 4, senior executives must learn agility and Syngineering, and agility looks very different in this culture. Executives need to understand, experience, and master enabling leadership and the intricacies of design thinking and prototyping. Rather than special sessions, these are best part of regular executive leadership meetings.

The sidebar has representative activities that might be used to move a Directive culture to Flexible. This culture doesn't rigidly work through the ten Syngineering deliverables, but the entries with a number in brackets will have many aspects of those deliverables in Part IV. Comfort Home in Chapter 9 used a variation of this approach.

After setting up Sensing, the sponsors initiate preparations for the critical

Flexible Roadmap

Begin to Sense
◇ Learn Flexible Agility
◇ Gather Information
◇ Assess Issues
◇ Decision to Act

Prepare to Prototype
◇ List Actions [1]
◇ Arrange Workshop [1]
◇ Socialize Materials

Prototyping Workshop
I. Introductions
II. Inspirational Futures [3]
III. Strategic Aspirations [2]
IV. Oper. Mod. Prototype [4-5]
V. List Actions [6]

Operationalize Prototype
[within Business Units]
◇ Roles & Accountabilities [7]
◇ Structure [8]
◇ Supporting Systems [9]

30-60-90-day Iteration
◇ Adjust Prototype [10]
◇ Resume Sensing

prototyping workshop. They often convene a facilitation team to help arrange the prototyping workshop. This workshop has sessions on inspirational futures, strategy, operating model prototype, and further actions. The executive sponsors then involve the operating units and functions in operationalizing the prototype. Checkpoints at 30, 60, and 90 days surface and resolve issues. Sponsors stay involved throughout.

Gathering Information

As with the Directive approach, this requires building a continuous sensing function. To symbolize the fluid nature of roles in this culture, these sensing groups should include anyone with skills and experience in this area, regardless of their current assignment.

Assess Issues

The involvement of executives allows them to role model and foster collaborative working as they link the various sensing groups together to interpret the information.

Decision to Act

As sensing builds a landscape picture that requires a Flexible culture, executives are rarely surprised. There will have been cries to move faster, but it's often not clear how to do that. The Flexible approach with its prototyping framework provides the bridge. If the executives can understand the approach and how radically different their roles will be, they can move to action: agree on prototyping and begin mobilizing.

Prepare for Prototyping

List Actions

In this culture executives set in motion the road to prototyping. These activities in other cultures are often called 'planning,' but Flexible cultures are proud of their action focus and avoid the 'p' word and its association with over-analysis and delay. They build an action list that maps out the workshop. It's important for participants to see different views on the compelling future, so they invite presenters to provide expert insights about the organization's landscape and innovative thinking about successful operating models.

Arrange Workshop

This activity has many features of Deliverable 1: Charter but is much more informal and action oriented. Executives often convene a team to facilitate and make arrangements. Working with this team provides an ideal laboratory for Directive leaders to experience Flexible!

Select Participants: The executive team begins selecting participants. They look for task-focused knowledge workers from all parts of the organization likely to be impacted. Ideally there are not only 'process exemplars' who have deep knowledge but newer workers as well. Invitees often include suppliers, partners, customers, and other third parties who have some control or influence over the work. Government regulators and industry professional associations may also be invited.

Facilitation Team: The executives often 'pass the baton' to a facilitation team. The executives' roles in the workshop are not to facilitate or approve decisions, but rather to be involved as fully engaged participants who take the lead in  identifying actions and committing to follow through. The facilitation team facilitates and makes all the arrangements. There are a number of tools and techniques they can use to improve the prototyping process: optimum room arrangements, methods for capturing contributions in real-time, and so on.

Socialize: Directive cultures have little experience with prototyping, especially design thinking. For this reason, substantial education needs to occur, before and during the workshop. The facilitation team circulates data about the organization and its work, articles from the invited outside experts, and prototyping guidance and suggestions. Participants are asked to read and assimilate the materials, discuss with others, and share their own articles and any information which might contribute to the success of the event, such as relevant trends and industry events.

Prototyping Workshop

Session I: Introductions:

The most senior and authoritative executive, the CEO, President, or Executive Director, describes with sincerity why change is needed, and the power of prototyping in convening the right representatives from all key players in a three-day workshop that builds an enterprise-wide prototype. Participants and the players and areas of expertise that they represent are introduced. This brevity mirrors this culture's action orientation.

Session II: Inspirational Futures

This culture handles strategy and diagnosis quite differently than Directive or Participative cultures. Instead of linear strategy development and gap analysis, it's based on painting a compelling picture of the future and identifying the conditions and actions that will cause it to happen. While they are not explicitly used, many of the outputs and ingredients of Deliverables 2: Strategy and 3: Diagnosis in Part IV are helpful in this session and the one that follows.

This session starts by anchoring participants in the customer experience. It uses videos or visual snapshots or testimonials or panel discussions or live interviews to make real and personal how products and services impact the lives of those needing them. In whatever fashion they are done, these snippets are designed to be uplifting, inspirational, and motivational. When done well, the room will be bursting with creative energy to get on with it!

Next, one or more of the senior executives ground participants in the enterprise's core purpose and reason for existence. This can be hard-nosed and edgy, or it can be personal and emotional, depending on the executive and how the culture sees itself. Either way, it's tied back to the customers' wants and needs and evokes the enterprise's intention to fill them.

Small groups are then tasked with visualizing the future organization that does so. This is often done with unexpected exercises that unleash the creative and visionary sides of people: oil paints and blank canvases, costumes and stage lights, musical ensemble  instruments, blank journals, sculpting clay, building blocks etc. these are just a few things that can do this. The desired outcome of this session is not an agreed final consensus view, but almost the opposite, a collection of images, sound bites, or tactile sensations that draw people in, cut through their normal automatic judgments, and transport them, if only for the moment, into the future. It does more: it embeds in their psyche the experience and the memory.

This entire session typically takes half of a day. The facilitation team arranges for 'documenters,' ad hoc or part of the team, to capture visual and written records of the session: streaming videos of discussions, photos of whiteboards, and verbatim transcripts of decision making. They post these online, so all employees have virtual access to the proceedings almost instantly. They are expected to review, comment, and participate. As comments roll in, they may patch in one or more of the responding employees to engage the entire workshop and further deepen and broaden the pull towards the future.

Session III: Strategic Aspirations

This 'future pull' draws participants naturally into "how do we get there?" As a way of focusing these inquiries, this next session begins with expert speakers, either from outside or within, who carefully describe the current and emerging business climate. While still encouraging the future vision, they use performance metrics, other data, analytics, and anecdotes, to illuminate the realities of what the organization is facing.

This doesn't need to be in the traditional format of dry speeches with endless PowerPoint slides. It can be virtual, multimedia, videos, or any combination. It can even be a 'road trip' if carefully orchestrated. The Comfort Home case study provides a great example. Their visit to a similar company in a different market stunned everyone on the trip. Here was a group of folks much like themselves, doing what they were only just start-ing to dream about. It moved them from intellectual 'should' to visceral 'must' and drove them urgently into action.

Participants are now ready to move into strategic design thinking. This is not to solve any problems that have come up, but to look for strategic solutions. What products and services will satisfy the 'functionality' our customers are hungering for? What have we learned about our business landscape that informs how we go about this? What provides our competitive advantage? The group process in this workshop is much more informal than in Participative conferences. The small groups, called 'villages' to emphasize the sense of community, develop ideas, and people rotate around and review and comment on each village. Gradually the groups combine themselves into larger groupings with shared views. Finally, a consistent strategy emerges.

This session typically takes a full day. Where it continues from one day into the next, some organizations have senior executives online into the evening and overnight to engage and energize those not present in a way that news flashes could not. The suggestions that result are often quite insightful and complement nicely the work of those present.

Session IV: Operating Model Prototype

This is the heart of the method. To those not familiar with it, the way a room full of senior executives and knowledge workers can, in a few hours, map out an operating model prototype may seem nothing short of miraculous. It's not. It's the group process on steroids, the steroid of choice being design thinking. It's a paradox: a totally unscripted exercise that's carefully designed to produce an outcome!

Participants are again placed in villages, but this time with intentionally vague instructions: don't ask what's wrong and how do we fix it, but instead what do we need to do to get where we agreed in the two previous sessions. They are not asked or even encouraged to use any specific tools or techniques. Some may work through the materials in Part IV on Deliverables 4: Core  Work and/or 5: Operating Model. Some may focus on technology, core work, and operating model requirements contained within these deliverables. Many just dive in and work. In every case, the groups use syntheses from the earlier sessions to guide their deliberations.

As the villages develop ideas and villagers rotate and mature them, patterns emerge. The power of these patterns is that they show up in a myriad of different ways. Written documents with bullet points speak to some villagers. Drawings and sketches speak to others. Still others respond consciously or unconsciously to the shifting energies, non-verbal, interpersonal, and multisensory cues swirling about. The sum total of all these threads ultimately lead participants to a shared operating model prototype, one they have each had a role in shaping, and one they are convinced will deliver on the strategy earlier agreed.

This is often called a 'wire frame' prototype, a coherent framework or skeleton yet with substantial room for filling in and putting flesh and muscles on the skeleton to be developed during the operationalizing iterations. Any indications that the culture might need to be an Adaptive rather than a Flexible one will come out of this session.

The session typically runs for about a day and as with earlier sessions, results are posted online, and feedback encouraged. Some of our clients are experimenting with interactive chat sessions, gaming-type instant rewards, and entertaining videos. They are finding that these can increase interest significantly over static text and photo websites.

Session V: Identify Actions and Close

In this final half-day or so the participants use their expertise to identify the actions needed to actualize the prototype. They typically begin by work group but rotate around to add richness. This is not planning in the sense of 'who does what when,' but instead simply naming 'what' needs to happen. They set dates for reconvening participants to review prototype iterations. After a final round of online engagement, the executives close the conference and operationalizing begins.

Operationalizing the Prototype

The executive sponsors turn to the business unit and functional leaders to operationalize the prototype, this culture's term for Customize. Individual groups apply the prototypes and tailor roles, structure, and systems to fit. Senior leaders ensure integration. The challenge for leaders is to play their new roles in providing resources and staff, and resist shaping the design details.

Individual workgroups take the high-level general actions from the workshop and turn them into concrete specific tasks and set them into motion. This culture does not explicitly use Deliverables 7: Roles and Accountabilities, 8: Structure, or 9: Systems, but most of the actions identified in the prototyping workshop will cover the same ground. The outputs and ingredients in Part IV can serve as a useful checklist. For particularly thorny issues, especially cross-business processes and systems, the executives sponsor smaller-scale prototyping sessions similar to the one used for the operating model.

While there are still hierarchical aspects to this Flexible culture, its accountabilities shift dramatically. Instead of reporting to and being held accountable by business or line managers, individual and group roles are accountable to the groupings around customers. With freely available information about every work product, group norms can enforce accountabilities without management oversight.

To accelerate the cycles, executives can identify individuals called 'integrators' to play a coordination role. These folks move between several teams and the wider group of stakeholders to address tensions, get resources, and share changes and learning across and within their groups. A group of integrators may be established as a coordination team, often including some or most of the facilitation team, and taking over their role in arranging and facilitating the reconvened workshop participants at the end of each iteration cycle. Where this coordination team satisfies a missing ingredient in the operation it may even be institutionalized in the design.

Engagement across and within work groups happens as needed and is triggered by continuously updated and transparent information flow. Alignment occurs throughout the iterations as the prototype is diffused to everyone in the organization. Integrators monitor and report patterns of emerging issues so they can be addressed.

30-Day Iterations

The original workshop participants convene at periodic intervals to address tensions and issues. The number of these depends on the complexity and magnitude of the changes but are often at 30, 60, and 90 days. The challenge for leaders is to play their new roles in providing resources and staff and to resist shaping the micro-design details.

Adjust

First Iteration Checkpoint: Here the coordination team reconvenes the original workshop participants, typically at the 30-day mark, to address all the tensions and issues that have come up. The operating model prototype is adjusted if needed. Support systems or other components that are seen to be misaligned can be similarly shifted to support the operating model adjustments. All participant discussions and proposed changes are shared online for comment, feedback, and action.

Further Iterations: The second cycle runs much like the first. The issues surfacing generally lead to smaller adjustments, but this is also where deeply-rooted systemic alignments can surface. If this happens, the 60-day progress and alignment meeting may need to include a specific session to address this. Any remaining cycles run much like the first two and the issues surfacing are addressed, and adjustments made. In the final adjustment meeting, the executive team will need to decide how to handle any issues that aren't resolved. Typically, they assign the accountability to one of the work groups.

Resume Sensing: Once the prototype is implemented things move on to the 'new normal.' Executives, business units, and functional leaders encourage staff to quickly adopt the new routines and use the hierarchy to flag emerging issues so they can be resolved before they escalate.

Reflection: Your Experience with Flexible?

◇ *Are you familiar with a change effort within a Flexible organization? They may be closer than you think: many healthcare providers have moved or are moving in this direction. The staff are often eager to talk. Ask them!*

◇ *How did it unfold? How was it similar to or different from the methods here? Did you do prototyping using design thinking?*

◇ *How did that work? How did operationalizing go; was the prototype picked up readily by the operating units? Why or why not?*

Chapter 7: Agile Adaptive Approach

This chapter describes the Syngineering approach for moving from a Directive culture to an Adaptive one. This is the hardest culture shift of all, so includes substantial education on Adaptive terms and practices. The Stratos case study in Chapter 8 used much of this approach and the messiness of their experience is representative of these shifts.

There are five sections. The first depicts the agile Adaptive culture and its key features. The second summarizes how Directive cultures headed to Adaptive learn the new culture and begin to Sense. In the third section they Take Action with activities much like Directive Mobilize but introducing Adaptive terminology. The fourth section describes how the central team, relabeled 'Change Circle,' generates or revises the operating model. The final section details how this is diffused across the organization as work units at all levels morph into Task Circles with rigorous accountabilities.

The Agile Adaptive Culture

How Adaptive Works

In its purest form, this culture operates through self-managed, cross-functional and interlocking teams frequently called circles or squads. Each circle has clear and rigorous accountabilities tied to customers'
needs with permeable boundaries into formal and ad hoc networks.

Sense and Respond: Change is not a project or initiative; agility is built into the organization's DNA. Each individual and circle focuses on tasks, which iteratively and incrementally build customer solutions. As tensions emerge, circles or ad hoc groups test solutions that are within their accountabilities, and involve others for things that are not. Customers help set resource priorities and develop 'good enough' solutions.

Enterprise Change: For tensions felt across the entire organization, a separate 'change circle' is often set up. They develop modifications to the operating model to reduce the tensions. Deploying this modified operating model is organic as change circle members move back to existing or new task circles and implement the modified or new accountabilities attached to this operating model.

Leadership Roles: This culture typically has no formally identified 'executives.' Authority is instead invested in individuals and groups via roles and accountabilities. There is often a general circle, which owns resourcing and assigns organization-wide roles and accountabilities. The traditional vertical management and supervision tasks are managed by task circles and their interlinked networks. Strategy is handled through regular work sessions open to anyone and scheduled on a regular cadence. In response to strategic tensions that have surfaced they develop new strategies or identify principles and criteria to be used by the accountable parties charged to modify the existing strategy. The individuals attending disseminate the results.

Rigorous Accountability: This culture emphasizes individual accountability and action. To the extent possible, every individual takes whatever actions they need to discharge their assigned accountabilities. Only when their actions overlap with other assigned accountabilities is coordination required. This is built into the way circles are interlinked via shared accountabilities into networks. Every individual and circle ensures that activities within their accountabilities are transparently coordinated and integrated. Specialized knowledge is distributed across individuals and teams. Systems are designed for transparency and alignment. The people who best thrive in this culture are resilient and adaptable.

Many of our more Directive clients and even some colleagues have trouble seeing how this culture can work. They fear anarchy and chaos if employees can "do what they want" without "close supervision and monitoring". It is only when they experience an Adaptive culture in action that they begin to see how every employee, every work group, every team, and every network, all operate under clear and interlocking accountabilities that are posted for all to see. Software packages like www.monday.com make it easy to track and modify accountabilities in real time on a platform that can encompass an entire enterprise. More than one of our clients have spent an afternoon in such an environment and seen exactly how it functions. One such place is Zappos.

Adaptive at Zappos

Zappos Online is one of the world's largest online shoe and clothing shops in the extremely volatile and somewhat complex world of online sales: instantly changing consumer tastes 'trending' in different directions hourly, coupled with frequent industry-changing technology shifts. In 2014 they faced the need to move more quickly without a lot of consultation. People in this Participative culture were focused on the vertical hierarchy and the horizontal functions, but in both cases, how to impress and get ahead. The rules were rigid and didn't allow for rapid change. The CEO concluded they needed an Adaptive culture.

Provocative headlines announcing "Zappos Eliminates Supervisors" were triggered by the move from 'approval by bosses' to 'approval by local work groups.' An Adaptive system of organizing called Holacracy helped eliminate managers and job titles. Teams became 'circles,' each assessing their own projects and the activities to achieve their goals. An employee might belong to

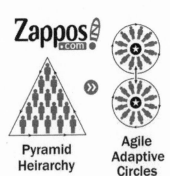

Pyramid Heirarchy

Agile Adaptive Circles

several fluid and self-organizing circles. Holacracy allows roles to easily shift, based on responses to emerging 'tensions' that are in shared governance among circles. No permission is required to restructure in implementing a new strategy. Employees assigned a project don't ask how the work should be completed; they are simply accountable to complete it. This is made transparent: an intra-net website shows what everyone is responsible for and anyone can respond to the resulting tensions if others are not performing.

Zappos is still 'in progress' and making adjustments, but overall, the transparency has enabled better communication across the old silos.

Whether Zappos can sustain Adaptive in the long run is unclear. But as the fashion cycle quickens and competition increases, it's certain that companies like it will continue looking for Adaptive ways of business.

Flexible to Adaptive

We focused the book on moving Directive cultures to one of the others. However, several of our colleagues have clients with successful Flexible cultures which are now faced with the increased complexity that justifies shifting to Adaptive. They are finding that

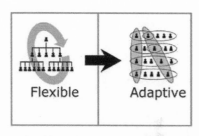

the involved leadership that sustains Flexible cultures and their prototyping actually makes it hard for executives to relax their control and empower interlocking networks with more distributed decision-making. This is much more of a fundamental mindset change than we had originally thought since it requires that leadership be reframed from positions and authorities to roles with authorities built into the accountabilities. Intensive practice, feedback, and coaching are necessary.

Several of these efforts involve large global companies with diverse operations. While it may be easy to visualize interlocking networks in a smaller entity, it can be daunting to scale this up to global enterprises. One specific challenge is performance metrics and compensation schemes that motivate the nimble entrepreneurial growth parts of the company and at the same time serve the sprawling manufacturing complexes that actually build the products. There's quite a bit of work still to do in designing such 'ambidextrous' organizations.

Adaptive Sense

Learning the Adaptive Culture

The jump to Adaptive is nearly impossible to do all in one jump without significantly changing everything in the organization. There are almost always insistent calls for change, but it will not be clear what's involved or how to do it. To imagine it at all, executives and the sensing circle will need to see and experience for themselves.

Reading about it can be a start. The Stratos Information Systems case study in Chapter 8 illustrates this shift. Its Directive culture was forced into it by unavoidable circumstances. To service the growing IT needs of changing government, the leaders of its service provider needed to transform their leadership and operations into an Adaptive culture. Other examples constantly surface in business journals.

Visiting an organization with some features of the Adaptive culture, even if not in the same industry, can be an energizing wake-up call. It can be awe-inspiring to see the ability to respond to changes in its environment built into the fabric of an organization where everyone is sensing and responding. ING, a large European banking institution, has recently completed this shift. It's the largest organization to date to make this culture transition successfully. The shift took two stages over a seven-year timeframe, but was well worthwhile. Customers are constantly surprised at the new responsiveness, and visiting bank executives can hardly believe that this is the same ING Bank they had known a few years ago.

Move to Action

Reading and visiting about this culture are not enough; leaders must experience it personally. How this is done depends on circumstances, but the sidebar shows the activities in a typical sequence. Sense looks comfortable to Directive cultures. Take Action introduces Adaptive terms like circle, resourcing, and the change lead role. Deliverables are not used explicitly, but the numbers in brackets provide an index to useful ingredients in Part IV.

Adaptive Roadmap
Begin to Sense
◇　Learn Adaptive Agility
◇　Gather Information
◇　Assess Issues
◇　Decision to Action
Take Action
◇　Resource the Effort [1]
◇　Change Lead Plans [1]
◇　Strategy Meeting [2]
Change Circle
◇　Sense Gaps [3]
◇　Core Work [4]
◇　Operating Model [5]
Task Circles
[via linked membership]
◇　Roles [7] & Structure [8]
◇　Support Systems [9]
◇　Adjust Changes [10]
◇　Resume Sensing

Directive leaders may need substantial coaching to fully accept the approach, but their growing acceptance can help them educate the whole organization and move towards Adaptive. The idea of circles is introduced throughout, but those tasked with sensing are often the first to experience these, becoming a sensing circle to pioneer the process. The emerging Adaptive culture is reinforced by rigorously defining this group's accountabilities. They work with executives to gather information and identify issues. Concrete evidence for the need to change culture makes the Move to Action less often an explicit decision and more like natural next steps.

Adaptive Take Action

Resource the Effort

With their knowledge of the aspired Adaptive culture, executives discuss to what extent they are ready to function as an Adaptive general circle, functioning through accountabilities. One of the most important of these is to provide strategic resources. They typically assign a lead change role (maybe you!) to assess the situation and determine concrete steps.

Change Lead Plans

The change lead moves into action with explicit leadership sanction as long as they function within their accountabilities. Where things are complex, this may involve consultation with other groups, often coming back to the executive leadership sitting as a general circle. They seek to create a clear framework of what needs to be done and who needs to do what.

The change lead determines how best to proceed: work individually, with one or two others, or convene a change circle. This is a representative cross-functional group from all levels of the organization. While superficially like a Directive design team, the term takes on growing significance as the process unfolds.

Strategy Meeting

The change lead and circle work together with the executives to convene an Adaptive strategy meeting. Often the change and sensing circles take lead roles and bring in information from Sense, but others with relevant knowledge are invited also. These highly confidential sessions review, evaluate, and revise strategy. They decide whether additional action is needed and if so, whether accountability rests with an existing group or individual. Many of these actions fall to the change lead and circle.

This is often where executives begin to see their roles based on specific accountabilities instead of position authority. Sometimes they even formally reconstitute themselves as a general circle and test how that works. They sometimes play around with redrawing work units as tentative circles to test how they work and what skills are required. This can be an extremely enlightening experience that begins to pull them into Adaptive practices.

Adaptive Change Circle

Collaboration needs to become the norm in this new culture, and the team dynamics concepts in Chapter 1 are a useful set of practices for this circle. They establish a routine set of daily operations and weekly progress meetings. As it starts its work, it needs to understand its new accountabilities, review and update the change lead's plan, and agree how they'll operate. Be-  cause of the routine cadence, this is mostly how the accountabilities will be shared and how activities will be coordinated. They also identify any tensions needing immediate addressing. Circle members typically have other roles so may have backlogs in their existing work or other availability conflicts.

Sense Gaps

Adaptive circles handle diagnoses differently than how we describe in Deliverable 3. Sensing has to a great extent already addressed this, and the tensions that led to the work have been validated by those in the leadership roles with the general circle and strategy meeting. Formal diagnostics are rarely undertaken here unless there is a major strategic shift, and even then, the strategy meeting likely covered this ground. The Adaptive culture emphasizes focused insightful action over deliverables, analysis, and checklists. If the original tensions and root causes are kept in mind, the actions will be fine.

Core Work

As the circle works it may consider the material in Deliverable 4: Core Work, not in a prescriptive way, but as a menu of possibilities. They often find it helpful to review the key technologies needed, the value chain and its fit to the strategy, and existing accountabilities versus those required by the changes. General workflows adapted for any strategy changes make things visible and are sometimes a revelation for this sort of Directive organization. If managed downward to employees for validation and upward to executives for concurrence and understanding, it can establish or enhance the credibility of the circle.

Operating Model

This is often developed as a prototype as in the Flexible culture. For Directive cultures not ready for this, the change circle can use the ingredients in Deliverable 5: Operating Model as long as they base it on generalized workflows instead of existing reporting units. They often take a first pass at drawing task circle boundaries and retain some higher-level units to ease the transition. This is a messy and chaotic process, but if the business truly requires Adaptive, it can pay off. The managers of these higher-level units will need to  take on new facilitation-style leadership roles, and involvement in these activities can help get them ready.

Task Circles

Task circles are the engines that enable or deliver customer products or services. The Adaptive culture diffuses the new operating model not by formal deployment but rather by simply having change circle members return to their task circles to initiate. At this point in the move from Directive, the change circle works with executives to organize local work groups into self-managed circles so this can happen.

Roles and Structure

Task circles use group process to define accountabilities to match the prototype operating model. They collaborate with other circles as needed, using some or all of the materials in Deliverable 7: Roles and Accountabilities, and Deliverable 8: Structure in Part IV. The change circle shifts to a coordination and integration role. Visualization and progress reports on walls or in virtual locations can help immensely.

Work unit manager or supervisor roles are redefined as 'lead-link' roles involving communication and facilitation. Those not willing or suited for the role are recognized for their expertise and moved into special assignments. The leaders of residual higher-level units often take on the role of facilitating and supporting groups of related circles.

Support Systems

Supporting systems like finance, people or human resources, and supervision systems by definition cross multiple circles but typically are assigned as accountabilities to specific circles. These circles harvest requirements from the other task circles and create solutions that fit, using some or all of the materials in Deliverable 9 in Part IV. The leaders of the residual higher-level units above the circles often take on the role of facilitating and supporting one of these systems circles.

Adjust Changes

The task circles move from testing to using their new roles, accountabilities, relationships, and systems as they move into the 'new normal' of delivering customer solutions. This starts with the product, services, and customers based on the latest iteration from the strategy meeting and general circle. They identify the roles needed, if necessary, resource them via the general circle, and take action to individually or jointly deliver. They evaluate and choose the best approach, whether project management, prototyping, or individual action. The choice is up to the accountable person or circle, subject to revision if tensions surface.

They also handle management chores like administration, coordination, and communication. There are no 'expert' circles: expertise in functions like finance and human resources are distributed into the work of each task circle and individual skill sets. This culture tends to avoid the use of titles and organization charts since skill sets, tasks, and capabilities are not necessarily hard wired to role descriptions.

Executives should be operating as a general circle providing resources, addressing cross-circle tensions, and creating new circles when needed. They don't wait for pain or opportunity to act but depend on Sensing. Regular strategy meetings address tensions in the organization's performance and determine whether an existing circle or network can resolve them or a new one is needed. The change circle at this point has completed its work, and members who have acquired good facilitation skills may move into roles that use this skill set in the new culture.

Reflection: Your Experience with Adaptive?

◇ *Are you familiar with an Adaptive change effort? They may be closer than you think: some of your electronic devices likely come from organizations thriving with this culture.*

◇ *How did it unfold? How was it similar to or different from the methods here? Were there accountable circles or their equivalent?*

◇ *How did that work? How did the translation to the task circles go?*

Part III: Case Studies

Part I introduces the fundamental concepts and Part II welds these into an integrated framework. Part III shows how these work in practice, using real case studies from our practice. Since disruptive technologies are driving volatility and complexity in even formerly stable industries, we have chosen examples that each started in a Directive:

Stratos Information Services, a provider of IT services to government agencies, explored several cultures before landing on agile Adaptive.

Comfort Home Services brought together three home product businesses into a network linked through shared Flexible cultures.

Wilderness Petroleum, a regional oil and gas producer, moved to a Participative culture which facilitated introduction of new disruptive technologies.

Each case came from each of the three major types of business: service, product, and commodities providers. The sidebar at right shows how the ten industry categories from Chapter 2 define these types. While your industry may not be directly represented, find a closely related case and see if it helps you apply Syngineering to your situation.

In each case, real people in real world situations applied Syngineering tools to resolve their business challenges. Each case has excellent examples of a few of the Part IV deliverables and templates. For Stratos deliverables 1, 2, 4, 6, 8, and 10 are exemplary. For the Comfort case deliverables 2, 7, and 9 are exemplary. For the Wilderness case, deliverables 1, 2, 3, and 5 are exemplary.

INDUSTRIES

Services
◇ Leisure & Travel
◇ Non-Profit & Education
◇ Finance & Insurance
◇ Healthcare & Medical
◇ Government & Agencies
◇ Information Technology — STRATOS

Products
◇ Aviation & Defense
◇ Consumer Products — CHS

Commodities
◇ Food & Agriculture
◇ Energy & Construction — WPC

Chapter 8: Stratos Directive to Adaptive

Stratos Information Services is the story of a city-county regional government spinning off its IT department into a stand-alone enterprise to remedy poor performance and lack of responsiveness. It illustrates how a bureaucratic Directive culture transformed to a more Adaptive one better suited to its increasingly complex and volatile landscape. This case study has five sections. The first, Sense, describes the situation facing the new Chief Technology Officer tasked with managing the spin off. The second, Mobilize, covers how a project team helped leadership understand the challenges involved in meeting customer needs. The third section, Frame, outlines how they engaged staff to develop a new customer-focused operating model. The fourth section, Customize, tells how new operating units and cross-business initiatives brought it to life. The fifth section, Task Circles, describes how Stratos coped with major iterations in the operating model and embraced Adaptive practices using interlocking circles.

Stratos Sense

Gather Information

Kyle was the new Chief Technology Officer or CTO for Middleburgh Regional Government or MRG, which governed a sprawling dynamic regional city-county government and its agencies. He faced a huge challenge. One of the new mayor's campaign pledges was to address ineffective agencies hobbled by antiquated IT systems. She had asked her old friend Kyle to straighten things out, but before he could start, MRG suffered a massive security breach and thousands of sensitive citizens' records were compromised. The resultant public relations nightmare triggered a study by an outside consulting firm.

They concluded that MRG needed new technologies for better security and service levels and the best way to do that was to outsource MRG's

IT operations and support. After consulting the various stakeholders and assessing the risks and benefits, the mayor got the legislature to approve spinning off IT into a stand-alone business to be called Stratos Information Solutions or SIS. While uneasy about forcing so many talented staff to move employment, she was convinced that the private sector had a much better chance of making the necessary changes. She gave Kyle six months.

Uncertain of the existing IT leadership, Kyle brought with him his chief of staff, Athena, whose focus on performance and efficiency made her a powerful ally in this transition. However, he knew he would need more. Before MRG he had experienced agile practices in an applications development company and felt that this might be a useful approach. Typical of his bold style, he reached deep down into the MRG IT technology innovation group and tapped a little-known associate, Suh (pronounced Sue), to spearhead the transition. Suh had worked on an agile software team and her creativity and talent had impressed Kyle.

Kyle, Athena, and Suh met with the mayor's office and committed to three initial activities: (1) Athena would lead an assessment of the current leadership, (2) Athena and Suh would review the existing 21 budgeted programs, and (3) Suh would lead the design of a new Stratos organization in alignment with the mayor's 'government that works' strategy. In her agile work, Suh had used Syngineering, and wanted to lay the groundwork for broad employee involvement, so they agreed to a brief employee survey to begin the design process.

Assess Issues

Leadership Structure: MRG IT had a hierarchical structure typical of functional Directive organizations. The leadership team consisted of Kyle, six functional IT department heads, four support function managers, legal counsel, and the chief of staff. The next layer was 21 program managers, most of whom reported to one of the department heads.

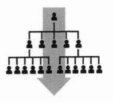

Leadership: As Athena completed her assessments of the 33 leaders, she and Kyle met with each one for feedback sessions. Here they provided coaching on weak points, usually functional and operational issues. While the clear intention of these interviews was to determine who would stay and who would go, Kyle and Athena wanted it kept quiet. As is often the case in Directive cultures, this secrecy bred uncertainty, suspicion, and distrust, especially among the department heads, and distracted many from focusing on their work.

Program Reviews: While Athena took the lead, Suh designed the process to ensure candid responses and exemplify more agile practices. MRG IT was used to one-to-one department head to program manager reviews focused on a 'what is wrong' mentality, typical of Directive cultures. Suh had each program manager instead bring five staff ranging from most positive to outright cynical. They met as a focus group to consider five questions: What's the purpose of your program? What's working well? What could be done better? What technology are you using? What additional technologies would help?

Assess Issues: Athena and Suh debriefed each program manager on their focus group results and incorporated any differences or missing content. They then met with the leadership team and developed three themes: erratic customer service characterized as islands of innovation and excellence lost in a sea of bureaucratic indifference, poor coordination between siloed work groups with poor hand-offs, and sporadic innovation under-appreciated and under-resourced. Even with the cloud of leadership assessment hanging in the air, this meeting laid the groundwork for engaging all levels and encouraging accountability.

Learn Agility

As Kyle, Athena, and Suh explored how to implement the three commitments to the mayor, they found that they had radically different views, especially on how to design Stratos. Kyle wanted to 'go agile,' which to him meant speeding up customer responsiveness, but he was not sure what that involved, other than more employee involvement.

Athena, on the other hand, gave lip service to Kyle's talk of agile, but only the speed and performance aspects. The whole agile concept of shared accountabilities made her nervous. The leadership assessments were all the data she needed to "fire, hire, and inspire." By dumping the entirety of the current leadership and bringing in a new cadre of leaders, she could use some systematic tops-down methodology to design the right pyramidal organization. She resisted listening to any alternatives.

Suh had recently joined MRG, frustrated by the glacial bureaucracy at her previous company. She liked collaborative and collegial work styles and the agile Adaptive culture fit her well. Kyle's enthusiasm and reputation for innovation had lured her into MRG. Suh wanted an approach that both fit their commitments to the mayor and also helped Stratos 'go agile.' She knew that the Syngineering concepts in Chapter 1 would work, but not how specific agile practices like backlogs, job estimation, story boards, scrum, and self-direction would scale.

Her earlier agile experiences with Syngineering had involved smaller organizations with cultures quite different from Stratos. How to apply here? How to scale up? How to work closely with Kyle and collaborate with Athena, who, while cordial on the surface, seemed threatened by Suh's approach? She saw that she needed to learn much more about Syngineering and role-model its concepts as she educated herself and Kyle, and in the meanwhile addressed Athena's opposition.

Move to Action

As Suh learned more about the four common corporate cultures, she became convinced that Stratos needed agile Adaptive. The design project would need to start with classic project management phases, broaden involvement with Participative conferences, experiment with operationalizing prototypes, and move into agile Adaptive task groups. The roadmap on the next page summarizes her musings.

To clarify her thinking, Suh worked on a formal charter using the templates in Part IV. The scope ingredient and its elements seemed well-defined: the order to outsource provided a shared understanding of the benefits, high priority, and sense of urgency. The involvement ingredient, however, crystallized her dilemma. Athena seemed wedded to a highly Directive approach, tightly controlled by Kyle and his confidants, with little or no engagement outside that circle of trust.

Kyle was clearly the sponsor and together with the mayor's office had the authority. However, Athena was a powerful force needing careful handling. Suh arranged to meet first with Kyle alone, and then both together. These conversations went well. Kyle emphasized that Athena as chief of staff had a central role to play in managing the current business. He contrasted that with the collaborative role Suh needed for designing the new Stratos.

Kyle admitted he was uncomfortable with the Co-Configuration landscape and its related Adaptive culture, yet needed to keep his promises to the mayor. While he sympathized with Athena's 'fire-hire-inspire,' he had grudgingly let go of the notion that ordering people to 'just do it' would bring about the needed changes. He had hoped the two could work out their differences, but now saw that their respective roles, managing the current, and creating the future, required vastly different skill sets and needed clear 'swim lanes' to distinguish the two.

He asked Athena to trust the process, and his leadership, and asked Suh to get started pulling together a design team, even though he was only just beginning to understand what would be involved.

Stratos Roadmap

Sense
- ◇ Gather Information
- ◇ Assess the Issues
- ◇ Learn Agility
- ◇ Decision to Act

Mobilize Phase
1. Charter & Plan
2. Revisit Strategy
3. Diagnosis & Criteria
- ◇ Decide on Culture
- ◇ Approve
- ◇ Announce
- ◇ Mobilize Conference

Frame Conference
I. Preparation & Intro
II. Core Work [4]
III. Operating Model [5]
IV. Deployment [6]
V. Plan & Engage

Customize
- ◇ Experiments & Pilots
- ◇ Roles/Accountab. [7]
- ◇ Structure [8]
- ◇ Support Systems [9]
- ◇ Customize Conference

Task Circles
- ◇ Adjust [10]
- ◇ Resolve Conference
- ◇ Resume Sensing

Stratos Mobilize

Deliverable 1: Charter

With all the information from Kyle, Athena, and the mayor's office, Suh convened a chartering team of herself, and two individuals she trusted, from Application Solutions and Cyber Security. With an Adaptive mindset Suh suggested that they draft the charter, but not finalize it. It would evolve iteratively as they engaged more people, and in fact the design team would have a primary role in fine-tuning the details.

Stratos Scope

Case for Change	Transition MRG IT from public-sector agency to private sector business. At stake is survival and the jobs it provides.
Boundaries and Givens	All 600 current employees and all current IT functions and associated support groups: legal, HR, finance, etc.
Goals and Objectives	We have six months to start Stratos and begin providing most of the needed functionality

Suh worked with the HR manager and public relations officer to develop an employee survey, sent to every employee in the organization. It had diagnostic questions which are discussed later in the diagnosis deliverable, but it also asked: "Name three candidates for an enterprise-wide design team: Who do you trust? Who gets things done? Who is already doing innovation or change?" Suh discussed the names with the program managers and picked 21, one from each program. This process tapped into the accumulated wisdom of the workforce to produce a design team covering the entire business.

Stratos Involvement:

Syngineering Approach	Start as Directive project, engage staff with conferences, experiment with operationalizing prototypes, and move into agile Adaptive task groups. See the roadmap above.
Resources & Staffing	◇ Design Team: A representative from each of the twenty-one programs covering all IT and support functions. ◇ Steering Team: The entire leadership team plus three of the most and senior respected program managers.

The 22-person design team reviewed the charter with the steering team. Their concerns led to spirited discussions about programs, employees, and customers. They agreed that the Adaptive culture's teamwork and interconnectedness would be a huge challenge and suggested a project motto of 'One Stratos' so everyone knew the destination.

The design team then worked on a project plan that dovetailed with the leadership assessments and program reviews, the other two mayor commitments. This was essential to keep the organization focused and balance current work against the change activities. During the planning, they became skeptical that the entire goal could be completed in six months. They added three months to Customize with the expectation that results should be showing up by then.

Stratos Plan

Engagement Needs	◇ The Drivers: Steering and design teams, and program managers need to be deeply involved and used to engage other groups. ◇ The Curious: They need as much information as possible without violating confidences or premature disclosures creating panic. ◇ The Hiding: Create safety for these veteran employees to speak up. ◇ The Frightened: Leaders assessed as "failing" but not formally told need to be engaged to keep them radiating their fear to others. ◇ Customer agency heads, the mayor, and citizens, need to be consulted, but only once the design work is underway.
Risks	◇ The biggest was not being able to shift to a more Adaptive culture. The mitigation was to involve as many employees as possible. ◇ The second was losing touch with customer agencies during the transition. Athena was tasked with ensuring this didn't happen.
Comms.	◇ Each design team member accountable for communications with their own program. Team agrees on key messages centered on outcomes. Feedback brought back at next meeting. ◇ Public information officer handled formal communications. ◇ Three design team members met weekly with the steering team.
Integrated Plan	Includes design team plus sub-teams for each 'One Stratos' theme: ◇ Customer Service: (a) clear service level agreements, (b) a voice for the customer, (c) integrated helpdesk, (d) increase system uptime. ◇ Coordination: (a) standard cross functional processes (b) automate internal collaboration and (c) identify and manage handoffs. ◇ Innovation: (a) integrate all agile methods across the enterprise (b) use technology to address organizational issues where possible.

The design team's alignment around a concise charter mostly devoted to actions and plans was not unusual; they had been thinking about their challenges for some time. They quickly reviewed with the steering team and observed how they had already begun moving away from experts each owning their sphere of knowledge towards more of a collaborative team. While interested, the steering team seemed listless as they superficially endorsed the revised charter.

Kyle noticed. He had the design team engage steering team members individually. Their silence had been opposition, but not against the project. They were terrified of losing power, authority, even their jobs. Kyle reconvened them a week later and spoke from a script he and Suh had crafted to invite openness. He admitted missteps in the leadership assessments and said he would put off acting until after the project ended. Decisions would be based on performance during the project.

This led to genuine dialogue. As the design team listened carefully, responded to their concerns, and incorporated the feedback, their opposition turned to open-minded curiosity. The steering team members left the meeting much clearer on what was needed, satisfied that the plan was realistic, and prepared to engage and inspire.

Deliverable 2: Strategy

Kyle reached out to several strategic thinkers to take a hard look at what might be needed for the new stand-alone enterprise. This included Kyle, Athena, Suh, the Chief Financial Officer, the Public Information Officer, and representatives from Strategic Requirements and Network Infrastructure departments. This group articulated:

Stratos Core Business

Purpose	Exceptional IT customer service at a competitive price.
Values	Efficiency, innovation, and exceptional customer service, effectively translated into behaviors and performance at all levels in the organization.
Capabilities	Existing application design and cutting-edge technologies need to be fully leveraged for competitive advantage.
Assets	Existing hardware and software including region-wide broad-band fiber-optic plus state-of-the -art data centers.

This strategy group described the landscape as shown in the table below and agreed with Suh's original assessment that it was moving rapidly towards Co-Configuration. They also agreed with her that the current culture was highly Directive and that the top-down structure was the main hindrance to the kind of responsiveness needed. This had been felt for years, had come out in the program reviews and employee survey, but had never before been rationally attributed to their structure, culture, and business landscape. This exercise helped them understand that Kyle's call for an agile Adaptive culture was exactly right, but they realized they needed to learn much more about it.

Stratos Landscape Review

Technology Trends	Increasing hardware and software complexity. Cloud computing changes the game. Applications exploding.
Markets, Social, and Customers	Different customer agencies each want their own tailor-made IT solutions delivered in real time.
Competitor Developments	Governments increasingly outsourcing IT. Mayor's office in conversations with several of competitors.
Regulatory & Government	New data privacy requirements just enacted in response to massive data breach.

The strategy group struggled to articulate the current strategy. While they had a statement written by a technology architect, it did not help prioritize activities or allocate resources. These decisions were clearly being made but without much coherency. Suh suggested that a good way to sort this out would be a prototyping mini-workshop involving a cross-section of the decision-makers, including the leadership team, the 21 program managers, and the design team.

Suh facilitated. She grouped them into groups of three to five pre-selected for maximum diversity and asked them to individually reflect and then discuss: What are we collectively trying to accomplish? How do we decide what we will and won't do when there are options? After much discussion, they boiled down to a few concise draft statements.

The workshop agenda had the program managers and design team members take these statements to their program teams for review and feedback. These teams were pleased to be engaged but skeptical that it would make any difference. It did. They were able to quantify the value of their technology infrastructure, link program budgets into strategic patterns, and define high-level customer outcomes.

The prototyping mini-workshop reconvened and easily incorporated the feedback, producing the table below. Kyle, Suh, and Athena took this result to the mayor, who endorsed it as aligned with the overall MRG strategy. This workshop provided tremendous commitment and buy-in and gave the design team exactly what they needed to move into the diagnosis.

Stratos Strategy

Products & Services	Help MRG agencies achieve "a strong economy; a world class education system; a healthy community; a safe place for residents; and a city prepared for the future" by: ◇ Excellent online experience ◇ Customized IT solutions ◇ Exceptional customer service
Value Prop.	Excellent IT solution delivery at competitive prices
Goals & Objectives	◇ Online Experience: Improve and expand agency and citizen online experience and clean up current databases ◇ Customize IT Solutions and support for each agency ◇ Service: excellent delivery at acceptable quality & rates.
Organizational Characteristics	◇ Work: Integrated, seamless processes for delivery quality and speed. Clear and effective security policies and procedures. Cost-benefit analyses determines custom design versus off-the-shelf. Technology governance for deciding on emerging technologies. ◇ People: Need skills to deploy and support emerging technologies and create a customer-focused organization ◇ Systems: Recruit, retain, and deploy skilled employees. Training, career planning, and budget to develop IT and leadership skills

Deliverable 3: Diagnosis

The employee survey provided substantial information. One section had included the diagnostic questions by component listed in Deliverable 3 in Part IV. Another asked for ways to improve those components with the lowest scores. Suh and the design team combined the compiled tabulations from these surveys with interview results, customer feedback, the program reviews, and their own experiences.

In composite, this revealed a rigid hierarchical bureaucracy with a highly polarized management vs. worker culture. Those in the access-restricted executive suites had little understanding of the work of their staff. Their staff lived in fear that as a result these same department heads were making poorly informed decisions damaging to their work with customers.

The design team grouped the diagnostic issues into six broad themes: They found the organization chart on the next page a helpful way to illustrate this. It shows the six IT functions (Security, Infrastructure, Wi-Fi, Applications, Strategic Requirements, and Lifecycle) and the four support functions (Technology, HR, Finance, and Communications). The numbers correspond to the six broad diagnostic themes:

Stratos Diagnosis: Synthesis Themes

1. Customer focus poor	No joint accountabilities or adequate training for total customer outcomes. This is not shown on the diagram since it involves each of the IT functions.
2. Siloism	Poor cross-functional collaboration; databases plagued by multiple, outdated, and inconsistent information. Several sub-theme branches shown on the diagrams.
3. Processes	No standard workflows or inventory of people's skills, which is why HR highlighted on the diagram.
4. Lagging Technology	Customers bypassed technology group for latest technologies, bypassing normal procedures and budgets
5. Outmoded Security	No consistent processes; accountabilities unclear; work groups understaffed, under-skilled and ineffective.
6. Misaligned Budget	Process owned by Finance but largely hidden from view and not aligned without a cohesive strategy. Work groups confusingly and opaquely named; real work done by twenty-one 'temporary' programs not on chart.

The design team presented the synthesized diagnosis to the steering team. They recognized the issues immediately, and fully endorsed the conclusions. They expressed appreciation for a synthesis of what had been rumbling around MRG for years but had never been coherently articulated, much less tied back to the cultures and behaviors!

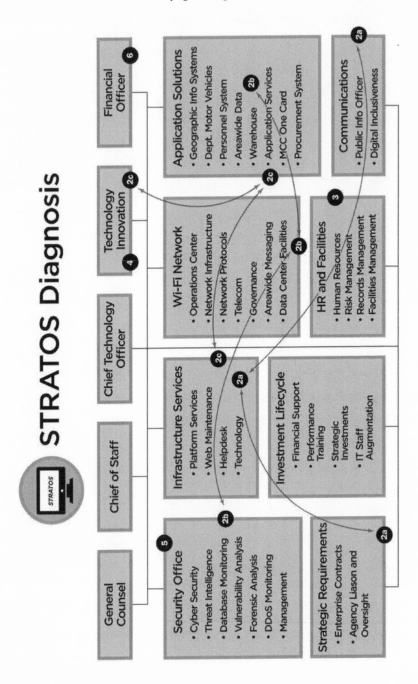

STRATOS Diagnosis

To determine whether the organization was ready for such dramatic change, the design team used their collective experiences:

Stratos Change Readiness

Change History	Numerous changes under different leaders mildly helpful, but few really helped customers or stakeholders.
Priority	Everyone agreed that this was a survival issue for IT
Organization Factors	Customers and most employees ready for change, except some department heads who did not see what to change

The diagnosis led very naturally into the discussion of criteria. The design team developed a draft, then reviewed with the steering team for additional input and approval. They came up with this table:

Stratos Decision Criteria

1. Security: must enhance procedures and effectiveness of cyber-security
2. Cloud: must ensure that the entire enterprise is ready for cloud services
3. Customer service: excellence delivery via one-stop customer experience
4. Collaborative technologies: incorporate and be able to adopt new ones
5. Customer relationships: must focus on building relationships
6. Cross-functional collaboration: agile teams with decision authority

Decide on and Approve Culture

Since chartering, many of the steering team had evolved into full sponsors who understood the diagnosis and knew where things were headed. They were 'in the know,' thinking strategically, invested in the process, and gaining Kyle's trust. Kyle and Suh were pleased and decided to press the issue of the desired culture. Suh led them through a description of the key aspects of each culture, especially Adaptive, with its rigorous accountabilities, explicit customer interfaces, processes to surface and resolve tensions, and collaborative networked dynamics.

They collectively agreed on Adaptive, even though Suh made clear that this culture doesn't just happen; it takes work and time. She took them through her original roadmap musings and suggested their next step be to broaden participation with a Participative-style conference to review strategy and diagnosis, followed by a Frame conference. They could then use Flexible-type prototyping to Customize, and then move to full Adaptive centered around task groups. The steering team members gave their support for a mini-conference on strategy and diagnosis to get the program managers fully behind the effort.

Mobilize Conference

The program managers were still largely in the fearful position from which the steering team had emerged. While they had been included in the strategy prototyping, it had felt pro forma and forced. They were still waiting for Athena's leadership assessment axe to fall. Kyle had come to disagree with Athena's assessment that they were as a group not performing well, and with Suh's urging, he now saw that they ran the real work and their buy-in was essential.

Kyle and the steering team hosted the collected program managers for a mini-conference focused on just that. As he had with the steering team, Kyle admitted that many of them had failed to pass. He acknowledged the shift in steering team members and made the same promise, to make any changes only after seeing their performance on the transition to One Stratos, starting now. They listened cautiously.

They then held a World Café session focused on the outcomes of the diagnosis. This is a participative group facilitation process explained in detail in Juanita Brown and Bill Isaac's book *The World Café*. It encourages an environment safe for expressing deeply-held views. The program managers' initial skepticism slowly gave way to a halting acknowledgement of the real situation, and their deep despair at having a meaningful role in developing the solutions. The department heads shared the steering team's realizations about how important the program managers were to the overall process and asked for their participation.

The response was mostly 'yes' but conditional on having meaningful roles in the process. The final session in the conference was to action plan how this could work. They concluded that the best way was to communicate the results so far to every program group and solicit participation in a Frame conference.

Announce

Design team members had been communicating only summaries at a high level, so after the mini-conference the attendees engaged those who had not attended on the detailed strategy and diagnosis findings.

Stratos Frame

Preparation

Suh was pleased at this progress and helped the design team transition to a conference planning team for Frame. With the steering team they decided the participants would be 12 steering team members, 21 program managers, 21 design team members, and additionally one more person from each program for a total of 75. Everyone in the organization was sent all the materials generated so far plus articles on the three Frame deliverables and collaborative group process. They were encouraged to read, discuss, and provide comments and suggestions to any one of the conference participants.

The planning team mapped out the conference, coached the steering team on their facilitation roles, and coached program managers on their participation. Their growing optimism was tempered only by Athena's dissatisfaction. She had tolerated Suh's culture change approach but was angry that things were now "spiraling out of control," with many of those she had assessed as 'failing' playing key roles in the process. Suh accepted that there was little she could do about this for now.

Session: Core Work

Kyle introduced the conference and expressed his confidence that this group would discern the operating model and deployment plan needed to start up the new One Stratos. He quickly put them to work.

The head of Technology Innovation gave a brief overview of the strategy and diagnosis, then introduced a World Café rotation process to identify the key technologies Stratos would need to enable this strategy. This is what they came up with:

Stratos Key Technologies

Operational Technologies	Dynamic real-time quality control tools to ensure that the systems delivered to agencies actually worked
Product & Service Innovations	The need for improved encryption was highlighted by an embarrassed confession that a public school third-grader had hacked into the school's grading system
Customer Focus Technologies	Cloud services: The current group was more focused on defending their hosting applications turf than developing technology for their customer's benefit

Next the head of the Investment Lifecycle department led an exercise to identify the work. MRG IT, like many functional government agencies, had never mapped its value chain. They started in tables by department. There were any number of disagreements on how things should work vs. how they actually did. Anecdotes about frantic users using unlisted mobile phones to have highly-skilled engineers reset passwords highlighted how broken things had become.

As they rotated, participants began to see that each department and program group was following roughly the five steps below.

Value Chain and Macro-Processes

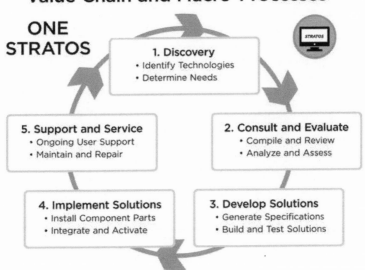

ONE STRATOS

1. Discovery
• Identify Technologies
• Determine Needs

2. Consult and Evaluate
• Compile and Review
• Analyze and Assess

3. Develop Solutions
• Generate Specifications
• Build and Test Solutions

4. Implement Solutions
• Install Component Parts
• Integrate and Activate

5. Support and Service
• Ongoing User Support
• Maintain and Repair

Each department focused on different applications, but this is how work actually got done informally on successful projects. Participants noted that this gave them a visual representation of the work involving ongoing support and service to both meet customers' existing needs and anticipate future ones. If these were adopted as standard macro-processes it could accelerate the move from the current stovepipes to an integrated One Stratos.

To that end, the tables were tasked with identifying hand-offs and coordination needs across workgroups and on to the ultimate customers. As they rotated, they realized that, while two departments (Security and Investment Lifecycle) set policy, most focused on (2) evaluate, (3) develop, and (4) implement. Further, while paying lip-service to (1) discovery and (5) support and service, no departments were actually accountable for carrying out these policies.

Session: Operating Model

The head of Infrastructure Services moved attention to the operating model. He outlined how the current Directive culture no longer suited their changed landscape and that an Adaptive culture was needed. He asked them to summarize component requirements from the diagnosis and core work. Here's what they came up with:

Stratos Operating Model Components

Work and Technology	◇ Enhanced technology and procedures for cyber-security ◇ Entire enterprise takes advantage of cloud services ◇ Use collaborative technologies and seek new ones ◇ Standardize cross-functional process flows and hand-offs
Assets [from strategy]	◇ MRG retains infrastructure, wiring, and radio links ◇ Stratos maintains, sustains, and makes best use of these ◇ Little-used broadband optical fiber network must be used
Leadership	◇ Cross-functional agile teams with decision authority
People	◇ Improved customer focus and relationship building skills ◇ Skills in collaborative behaviors and Adaptive practices
Systems	◇ Align people and programs with budgets ◇ Real-time quality control for customer delivery ◇ Cross functional performance measures and rewards.

The challenge was to develop a reporting and coordinating structure that linked departments with shared customer requirements and effectively prioritized work. Participants were provided the guidance from Deliverable 5 in Part IV. Each table of participants was given one of the five structure options in the diagram at right and asked to develop and assess a Stratos structure based on it.

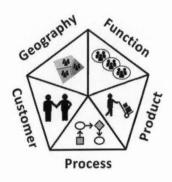

The tables converged on these conclusions:

◇ MRG agencies were all centrally located close to customer agencies; this quickly eliminated the geographic grouping.

◇ Processes as identified in the workflow diagram were so generic across the numerous groups that this grouping seemed irrelevant.

◇ Given that the current functional groupings each provided specific products to customers, these two groupings were combined as a single alternative.

◇ They had plenty of experience in the current functional grouping, but the workflow had uncovered unexpected bureaucratic detours which showed the downside of this grouping. Functions could not resolve many of the coordination problems on their own.

◇ This left only a radical shift to customer grouping. After the first rotation, most tables used their time mapping out this grouping centered around the customer agencies of Public Safety, Health, Education, and Economic Development.

They ran into two major issues: design and politics. The design issue was how to accommodate functions that each of the customers needed: infrastructure, security, digital network, and so on. There were strong arguments for keeping these functions intact. The political issue confronted the steering team with a critical question: How radical a change could the organization accommodate? They were intrigued by having a separate work group for each customer, but their interest shriveled when they realized that the leadership team would need to evolve from a functional one to a customer one.

Seeing the body language, Suh asked the steering team to huddle in a 'fishbowl' in front of the conference. It only took a brief moment for several leaders to acknowledge their concerns. Few of them had much experience in customer delivery. They were technical experts with little idea what their customer agencies actually did and how IT might enable it. A customer grouping was too much of a stretch for the current leaders to handle. Kyle then asked the tables to all work on an option that preserved a number of the existing functions while providing some way to give more focus on the customers.

The hybrid grouping that emerged in the diagram on the next page was a classic 'front-room / back-room' model and looked much like the Core Work diagram from the previous session, titled 'Concept of Operations'. The main existing functions would remain in place as a 'back-room' mostly unseen by the customers.

They moved the departments around a bit and created the integrated 'should be' workflow below. The new 'front-room' would be a department solely dedicated to ensuring these back-room functions actually delivered what their customers needed. Since this merely expanded the leadership by incorporating a department head for Customer Experience, this hybrid was received by the steering team with relief, and enthusiastically adopted.

This marked the real turning point in the project as the department heads began seeing the entire system. Each of the seven departments was clearly indicated and shown against the backdrop of the actual work and information flows. The value chain showed up explicitly, as did the need for collaboration and cooperation.

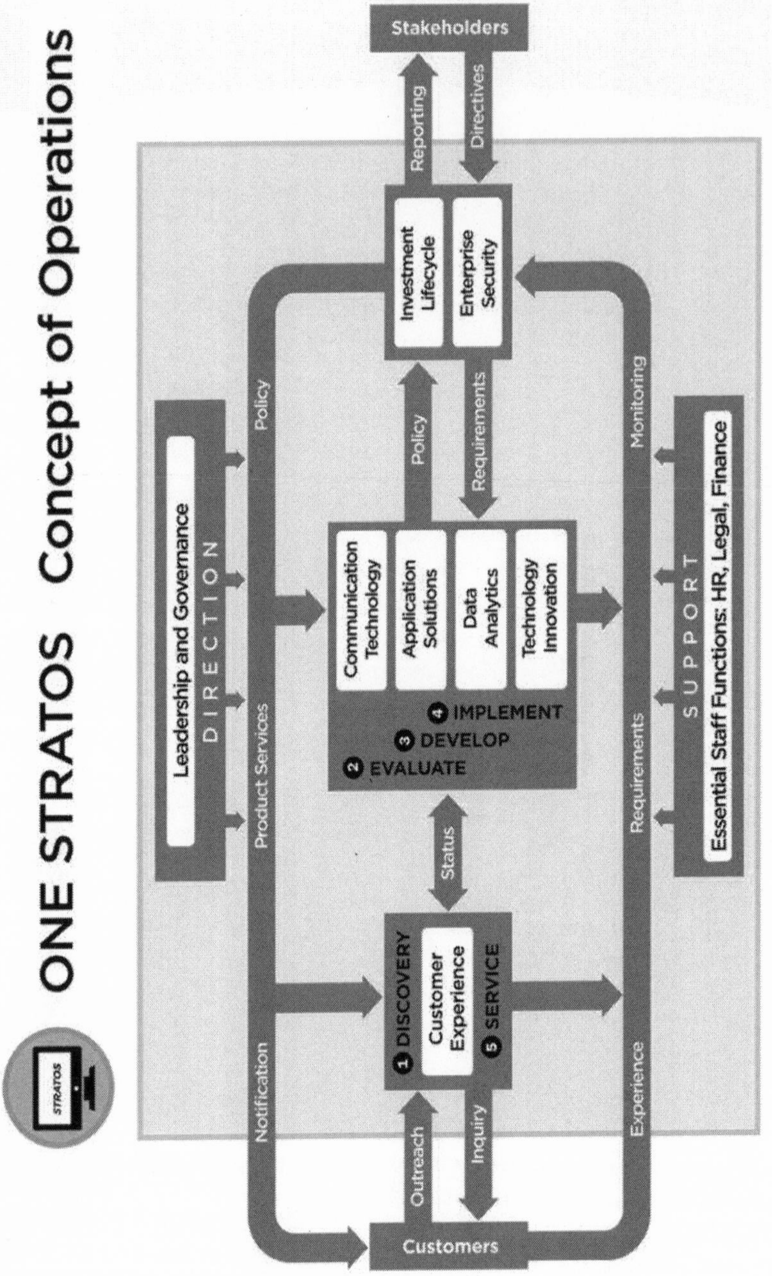
STRATOS
ONE STRATOS Concept of Operations
Stakeholders
Reporting
Directives
Investment Lifecycle
Enterprise Security
Policy
Requirements
Leadership and Governance
DIRECTION
Policy
Product Services
Notification
Communication Technology
Application Solutions
Data Analytics
Technology Innovation
2 EVALUATE
3 DEVELOP
4 IMPLEMENT
Status
1 DISCOVERY
Customer Experience
5 SERVICE
Outreach
Inquiry
Customers
Monitoring
Requirements
Experience
SUPPORT
Essential Staff Functions: HR, Legal, Finance

Session: Deployment Plan

Participants were eager to draw organization charts, but the head of Applications Solutions led them in a more methodical approach. They sat in tables by department and cataloged the significant changes that needed to occur, starting with technology, the core work, component requirements, and characteristics of their new operating model. After several rotations, the final list totaled 17 major changes. Next the tables took these changes and grouped them into the six major prioritized cross-functional initiatives below, quickly named the six C's:

Stratos Prioritized Initiatives

1	Cyber Security	4	Collaborative Technologies
2	Cloud Services	5	Customer Relationships
3	Customer Service	6	Cross-Functional Collaboration

The level of energy in the room surged as people sat around 13 tables, one each for the six initiatives and seven business units. They were asked to decide how the new operating model and its initiatives would be implemented. The increased energy turned out to be in anticipation of reallocating the programs from the old six departments to the seven new operating model business units. The discussions grew heated as each department head protected their own turf and programs. After an hour of haggling the head of Applications Solutions stepped in. He suggested that the reallocation of programs be deferred to Customization, and that the conference describe how it would be done but not the details of which program went where.

The tables settled down and mapped out the deployment approach:

◇ Dedicated cross functional teams would implement the initiatives

◇ Existing leaders would plan the creation of the new business units;

◇ Each support function would implement their own changes

◇ The leadership team would coordinate.

They assigned accountabilities to the existing departments as follows:

◇ The Security Office led the (1) Cyber Security initiative and the creation of the Enterprise Security business unit

◇ Infrastructure Services led the (2) Cloud Services initiative and to-gether with Wi-Fi Network created Communications Technology

◇ Since there was no existing Customer Experience unit, several staff members with those skills were asked to lead the (3) Customer Service initiative and help create the new business unit

◇ Technology Innovation led the (4) Collaborative Technologies initiative and created the new Technology Innovation unit

◇ HR led the (5) Customer Relationships initiative and changes to HR

◇ Applications Solutions led the (6) Cross-Functional Collaboration initiative and also the creation of the new Applications Solutions and Data Analytics business units

◇ Investment Lifecycle led the creation of Business Operations

◇ Communications led the changes required in its unit.

If you are confused by these bullets, you are not alone! As the steering team met for a 'fishbowl' discussion to formally approve deployment, it was fuzzy to them, also! Finally, Suh put up this chart which shifted focus away from the current leaders and turf, over to a shaded picture of how they needed to work together to create the new organization.

Stratos Deployment Accountabilities

Initiative:	Customer Experience	Enterprise Security	Technology Innovation	Data Analytics	Application Solutions	Communication Techn.	Business Operations	Communications	Human Resources	Finance and Budget	Leadership Team
1. Cyber Security		**A**	R	R	C	R		i			R
2. Cloud Services	i	R		R		**A**	R				R
3. Customer Service	**A**				R	R	R	i	R		R
4. Collaborative Technology		R	**A**	R	R	R	I	i			R
5. Customer Relationships	R	C	C	R	R	R	C	i	**A**	C	R
6. X-Functional Collaboration	R	C	R	C	**A**	R	C	I	R	C	R
Business Unit Creation	**A**	**A**	**A**	**A**	**A**	**A**	**A**	**A**	**A**	**A**	**A**
Integration and Coordination	C	C	R	C	R	C	R	C	C	C	**A**

A = Accountable
R = Responsible
C = Consulted
i = Informed

For example, she observed that the new Communications Technology needed to be a collaborative creation of the existing Infrastructure Services and Wi-Fi Network departments. She said that one feature of Adaptive cultures is being able to hold tensions like these and let the parties involved resolve them. There was little the conference could do until these groups got together. With that in mind, the steering team approved deployment using the accountabilities in Suh's chart above.

Session: Plan and Engage

Since existing department heads were tasked with the initiatives and business unit creation, the bulk of this session focused on how the program managers and planning team representatives would engage their teams. They decided on walkthrough sessions, as described in the Participative approach in Chapter 5, to present the operating model and deployment plan and solicit involvement in the new business units and initiatives. The rotations in this session started from tables by existing departments and ended up by the new operating units. Several tensions emerged around ownership and turf. These were acknowledged, documented, and deferred to Customization.

Suh suggested that Framing completion fulfilled both design/planning team and the steering team accountabilities. Moving forward, the leadership team should assume coordination of the change effort along with leading the business. The steering team agreed but asked that the planning team continue meeting during Customization to provide support and advice. They agreed and, with an eye on the Adaptive culture, asked that they be relabeled the 'coordination circle.'

Stratos Customize

Experiments and Pilots

Cross-departmental design initiatives were given the highest priority since they were critical to moving to more collaborative behaviors.

◇ Each kicked off a team (called a 'circle' to introduce Adaptive terms) with membership described in the accountability matrix above.

◇ Each circle outlined in detail the desired outcomes and their required changes: new work groups, new accountabilities for existing groups, internal linking mechanisms, and/or networks including externals.

◇ They then assigned accountabilities for the changes to the relevant groups and monitored their performance.

The cross-functional coordination initiative faced significant issues. A key characteristic of Adaptive is aligning work around customer needs, and they had assigned these accountabilities to the new Customer Experience business unit. The staff working on this had an uphill battle in an organization not accustomed to satisfying customers. As a stopgap measure, the initiative adopted the Adaptive practice of formal accountabilities for the still Directive work groups. They negotiated agreements regarding handoff effectiveness, timeliness, and service quality in meeting customer expectations. These operating agreements made accountabilities transparent across departments and programs. It was a bit of a bureaucratic fix for this behavioral issue, but one that is often needed in Directive cultures seeking to move into Adaptive.

One of the experiments was to try Flexible-style prototyping to speed up the changes at the program level. The Agency Liaison and Oversight work group volunteered to try this out, which made great sense since it was  closest to the customer agencies. They met for a full-day prototyping workshop with representatives from the various customer agencies. The results were enlightening but disappointing. The work of this program turned out to be that of the entire organization in a microcosm. A robust prototype would have required participation and collaboration from every group across the enterprise. There was neither the trust nor understanding of the system for this to happen yet.

Collaborative Leadership: The existing department heads began work on the new business units using the table on the next page. To make any progress they needed to reallocate the 21 programs to the new constellation of business units. This exercise had severely tested the executives in the Frame conference as each leader protected their own turf. They now dedicated a leadership team meeting to finish.

Several hours of haggling yielded no movement. Finally, the head of the Applications Solutions department spoke up. He was accountable for the cross-functional collaboration initiative and shared his views from that effort. Turf protection and silo mentality were deeply rooted in the psyche of MRG and had to end if Stratos were to succeed. He concluded that the leadership sitting around the table had to put aside their blinders for there to be any hope.

He observed that half of his department was needed for the new Data Analytics department, but he had refused to part with it because no one else would release any of the programs he needed in his reconfigured department. He confessed that he knew he was on Athena and Kyle's leadership 'cut list' and acknowledged that over time he had simply lost interest in his job. Given that he was on his way out, he challenged the others to help him create a new Applications Solutions department that his successor could make work. After a stunned silence, the logjam began to break, and the leadership team quickly distributed the 21 programs across the new operating model business units.

Old Departments/Functions	ONE STRATOS Business Units
Infrastructure Services	Merge together to form Communications Technology
Wi-Fi Network	
Security Office renamed as:	Enterprise Security
Application Solutions splits into two new business units:	Application Solutions
	Data Analytics
Strategic Requirements folded into:	New Customer Experience
Investment Lifecycle renamed as:	Business Operations
Technology Innovation function	Technology Innovation business unit
Chief of Staff function	Chief of Staff function
Financial function	Financial function
General Counsel function	General Counsel function
Human Resource function	Human Resource function
Communications function	Communications function

Deliverable 7: Roles and Accountabilities

With most department heads focused on the initiatives, design work on the new business units and the support functions fell to the program managers and work experts. To provide a common approach, the coordination circle convened a mini-conference. They reviewed the strategy, diagnosis, core work, operating model, deployment, and the allocation of the programs among the business units. They described the progress and plans for each of the initiatives and then laid out the work facing the program managers and their staffs in building their new One Stratos units. They piloted with one workgroup.

Procurement Applications Example: The coordination circle had picked this workgroup to apply the Syngineering Customize Deliverable 7: Roles and Accountabilities and Deliverable 8: Structure. They could then use this experience to provide a template for the other workgroups. It was the largest workgroup in the Applications Services program of the restructured Applications Solutions business unit. They didn't call this prototyping at the time, but it turned out to be a good example of building a process prototype.

Procurement Technologies and Work Mapping: Three technologies were critical enablers for the Procurement Applications workgroup: real-time quality control, enhanced security encryption, and cloud computing services. They built these into the process mapping, focused primarily 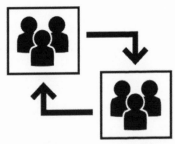 on inputs, outputs, connections, and interdependencies. There were three major interdependencies, each of which they had recognized before but had not recognized their enabling nature:

◇ Most important was the connection with the Contracts work group in the Relationships program of the new Customer Experience business unit. This group suggested that Procurement consider organizing by customer agency and the products offered to each.

◇ Security had become 'mission-critical' because of the recent systems breaches. Enterprise Security had to become intimately involved.

◇ The Procurement software ran on mainframe computers accessed through the cloud, involving the Cloud Infrastructure program and the Mainframe work group of the Platform Services program.

Procurement Individual Role, Skills and Numbers Example:

◇ Five software engineers for developing and maintaining cloud and mainframe software in collaboration with the other programs

◇ Five web-based roles with the capabilities for developing and adapting the needed user interfaces

◇ Five customer-service specialists for understanding and delivering customer needs in collaboration with Customer Experience

◇ Two procurement specialists who understand the supply chain and best practice principles of supply chain management

◇ Three finance experts who know the entire financial cycle from order to pay and the specifics of supply chain finance

◇ Three database experts specializing in supply chain management, inventory control, and customer ordering data.

Procurement Numbers: The above estimates were based on current workloads, which were not customer focused and did not take into account future needs. The employees working on this had compared their needs with nearby city, regional, and state governments. Differences in how the groups operated made quantitative comparisons suspect but suggested that web capabilities, customer service, and database were understaffed. The other three skills seemed to have adequate numbers.

The Issue of Jobs: Most public sector staffing numbers are tied to budgets and difficult to change. Staff immediately saw that if the new Stratos were free to streamline budgets and cut num-bers, this would be a threat to their jobs. However, the coordination circle estimated that with vacant mayor's office slots, reassignments, and employees eager for outplacement packages, there would be no surplus staff. They recommended keeping the estimated number of staffs about the same, recognizing that they would probably have different skills, for example more customer focus and fewer outdated technical specialties like mainframe architecture. Kyle addressed the organization and promised that no one would lose their jobs as long as they were willing to transition to new roles. This was a major plus for the project, and the organization breathed a sigh of relief.

Deliverable 8: Structure

Procurement Applications Example: Many of the Stratos work groups looking at their mandates were satisfied that existing groupings were optimal or at least adequate. Procurement Applications was different. They were organized into the six functional skill groups above but decided to take the Customer Experience advice to organize around products and customers. This diagram shows how:

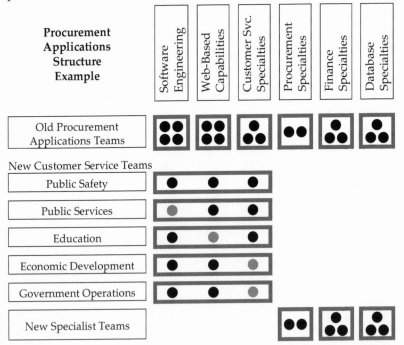

Staff from the old functional teams were redistributed into five customer service teams, each with a software engineer, a web-based application expert, and a customer service specialist. The three expert teams stayed the same: Procurement, Finance, and Databases. The four vacancies were shown grayed out.

Creating Customer Experience: The biggest change in the operating model was to offer a seamless customer experience. The customer service initiative had recommended a customer coordination council, but the initial design looked like an advisory network without authority. This reinforced the need for the formal business unit, but with no visionary leader to lead its creation, its design effort lagged.

Creating Technology Innovation: This critical design was led by a knowledgeable 'outside-the-box' activist from Application Solutions. He recruited two like-minded individuals and these visionary 'techies' got to work. To attract experts in emerging and future technologies, they needed an Adaptive organization that supported innovation. The leaders would have to move away from directing activities and towards resourcing and connecting efforts. They estimated a critical mass of six professionals: the three existing ones plus three new additions. Kyle's leadership agreed, so despite the hiring freeze, they petitioned the mayor's office for an exemption which was immediately approved.

The three visionaries continued designing and made the significant decision to have a 'no title' culture; they would each be 'innovation associates' with leadership roles rotating periodically. Kyle's leadership were concerned, saying that this was too 'out there.' However, in the rush of events, they didn't explicitly veto it and were rapidly consumed by other activities. The Innovation department thus began life as a truly staff-directed entity and by the time leadership took notice, it was too well established to turn back! It turned out to be an excellent example of the Adaptive culture: staff working together, clear accountabilities, and deciding on their own how to structure their group's work.

For Applications Solutions, Business Operations, Enterprise Security, Data Analytics, and Communications Technology, existing department heads and program managers used the Procurement Applications templates to map out work, staff needs, and team structures. The resulting map of the organization is shown on the next page.

◇ White units with circles are the seven business units

◇ Shaded squares show the 21 programs

ONE STRATOS
Customer-Functional Hybrid

Stakeholders
Citizens, Mayor's Office, and Legislative Body
Ⓒ

BOARD OF DIRECTORS

CEO

Ⓒ Customer Experience
- Relationships
- Web Maintenance

Ⓒ Communication Technology
- Platform Services
- Cloud Infrastructure
- Network Infrastructure
- Messaging
- Data Centers

✲ Innovation
- Technology Innovation

Ⓒ Application Solutions
- Application Services
- Human Resources
- ERP Systems
- Helpdesk Technology

✲ Data Analytics
- Geogr. Info Systems
- Data Warehouse

Ⓒ Enterprise Security
- Cyber Security
- Incident Management
- Operations Center

✲ Business Operations
- Financial Support
- Records Management

Generalized Work Flows

✲ CHIEF OF STAFF
- 🖿 Human Resources
- ✦ Property Management
- Public Information Officer
- ✦ Risk Management

✲ FINANCIAL OFFICER

GENERAL COUNSEL

- ■ = Business Units
- ● = Programs
- Ⓒ = Customer Coordination
- ✲ = Enterprise Health

Government Agencies
Customers
Ⓒ

◇ The letter "C" shows units on the customer coordination council, including agency customers and a representative from the mayor

◇ Stars show members of the enterprise health council, business unit heads who met to coordinate the internal health of the enterprise.

They immediately put it to extensive use, as an organization chart, as a diagram of how the work flows, as a map of the various relationships, and as a picture of the emerging heart and soul of the enterprise.

Deliverable 9. Systems

As shown in the diagram, the design brought together the HR function, the Public Information Officer, and various other functions under the Chief of Staff's office. While disappointed at the 'demotion', they saw the benefits of the grouping and got to work. Their focus was on broadening involvement and aligning reward systems to reinforce the new culture. To capitalize on the momentum, they convened the same 75 Frame conference participants to a systems conference.

Management and Finance Systems

◇ There was great pain over the budget process, and the conference outlined some simple fixes to align it with how funds were actually spent and by whom. The Chief Financial Officer and two volunteers agreed to flesh out these ideas and implement this.

◇ Strategy would be more important for an independent Stratos, and the conference advocated expanding strategy decisions from experts to a diagonal slice from senior leaders down to program managers.

◇ The conference recommended shifting focus from command and control to enabling relevant decision-making at the program level. A small group was charged with building a prototype.

HR/People Systems:

◇ Leadership Compensation: Leader salary and bonuses had been set by the direct supervisor, adjusted by the next level up. The conference proposed having 40% tied to cross-functional collaboration. The steering team agreed to a 25% pilot.

◇ Employee Compensation: In addition, rewards for all staff were added for effective team work in addition to individual effort.

◇ Collaborative and Virtual Working Systems: MRG IT had only a primitive set of collaboration and virtual working technologies. The collaborative working initiative researched customers, internal work groups, and current technology then brought into the conference two new but tested systems that participants agreed filled the needs. Training on these systems was to start as staff were learning their new role accountabilities.

◇ Recruiting: While the work mapping had made clear that younger employees exemplified many of the desired qualities of greater speed, adaptiveness, and collaboration, they mostly refused to work for MRG-IT. The conference found it was mostly because of rigid and antiquated personnel policies: low pay, incentive rewards non-existent, no investment plans, minimal vacation, and no time off for anything short of terminal illness. The conference helped HR scope out improvements.

◇ Training: The conference listed security protocols, customer relations, and technical innovation as key skills needing enhanced training, but concluded that the biggest need was cross-functional leadership collaboration and transparency. In the end, they could not agree on whether training could accelerate these behaviors.

Customization Conference

At this point it became clear that the issue was much deeper than systems and training. Not nearly enough had been done to explicitly encourage and reinforce Adaptive behaviors. The systems changes would help, but there was still a culture of hierarchy: individual to team leader to work group supervisor to program manager to department head. One program manager called it, "worshipping the vertical."

With Suh's advice, the leadership team decided to ask the conference to explore an Adaptive interlocking circle framework. Work teams would become task circles, nested within several larger circles that took on the accountabilities that had been departments, programs, and workgroups. Department heads, program managers, work group supervisors, and work team leads all stayed in place, but their roles were renamed 'lead links.' A new communications network was set up to connect the representative or 'rep links' across the circles. The leadership team itself became a general circle of 'lead links.'

Conference participants started in enthusiastically but found the task substantially more complex than they had envisioned. There were numerous moving parts. Individual roles and behaviors, all four levels of circle, and the general circle were all mutually interdependent. The conference mapped out an interlocking circle framework, but it would need changed behaviors to bring to life.

Stratos Task Circles

At this point in the project, everyone realized that the amount of change was far beyond what anyone could have imagined at the beginning of the project. Every employee was leaving the safe cocoon of MRG and moving to a private sector enterprise. The cross-department initiatives were recommending changes in almost everyone's work. Departments were changing. Systems were changing. Programs were changing.

Deliverable 10: Adjust: New Accountabilities and CEO

The leadership team leaped into the gap identified at the systems conference. With powerful support from Suh and the coordination circle, they were suddenly everywhere, encouraging, cheerleading, and communicating, and enlisting everyone from program managers down to individual employees in learning the new accountabilities across the entire workforce. They set a 'Go Live' date for all of this to be completed and to switch on the new operating model.

The coordination circle continued its role helping to resolve the inevitable tensions arising from individuals testing their evolving understanding of the revised individual and circle accountabilities. They monitored and resolved tensions that other circles were unable to address themselves, escalating to the general circle the ones they themselves couldn't handle.

Constituting the circles and distributing accountabilities to every employee took much longer than anticipated in the deployment plan as genuine issues led to refinements, which rippled across the organization. The change circle and general circle bowed to this reality and revised the deployment timeline to delay Go Live.

With Go Live a month away, Kyle privately told Suh that he and Athena were leaving! While he shared some of Athena's frustrations, his major reason was that the new Stratos was not what he had signed up for. The mayor's accommodation to political realities had shelved her campaign promise of a wired city, what had attracted him in the first place. Heavy lobbying from cable providers had changed her mind on broadband access. Kyle's relationship with the mayor had grown increasingly distant and he was convinced that being CEO of the new Stratos could only damage it and its relationship with MRG.

This is not an isolated occurrence: government political appointees leave on average every 18 months, only a bit shorter than in the private sector. A benefit of Syngineering is having a consistent logic for moving ahead when this happens. Kyle had given the new Board of Directors ample warning, and they were well into the search for a new CEO. The board had been impressed with the rigorous process and unified leadership, and asked them to continue the change effort in the interim.

Kali, the new soon-to-be CEO, came in from a major consulting house where she had led a very successful software implementation practice. Former colleagues called her 'harsh but fair' and she wasted no time in showing both characteristics. Ignoring the circle terminology, she called a leadership team meeting her first day. She said she would be meet individually with each department head and program manager. She would be completing the leadership house-cleaning that Kyle couldn't or wouldn't do. She dismissed the coordination circle and asked Suh to rejoin the innovation effort instead of frittering away her time on 'the change.'

As the dejected leaders drifted away, Suh suggested that they had come way too far to just give up and roll over. She advocated keeping staff focused on preparing for Go Live, even as Kali made the rounds with her individual briefings. Why not let the results of their change efforts speak for themselves? If Kali ended up canceling things, they would have at least tried. Each of them reluctantly agreed.

Deliverable 10: Adjust: Go Live

Kali met again with the leadership team two weeks ahead of Go Live. She had dismissed the Enterprise Security head for poor performance and was bringing in her own person. She was also setting up an IT Standards program, in her mind a critical missing function. She then bluntly confessed that she had been stunned by the one-to-one discussions with leadership team members and program managers. There was near-unified enthusiasm for the new operating model and agreement on the detailed designs. She had never seen anything like it!

She even acknowledged that the new design seemed solid. However, she was concerned that it didn't go far enough, specifically the lack of authority in the customer coordination council and new Customer Experience department. Still, she had carefully con-
sidered the timeline and concluded that further delay would hurt more than it could help. She agreed to go with their design with the implied threat that if and when she thought it wasn't work-ing, she would pull the plug.

So, at the delayed Go Live, Stratos Information Solutions started life: legally, contractually, strategically, and operationally. After a massive all-staff luncheon, people started to work. During the first few days, the new and the old units operated carefully in parallel to avoid dropping any important customer commitments. The priority for each task circle was migration to the new accountabilities.

Deliverable 10: Adjust: Emerging Issues

Tension grew immediately out of Kali's insistence on departments, programs, work groups, and teams instead of 'circles'. However, a chance encounter changed her mind. A former colleague, in the midst of a technology company transformation to Adaptive, talked glowingly of circles, links, and accountabilities. Kali acquiesced to Stratos labelling councils, work groups, and work teams as task circles, but refused to give up on the labels 'leadership team,' 'department,' and 'program.'

Three other tensions needed attention: process standards, IT standards, and procedures to evaluate and bring in new technologies. All three were lagging. The leadership team assigned these to the enterprise health council and asked for a plan for resolving each tension and weekly updates on progress. Kali listened and didn't intervene.

The huge lingering issue was customer focus.

◇ It was apparent from the start that the customer coordination council was inadequate. As a stopgap, Kali took over its leadership. She dismissed its members and asked the department heads to each name a personal representative to serve with her. The revitalized council immediately brought together dissatisfied and frustrated customers and the functions responsible into an honest dialogue of who was to do what to resolve the issues.

◇ The Customer Experience department continued to languish with inadequate staff, skills, and leadership attention. Kali asked her old consulting colleagues for help. They observed that world-class customer focus involved dedicated groups shepherding the customer's needs and interests. Kali noted that the new organization map didn't even have any customer agency names!

◇ Kali moved in various specialists from other departments to design five new 'front-room' Customer Service departments: Public Safety, Public Services, Education, Economic Development, and Government Operations. She had this group staff them, streamline the resulting slimmed-down 'back-room' departments, and transition to the new structure. No one bothered to tell Kali that this was exactly what the Frame conference had originally proposed and that the Kyle-led and Athena-led leadership team couldn't support. It hardly mattered; Kali was driving a transformation to a customer-focused organization.

Kali readily accepted the concept of 'tension meeting' in ongoing business operations. Her mantra became, "if you see something, say something!" Individuals took issues to their task circles, escalated as needed to programs, departments, and the leadership team. This became a robust and tested Adaptive way of working.

Deliverable 10. Adjust: Closure

Several former coordination circle members serving on the customer coordination council suggested to Kali that reviewing the change effort might yield useful insights. It was planned as a collaborative exercise conducted with most of those who had attended the Systems & Customization conference in a similar World Café style format.

It played out a bit differently than planned, heavily influenced by Kali. She introduced the review by acknowledging the hard work involved but reminded participants of the flaws in the design and congratulated herself for taking a leap of faith at Go Live and for introducing several critical corrections that, in her opinion, allowed it to succeed. The discussions were guarded, but still came up with some intriguing lessons. Here is a summary of what resulted, with some editorial comments of our own.

(1) Leadership was critical. Kali couldn't admit it, but Kyle's pressing for action started the effort and kept it going, even as he was uncertain about specific steps. He maintained current operations while fostering change experiments and tolerated their disruptions. Kali's forceful presence provided the corrections needed for success.

(2) Iterations were required. Stratos experimented with Participative conferences and Flexible prototyping before settling into Adaptive practices. The operating model compromise to leadership concerns was revised as it became clear that formal customer groupings were needed.

(3) Having a structured approach was essential in moving forward. The initial deliverables satisfied the Directive culture. Workflow mapping grounded the design in reality. Deployment planning assigned clear tasks and accountabilities. Adaptive behaviors and language were introduced gradually and prepared the way for Adaptive practices.

(4) Staff and leadership education and involvement harnessed the entire system. Enlisting department heads and program managers was

the critical first step. When interpersonal conflict risked the entire effort, it was carefully addressed. Staff conferences brought in expertise needed to fully understand the organization.

(5) Systems needed radical revision. Government agency command and control systems were ill-suited for collaborative Adaptive working. They needed to recruit and support collaborative working of very different skill sets.

Epilogue

The Stratos case study shows Syngineering applied to a medium-sized government service provider to shift a hierarchical Directive culture to a more Adaptive one. This is a common trend among technology organizations facing ever more complex and volatile landscapes. The state of Georgia's outsourcing of its IT function to IBM and AT&T is a good public example.

A year later, Suh invited members of the long-disbanded coordination circle to lunch. Things were going surprisingly well. The five new Customer Service departments were still getting oriented but had already cut the volume of complaints to a tenth of former levels. They had learned that often just listening empathically can diffuse anger and lay the groundwork for true collaboration.

Of the original 21 members, 12 were still with Stratos, two leading new Customer Service departments! The 'cut-list' Applications Solutions head not only kept his job but also, after freely donating the right staff to the new customer departments, became Kali's main ally. Others weren't so fortunate; Kali fired many of those identified by Athena. The lunch crowd gave Kali mixed reviews. Stratos was working, and her skills had played a big role. However, her harshness was fueling fears of job losses, declining staff morale, and the departure of key staff. Time will tell whether she will fully embrace the Adaptive culture.

Chapter 9: Comfort Directive to Flexible

CHS

Wood Home Services was a regional home air-conditioning and heating company not yet fully aware of the impending revolution from the convergence of real-time monitoring and connected handheld devices. Their case study shows how a highly Directive family business became aware of technology threats and joined with similar but complementary businesses to meet the challenge. It has five sections. The first, Sense, outlines how the three businesses got involved with each other and glimpsed the future. In the second section, Prepare, they got ready to move to a Flexible Culture. The third section, Prototype, details how sponsors and work process experts created a prototype networked operating model. The fourth, Operationalize, describes how they customized and implemented the prototype. The fifth section, 30-Day Iteration, details how they adjusted to achieve coherency.

Comfort Sense

Gather Information

Wood Home Services: Shawn, Chief Operating Officer (COO) at Wood, was grappling with changes facing his services business. Wood was a medium-sized minority-owned company led by his uncle Red Wood. It began in 1865 delivering coal, transitioned in 1945 to fuel oil, and moved again in 1975 into heating and air-conditioning. They now had three primary businesses: (1) emergency furnace and air-conditioner repair that brought in business, (2) profitable preventative maintenance they were trying to grow, (3) a legacy residential fuel oil delivery business that they were trying to exit. Business was spread over two large metropolitan complexes and the country and suburbs in between. Performance was flat and the anticipated growth had so far failed to materialize.

Landscape: Shawn had spent high school and college summers on Wood maintenance crews, then established himself as a knowledgeable, capable, adaptable, and well-liked executive. Recent conversations with MBA classmates convinced him that the digital revolution was going to change his industry dramatically. Wood might already be in trouble and things could get worse soon if action wasn't taken. His understanding of Syngineering led him to conclude that the business landscape was moving from stable Mass Production into the more volatile Mass Customization.

Wood's Culture: Shawn reflected on how things worked at Wood. Red was the latest in a long line of family patriarchs who had built Wood into a success. Besides Shawn, the two other senior managers were both older family members, perplexed by the exploding new technologies. None of Shawn's generation worked at Wood: the ash and soot of furnace maintenance held little attraction. The tight-knit family arrangement tolerated open discussions, but no one doubted how the hierarchy worked and who had the final say. It was a classic Directive culture.

Needed Culture: Shawn knew that the Mass Customization landscape favors a Flexible culture but wasn't sure exactly what it might look like at Wood, or how to get there. He neither wanted nor could afford a big consulting project. He wanted something more down-to-earth that he could manage. He wondered what he could learn from competitors, customers, and former customers about future opportunities in the industry. This might help him assess Wood's situation and issues.

Assess Issues

Stagnation: Despite the push for maintenance contracts, the business was stagnant; worse, customers were asking questions that technicians could not answer. What's the best way to cut my energy costs? How can I use these smart meters my utility put in? Can I control my furnace from my smartphone? Can you program it? Can you install sensors to turn things off when no one is home? Can you tie that into our home security system? Would it be worth installing solar panels? How would I do that? What about geothermal?

Losing Customers: This was happening as fast as new customers were gained, in two ways. Many were switching to cleaner and cheaper gas-fired boilers. Wood sold the equipment, but had no capabilities to handle the complex permitting, plumbing, and carpentry involved in installation. Frustrated customers moved to competitors who offered integrated gas boiler installation. Those looking for alternative energy found nothing at Wood, and while the growing rows of solar panels on residences and office buildings proved solar had moved into the mainstream, they did not benefit Wood at all.

Approval to Engage: Before doing anything further, Shawn needed to speak with Red. He brought it up one evening when both were relaxed, and was totally frank that he had no answers, just questions. He asked for some latitude to explore these concerns. Red's answer surprised him a bit. Red started with the well-worn family story, about the 1973 oil embargo and the company's shift into maintenance. What he had not heard before, though, was how resistant the family elders had been. Red promised himself not to repeat that. He spoke of his tremendous respect for Shawn's education, work ethic, knowledge of the industry, and business intuition. He was sensing the same winds of change that Shawn was and glad that he had taken the initiative and asked! They agreed Shawn would lead a special project to explore these threads.

Talking with a Competitor: Shawn set up a meeting with their biggest competitor: Joe's Furnace and Heating Company. He expected Joe to be guarded but found him surprisingly open. Joe was an opportunist with a natural talent for spotting business openings and customer service. Early in the latest gas boom he saw that home owners didn't know how to access natural gas heating savings so shifted his small furnace repair business over to natural gas boiler installation. He offered the complete package: he could walk through a house, ask a few questions, price and deliver a fully operational natural gas heating system, including permits, leaving a satisfied homeowner.

With his collaborative nature and folksy demeanor, he had accumulated a close-knit community of expert plumbers, rotating equipment specialists, carpenters, masons, utility liaison agents, and inspectors. Business had been booming but showed signs of plateauing. Joe confessed that he hated juggling costs, quality, and customers, and it had proved near impossible to train anyone else in his unique way of scoping and pricing projects. Work was not fun anymore. He loved running his own business, just not the administrative hassle. He was considering hiring a senior operations manager to turn things around. He had always admired Shawn and bluntly asked him if he would like the job!

Talking with a Trusted Colleague: With a bit more understanding, Shawn then spoke with an MBA classmate, Dawn. Shawn had always appreciated her initiative, business insights, and strategic views. After catching up, Shawn asked how her business was going. She had started her own solar panel installation business and patiently and carefully built an effective marketing effort, which now fed several installation teams. While pleased at her business's growth and vitality, Dawn was worried that further growth would require more structured ways of working. She understood the need but wrestled with 'how.'

Shawn shifted the conversation to the future of the home services industry. Dawn passionately argued that the 'renewable revolution' was happening but was also surprisingly realistic and objective about the current energy landscape and the continuing role and importance of carbon fuels. Shawn was intrigued and energized by the discussion.

Learn Flexible Agility

Collaborative Vision: Shawn was inspired enough to invite Joe and Dawn to talk with him about the 'state of the industry.' While Joe was initially irritated by Dawn's presence saying, "You greenies are ruining America," Shawn watched Dawn skillfully listen, empathize, and engage. She wasn't just pretending, but was genuinely interested in Joe's business and its parallels with her own business journey. She and Joe were soon talking honestly about their frustrations, hopes, and dreams. She supported his thoughts about needing an operations manager and shared her concerns about her own company's growth. Shawn moved the conversation to the industry as a whole.

The three of them reviewed the current state and what was emerging. Joe brightened as Dawn talked realistically about oil, the gas boom, the role of renewables, and the major issues with the power grid and infrastructure. They gradually began to speculate about the future. Then a chance comment about the threats from 'nightmare competitors' made them realize it could just as easily be them! What if they joined forces under an umbrella of giving people more control over the comfort of their home environment? People could choose energy suppliers, heating and air conditioning systems, smart meters, security and control systems, and much more. Shawn doodled some thoughts on a napkin with the label "Comfort dream."

New Business Models: Shawn pulled together as much as he could find on emerging business models in home services. From the generic value chain below, he realized that gas boilers and solar systems were just two examples of new offerings on a product development pipeline that could sustain a business. He also saw that Dawn's marketing expertise, Joe's delivery excellence, and Wood's invoicing, payment, and customer relations were quite complementary. As he researched this, he came across references to a company in a nearby market that seemed to be moving in this very direction.

SERVICES

Site Visit: Shawn asked Joe and Dawn to meet with Red to discuss an exciting opportunity: to visit the company he had read about. Red was impressed with the work this trio had done and readily agreed to accompany them. Together they thought through who to take. Dawn invited her marketer and social media savant as well as her power grid connectivity guru. Joe brought his best installation team lead and rotating equipment specialist. Shawn invited the most experienced Wood estimator and the young IT whiz who was continually complaining about Wood's antiquated IT systems.

The Wood-Joe-Dawn visitors were stunned at what they saw. What they were thinking was a future dream was here in place and working!

They were excited at the possibilities yet fearful that someone else in their region would get there first. It shifted their nagging sense that something might be wrong into a real data-driven sense of urgency. In the middle of the day Red disappeared. The CEO had measured him as a true equal and gave him some blunt peer-to-peer advice. He emphasized that anyone could do what his company had done: here were no real secrets, just commitment, collaboration, and hard work.

Flexible Approach: Back home the visitors excitedly debriefed what they had seen heard, sensed, thought, felt, and imagined. Red was a changed man who had seen the future: a dynamic collaborative community with a common purpose and high sense of trust. As Shawn reviewed the Syngineering concepts, they realized that they had seen a mature Flexible culture. Prototyping provided an effective way to respond to rapidly changing technologies and customer expectations. In contrast, their three cultures were highly hierarchical, even if benevolent. How to change? They reviewed the approach in Chapter 6 to shift from a Directive to a Flexible culture. While pleased that it used prototyping to get there, they didn't really know what it meant.

Prototyping: They learned that this is an 'experiment' where a cross-section of the most knowledgeable people come together and quickly design a new product or service or process or organization. The relevance to their 'Comfort dream' was clear. Prototyping uses a process called design thinking which focuses on creating solutions that would probably not occur to traditional management, and immediately acting on them.

Flexible Leadership: The 'Comfort dreamers' learned that there are two key differences from traditional Directive change approaches. First, decision making shifts from hierarchical approval of staff recommendations to trusting knowledgeable staff to develop creative prototype solutions. Second, management focus shifts from supervision and control to setting the strategic directions and then providing the resources and ensuring that the prototypes are implemented.

Decision to Act

Shawn, Red, Dawn, and Joe took what they had learned and sketched out the roadmap in the sidebar below, incorporating what they had learned about Flexible. The numbers in brackets linked to specific deliverables in Part IV, several of which they used. Joe, Dawn, and Shawn were ready to act, but Red needed to speak with his other senior executives. He convened his board: the other two family members (Office Manager and Sales & Marketing) plus Shawn and the Legal Counsel. Shawn described where their industry was headed, and how the Flexible culture addressed many of their issues. The board was most concerned about what the result would look like. Would this be a merger? Take-over? Who was in charge? Shawn's plea to 'trust the process' didn't help and served only to add to the uncertainty in everyone's mind.

Red sensed the fear and stepped in. He took them back to 1975. They had been young, ambitious, and pushed hard to move into home heating and air-conditioning maintenance. He reminded them of the resistance they had faced, and the critical importance of what they accomplished. He observed that they were at a similar choice point and asked if they wanted to 'stand in the way, or help open the door'? As they talked, each admitted to sensing the need to change and move faster, but not knowing how. Flexible prototyping was uncomfortable and a major stretch from their current operation, but they saw the passion in Red's eyes and were satisfied that they still had a central role. They agreed to begin.

Comfort Roadmap

Sense
◇ Flexible Agility
◇ Gather Information
◇ Assess the Issues
◇ Decision to Act

Prepare to Prototype
◇ List Actions [1]
◇ Arrange Workshop [1]
◇ Socialize Materials

Prototyping Workshop
I. Introductions
II. Inspirational Futures [3]
III. Strategic Aspirations [2]
IV. Op. Mod. Prototype [4-5]
V. List Actions [6]

Operationalize Prototype
[within Business Units]
◇ Roles & Accountabil. [7]
◇ Structure [8]
◇ Supporting Systems [9]

30-60-90-day Iteration
◇ Adjust Prototype [10]
◇ Resume Sensing

Comfort Prepare

List Actions

Red, Shawn, Joe, and Dawn were already operating differently from before and exhibiting some Flexible behaviors. Shawn had sensed a need and initiated the collaboration, seeing things from a systems-view. Joe offered challenging support, asking 'how' things would work. Dawn offered challenging support asking 'what' and 'why.' Red was the key authority figure for the conservative Wood family business. They had settled into this pattern: Shawn the initiator and integrator, Joe the tactician, Dawn the strategist, and Red the sponsor and spiritual leader.

These four realized that they need broader involvement. They called it a network to signal something very different from the status quo. The 12-member Coordination Network included the entire group that had made the site visit, the Wood personnel (HR) and Customer Relationship managers, and a few others. It mirrored the employee mix across the three companies. They formed four sub-networks:

◇ Customer network, led by Joe's installation team lead, was formed to bring the voice of the customer into the workshop

◇ Technology network, led by the Wood IT whiz, would explore emerging technologies and their impacts on current and future business

◇ Facilitation network, led by the Wood personnel manager, would help to develop the workshop agenda, handle logistics, and facilitate

◇ Engagement network, led by Dawn's social media marketer, would document the proceedings, circulate materials, and solicit feedback.

They wanted their behaviors and methods to reinforce the move to the Flexible Culture and committed to "trust the process" and use group process to have unanticipated outcomes emerge. While still not clear how things would sort out legally, the coordination network began calling their enterprise Comfort Home Services.

Comfort

Workshop Arrangements

Inspirational Futures: To engage participants' creative sides they decided to include positive and aspirational aspects. The customer network began interviewing existing customers, formerly loyal customers who had turned elsewhere, and people with no connection with any of the companies. Most were interested in energy supplies, solar and alternatives, and also smart homes, tied to the growing presence of electronics. Why can't my home be as well-designed, easy to use, affordable, with as good customer service as Amazon, Apple, or Google? They lined up some of those interviewed to attend.

The technology network considered the looming disruption in their business and found it was centered around the 'smart home,' integrated systems with automated sensors monitoring energy, security, and the home environment. They came to understand that despite their ideas and enthusiasm, they had little expertise in this realm. They hired a 'smart home' consultant and a security systems consultant to help bring perspective to the workshop.

Design Workshop Sessions: The facilitation network designed sessions keeping in mind two ideas: (1) design thinking, looking for sustainable solutions rather than traditional incremental problem solving, and (2) leaving the 'how to' of implement- ing solutions to operating managers and staff, since it involves significantly different skillsets from design. They turned the roadmap into five sessions over three days.

I: Introduction: senior executive briefing and attendee introductions

II (½ day) Inspirational Futures: customer experiences, core purpose, technology vision, and engage as many staff as possible

III (1 day) Strategic Aspirations: expert speakers describe the state of the business, small group 'villages' iteratively develop strategy; extract decision criteria, and continue engaging other staff

IV (1 day) Enterprise Prototype: villages develop an operating model prototype; continue engagement in real time

V (½ day) Identify Actions and Close: list high level actions to operationalize the prototype and confirm the schedule.

Socialize Materials

Select Participants: The coordination network looked for task-focused knowledge workers from all three companies. They sought not only 'process exemplars' but newer and younger workers and included a number of small intact work teams. This resulted in 40 employees, covering every capability and skill set. They also invited the customers interviewed by the customer network and the smart home and home security consultants. To bring in challenging external view, they invited an experienced government inspector, the owner of one of their major suppliers, and a representative of a national home services professional association. They ended up with 60: 40 employees, 8 external invitees, and the 12 coordination team members.

Workshop Logistics: The facilitation network handled invitations, scheduling, meeting hall design, session mechanics, and so forth. They learned the importance of dedicated spaces that can be reconfigurable to optimize design thinking and set aside several rooms at the Wood offices. The engagement network geared up to document and communicate results via real-time video-streaming, blogs, and so on.

Educate Participants: The engagement network agreed that significant education was needed on the Flexible culture, prototyping, and design thinking to shift people's mindsets away from following leaders to being leaders in the creative process and away from solving specific problems towards developing broad solutions focused on customer needs. They circulated a combination of articles and YouTube videos, on the Flexible Culture and its practices plus aspects of security, energy, and the smart home concepts. Invitees were asked to read and assimilate the materials, discuss with others, and to experiment with design thinking prior to the workshop.

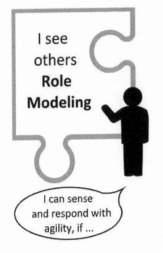

Educate Executives: The four executives brainstormed how to role-model collaboration, support participants, foster openness and innovative thinking, and lead identification of actions and commitment to follow through. While several expressed concerns that it was too much too fast, they agreed to 'be Flexible' and trust themselves, their people, and the process. The facilitation team brought in articles on 'Work Information Networks' and Stu Winby's 'Decision Accelerator' which describe the principles of design prototyping: organizations as information processing systems, and people as nodes of information exchange (instead of management structures).

Comfort Prototype

The selected 60 convened for a three-day workshop.

Session I: Introduction

Red set the tone by encouraging everyone to be themselves, listen to each other, and be influenced by what they experienced. If they did this, together they could create a great future for the new enterprise that emerged.

Session II (half-day): Inspirational Futures

Changing Expectations: The customer network introduced a loyal Wood customer who sang their praises for service and quality but had to go elsewhere when he wanted a smart home system. The smart home con-  sultants showed video clips showing different configurations of home systems and what the owners loved about each. Finally, participants plugged into virtual reality headsets that seemed to be a recording but turned out to be a real-time feed from a tour guide at the site-visit company. This virtual tour brought participants into the future-oriented mindset the executives had been living in since the visit. People like themselves were already doing what they were only starting to think about. It galvanized the entire workshop from an intellectual 'should' do to a powerfully visceral 'must' do!

Future State: Participants returned from a break to find creative crafts materials: oil paints and blank canvases, costumes and stage lights, musical ensemble instruments, blank journals, sculpting clay, building blocks, and recording cameras. The instructions were simply: visualize the future Comfort. The creative energy that this unleashed was awe-inspiring. Participants developed scale-model smart homes, paintings, poems, and videos. The images, sound bites, and tactile sensations cut through normal automatic judgments and transported people even if for a moment into the future. Far more than written reports or bulleted slides, these items embedded feelings, sights, tastes, experiences, and memories into their psyche.

Engage Staff: The engagement network posted artwork, videos, and evocative writing. The more extensive materials went on the internal networks and particularly striking examples went up on all three companies' Facebook and LinkedIn pages cross-posted to YouTube, Tumblr, and Pinterest. Notifications to all staff and selected customers went out via e-mail distribution lists, Twitter, Snapchat, Skype, WhatsApp, and Instagram. Insightful comments rolled in. Virtual access to the workshop sent the clear message that shaping the change and improving the work was part of everyone's responsibility and that ultimately, all employees would be involved in the process.

Session III (1 day): Strategic Aspirations

Industry Landscape: Shawn led off, describing the current performance of each of the three companies: Wood's stagnation, Joe's revenues just beginning to plateau as the market saturated, and Dawn's explosive growth. Several employees told stories about the realities 'behind the numbers' and helped participants understand the other two companies. Then the national home services association representative gave a statistical tour from a national and regional market perspective. The trends were disturbing: Wood's stagnation signaled a slow decline; Joe was soon facing the same thing; and Dawn's continued growth, while encouraging, was just an earlier stage of the same well-known product development S-curve. Shawn asked tables to process all this and built the landscape picture below from their outputs.

Technology Trends	Cheap mass-produced cameras and meters driving a revolution. Renewable energy markets increasing.
Markets, Social, and Customers	Changing customer expectations. Each company has a reputation for excellence but over limited offerings.
Competitor Developments	Site-visit company operations available to anyone, but require the vision, commitment, and investment.
Regulatory & Government	Green energy incentives and grid connectivity standards balancing the energy picture. Data privacy a concern.

Core Business: Red asked the participants to ground the new enterprise in its core business, tied to customer needs, shaped by the previous sessions. They fitted the results of these discussions into this matrix.

	What We Have to Keep	What We Need to Add
Core Purpose	Solar panels, gas boilers, and heating and cooling	Full home control: energy, security, & temperature.
Core Values	Do it right the first time; meet the customer's needs	Offer the latest technology tailored to customer needs
Core Capabilities	Estimation & installation, social media marketing	Smart home, security, and other monitoring expertise
Core Assets	Skilled crafts tools; high credibility with agencies	Smart home analytics and connectivity software

Strategy for the Future: Dawn the strategist moved participants into strategic design thinking, which is to look beyond immediate problems and find solutions in the strategy. She asked: "What products and services would satisfy the functionality our customers are asking for? How does our landscape affect this? What would provide competitive advantage?" Dawn placed participants into small groups called 'villages' to discuss. After some time, people rotated around to review and comment on other villages. The engagement network busily posted intermediate thoughts on the internal network.

As participants broke for a group dinner, Dawn volunteered to stay online into the evening to engage staff as they commented. Several spirited discussions strongly reinforced the thinking of the villages. The next morning, Dawn reviewed these, and had participants continue the conversation as combined groups. The thoughts below emerged:

Value Proposition	Offer complete control over the home environment using current technology to satisfy customers at acceptable cost
Products & Services	Integrated product line anchored in air-conditioning, heating, and solar systems, extending all the way to a fully wired home. Fuel oil clients encouraged to replace.
Goals & Objectives	Within one year: stabilize Wood's and Joe's revenues, continue Dawn's increases, and offer new services.
Organizational Characteristics	Add full smart home capabilities: metering, systems, and home security. Add alternative energy expertise. Create a new product and service development function.

Session IV (1 day): Enterprise Prototype

Scope: Shawn introduced this key session. He laid out the boundaries. Scope would be all of Wood, Joe's, and Dawn's as a network of three separate legal entities with interlinked work processes. Administrative processes could possibly be centralized with built-in best practices from each company. The Wood family management structure and Joe's and Dawn's investor arrangements were totally off limits. There could be no large cash outlays, or mergers, or acquisitions.

Instructions: He asked participants to use the session outputs so far, especially those growing out of strategy. He grouped them into villages of maximum diversity of parent company, skill set, and job function. After drawing a simple three-balloon sketch of Wood plus Joe's plus Dawn's with lines representing networks, he asked each village to sketch out an operating model of how work would get done. He did not suggest any specific approaches, just asked them to build the operating model prototype.

Village Dynamics: Each village developed its own personality. Some took the results from earlier sessions and followed them to their logical conclusions. Some took Shawn's sketch and filled in the details. Some identified the technologies, defined the core work, and explored the operating model  characteristics these suggested. As attendees rotated and matured ideas, they responded consciously or unconsciously to the non-verbal, interpersonal, and multisensory cues swirling about. The patterns emerging showed up in a myriad of ways. Some villages posted written documents with bullet points, some posted drawings and sketches, others featured vignettes of different facets of the new enterprise.

Macro-Process Mapping Village: One village included an engineer and planner-scheduler intrigued by the phrase 'how the work gets done.' They drew a simple high-level work flow for the new Comfort which took on a life of its own as different capability groups rotated in and added expertise and perspectives. The remarkable diagram below emerged. There were several significant features:

◇ There were four macro-processes: innovate, order, deliver, and pay

◇ Customers, not on Shawn's initial diagram, ended up prominently on the top row to mirror the values and proposed strategy

◇ Innovate was added as a key set of processes for the strategy

◇ Finance insisted that pay be elevated from 'administrative support'

◇ Innovate and deliver were deemed advantage and shown in black

◇ Order and pay were deemed enabling and shown as lighter gray

◇ Project coordination was added as a capability to remedy various communications shortfalls between workgroups.

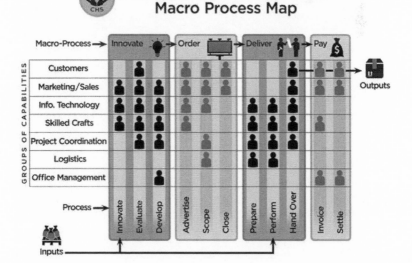

Part III – Chapter 9: **Comfort** – Section 3: **Prototype**

While not a major focus of the session, this graphic was quite useful. It showed the organization as a whole, and it helped people see where they fit. It helped everyone visualize the operating model prototype and provided the list of work processes and capabilities groups that were needed as the business units operationalized the prototype.

Engage Staff on the Operating Model: In late afternoon, each village illustrated their operating model thoughts so far. Their diagrams were posted by the engagement network on the internal network. Employees not in the workshop were by now quite aware of the engagement and were waiting. Both Red and Joe stayed to chair the evening chats. They harvested a rich selection of comments, observations, and suggestions.

Villages Converge on the Operating Model Prototype: Participants led off the third morning reflecting on the first two days and hearing Red's and Joe's chatroom experiences. The villages continued working and over the morning converged on the prototype operating model below.

This 'wire frame' prototype is a coherent skeleton with substantial room for filling in flesh and muscles. It had these features:

◇ Temperature Solutions for heating, cooling, and complete delivery systems and ductwork were provided by coordinated teams from Wood's and Joe's installation and maintenance business

◇ Energy Solutions were Dawn's existing teams with added specialists in alternative energy sources and integrated energy systems

◇ Central Functions were based on the existing Wood central groups, augmented by staff from Joe's and Dawn's seconded in

◇ A new development function covered the innovate macro-process

◇ A new Monitoring Solutions handled the new smart home offerings

◇ The three legal entities were a given until operationalizing brought relationships, behaviors, and systems to life.

The leaders, especially Red, were a bit surprised as composite groups like Temperature Solutions emerged. As each village reached the same conclusions, he came to accept the logic and unity behind the results.

Three critical success factors were identified:

◇ Build a Comfort brand and bring in the good customer relationships

◇ Adopt the needed technologies and bring in the right IT people

◇ Create an effective development function to handle the Innovate work

Session V (½ day): Identify Actions and Close

Introduction: Joe the action figure introduced this session to identify the actions needed to implement the operating model. He explained that once the workshop was over, the prototype would be operationalized by the business units and functions under the direction of the senior leaders. Workshop participants would reconvene for one day sessions at about 30, 60 and 90 days to work out impediments that could not be resolved through management or individual action.

Village Small Group Process captured thoughts on what was needed and rotated around to integrate. The actions fell into these categories:

◇ Monitoring Solutions: It was clear that IT needed to sit here but permeate the entire organization. This required new skills and leadership. The smart home and security consultants helped the villages understand the important initial actions.

◇ Central Functions: Several overnight online comments expressed concerns that central functions were actually the glue that held the existing companies together; pulling them out risked extinguishing each company's heart and soul. Villages agreed but decided that glue sticks two ways. Centralizing could both reduce operating expenses and pull the enterprise together. This was high priority.

◇ Marketing: This involved bringing together three different groups and was deemed high priority. The development function was slated to ultimately provide competitive advantage, but forming it was a lower priority in the face of the mountain of other work.

◇ Establishing Temperature Solutions around Wood and Joe's

◇ Establishing Energy Solutions around Dawn's existing business

◇ Coordinating and keeping the whole enterprise on track required identifying the needed roles and accountabilities, establishing the relationships and linkages between them, and revising the support systems. The coordination council agreed to take on.

30-Day Iterations: The workshop ended March 15, after furnace season was over and with three months before air conditioner season. Joe said that the workshop would reconvene at 30, 60, and 90-day mileposts to examine progress, identify tensions, and synchronize activities.

Close and Engage: The coordination council members summarized the action lists and made adjustments as discrepancies surfaced. Closing was simple: each participant gave their 15-second 'elevator speech' for co-workers who had not attended. What did people need to know? Important outcomes? Priorities? The action lists and several of the elevator speeches were immediately posted online. Employees were asked to reach out to coordination council members with feedback, suggestions, and offers to help. An interesting sign of the new energy was the number of small groups that kept going far into the evening.

Comfort Operationalize

Individual coordination team members began marshaling resources to address the six action categories. This resulted in five efforts plus the coordination team. They called these five 'workstreams' to match the Flexible culture, after rejecting the Directive 'project' and Participative 'initiative.' While they chose not to use the agile term 'scrum teams' they did use the term 'sprint' for the 30-day chunks of work. The workstreams were focused on operating model units, the three delivery units (Temperature, Energy, and Monitoring Solutions), the Marketing and Sales unit, and the Office Management unit. Operations and Logistics were addressed by the Temperature and Energy Solutions workstreams. The mix of operating unit and cross-unit work streams is typical of those found in Flexible operationalizing.

Roles/Structure: Monitoring Solutions

Smart-Home Pilot: The technology network took on the effort to build Monitoring Solutions, sponsored by Dawn and led by Wood's IT whiz. Their consultants recommended they build a smart-home pilot as an alternative to study and planning. Dawn volunteered her home. The workstream convened a product-focused smart-home mini-prototyping session in Dawn's home and invited several staff from the other workstreams to provide the needed skill sets.

Dawn's home was already outfitted with state-of-the-art solar. Since this involves isolating the home electrically, it's not hard to move from there to an integrated home system. The smart home and home security consultants helped the workstream, including Dawn's power grid guru and solar panel installation team, Wood's IT whiz, and Joe's craft masters, to cobble together a functional 'home-grown' system. Each company offered up some of their meager development budget to fund the equipment purchases. After numerous glitches in component suitability and

system security, by mid-April they had a rough working version.

The roadblocks they encountered turned out to involve more adapting systems to specific situations than inadequate knowledge about hardware and software. Every room, every house, every family, and every neighborhood were different: door and window geometry, wall and ceiling architecture, children's ages, pets' types and numbers, background sounds, Wi-Fi blocking pipes: each changed the equation.

Roles and Skill Sets: With a little electronics education, Joe's craft masters turned into better smart-home technicians than the IT experts who were all about electronics instead of 4 x 4 timbers, glass breakage frequencies, or abandoned 1900s gas pipe networks. This informed the workstream's effort to staff the IT function. They centered their search on people with IT expertise but also practical real-world experience. To their delight, they found that their ideal recruit actually had more affinity with their business than those with more theoretical knowledge.

Structure: Customer Solutions Teams: This workstream puzzled over how to group employees. Having fixed installation or maintenance teams made little sense with the work for each project so different. What they needed were groups like the pilot, ad hoc project teams with just the skills needed. They decided to maintain a core of IT systems specialists to work with customers, scope out projects, and then pull others from across the three business units into what they started calling ad hoc customer solutions teams.

Roles/Structure: Temperature and Energy Solutions

Workflow Mapping: The workshop macro-process map showed that Temperature Solutions and Energy Solutions had many activities in common. The two workstreams agreed to work together, sponsored by Shawn and led by Dawn's operations manager. As a first step they decided to add detail to the workshop mapping, focusing on the Deliver macro-process. This would help determine staffing and skill needs, standardize the work across the new enterprise, and determine how the centralized Operations and Logistics would fold into the work.

Shawn, Joe, and Dawn convened a prototyping mini-workshop. They invited one installation or maintenance team from each company, the entire Operations and Logistics staff, the leads from all the other teams, each of the craft masters, plus a smattering of sales, operations, logistics, and finance staff. Once assembled, they were asked to start with the macro-process map developed at the prototyping workshop and focus on detailing the deliver macro-process. They came up with the simplified diagram on the next page.

Please note that Comfort used a somewhat different definition of the RACI items than Stratos. For the initiatives in Stratos it was critical to identify who had the accountability for driving and delivering the initiatives. For the work process in Comfort it was more important to see who had the power to authorize the work.

Things kicked off with an order from the order macro-process. This could be to install a boiler, repair a solar panel, overhaul a security system, or a similar order from a customer. The customer relationship capability, which solicits and takes the order, is paired with the customer to emphasize the strategic focus.

COMFORT HOME SERVICES
Delivery Macro-Process

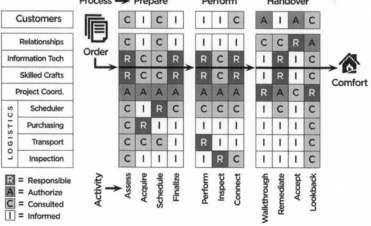

	Prepare				Perform			Handover			
	Assess	Acquire	Schedule	Finalize	Perform	Inspect	Connect	Walkthrough	Remediate	Accept	Lookback
Customers	C	I	C	I	I	I	C	A	I	A	C
Relationships	C	I	C	I	I	I	I	C	C	R	A
Information Tech	R	C	C	R	R	C	R	I	R	I	C
Skilled Crafts	R	C	C	R	R	C	R	I	R	I	C
Project Coord.	A	A	A	A	A	A	A	R	A	C	R
Scheduler	C	I	R	C	C	C	C	I	C	I	C
Purchasing	C	R	I	I	I	I	I	I	I	I	C
Transport	C	C	C	I	R	I	I	I	I	I	C
Inspection	C	I	I	I	I	R	C	I	I	I	C

R = Responsible
A = Authorize
C = Consulted
I = Informed

Comfort

The new project coordination capability oversaw the first activity, Assess, shown as a vertical column. They signed off in the Authorize task. The beefed-up IT and existing skilled crafts capabilities performed the Responsible tasks to evaluate the factors affecting feasibility of the order. Other capabilities, including customers, were Consulted as needed.

The mini-workshop worked through all three processes and associated activities and tasks. The mapping strongly reinforced the importance of project coordination, IT and skilled crafts capabilities, and clearly showed how logistics capabilities folded in. It pleased participants to see how a few boxes and arrows could convey so well their actual work as they delivered each customer a comfort home.

Implementation of this mapping took two paths. The first was to post it immediately online as the standard. They used a wiki-style open access editable format, kept open on a large screen in the operations rooms of each of the three companies. Editing by staff was initially quite heavy but settled down after a few days. The commentary shifted from the map itself to documenting the actions required for each product.

Roles and Accountabilities: The second path had each installation and maintenance team use the process map to define roles, accountabilities, and estimated numbers needed by their team. They were asked to coordinate with the capabilities housed in operations and logistics. As each team explored these interdependencies, it reinforced the project coordinator role and suggested a team structure.

Drawing from the Monitoring workstream, they adopted the customer solutions team model. Each team was initiated by a customer sales representative who had originated an order, and was led by the project coordinator assigned to that order. As the order progressed, a designated planner/scheduler was added, and then the installation or maintenance staff designated to the work. This solved several shortfalls that the three businesses were experiencing.

They used the workflow maps to group capabilities into specialties and functions, determine roles based on similar tasks, set accountabilities for those tasks, and estimate numbers. Three of the roles changed radically and illustrate the development of roles and accountabilities:

The customer relationship specialty had three capabilities, one for each business unit, and was itself part of the Marketing and Sales function. The customer relationship manager role kicked-off the delivery macro-process and solutions team with an order. Accountabilities:

◇ Interact with the customer and extract what they really need

◇ Understand products and services, including integrated solutions

◇ Initiate the project and work closely with the project coordinator

◇ Help the customer solutions team meet the customer's needs

◇ Lead the total customer experience: progress vs. expectations

Project coordinators handled tasks related to planning and delivering customer solutions. This role shifted from traditional hierarchical 'supervisor' issuing orders, towards an integration and coordination role. Its accountabilities included:

◇ Feasibility of proposed solutions: outcomes, timing, profitability

◇ Own the project plan, which integrates the activities of all involved

◇ Manage the project and coordinate the customer solutions team

◇ Deliver the finished solution to the customer's satisfaction.

The IT function had three specialties: applications, infrastructure, and data. One of the applications specialties was home security, and the new home security applications role, housed in Monitoring, provided expertise on Comfort's products and services and helped select, install, and maintain those chosen. Their accountabilities:

◇ Understand the integrated security system: software applications, hardware and connectivity infrastructure, and data capture

◇ Select the right applications to meet customer requirements

◇ Represent the other security specialties (infrastructure and data) on the customer solutions team and coordinate with them as needed

Structure: With roles, accountabilities, and numbers defined, the workstreams turned to defining work groups. This was easier than expected. Each of the two business units had mandates for installing and maintaining various products, which led to these units and roles:

◇ Installation teams handled skilled crafts, IT, and delivery

◇ Maintenance teams did routine check-ups and emergency repairs

◇ Project coordinators ensured integration and adequate resourcing
◇ Craft masters provided expertise and mentoring in the skilled crafts

Systems: Office Management

This workstream, led by Wood's personnel/HR manager, worked on the central services work unit. They quickly realized the need for interconnected systems to knit the companies together. Each of the separate enterprises had evolved different informal ad hoc practices, none that could scale up to the combined effort. They needed progress reporting, management reviews, and employee recognition. They convened a prototyping mini-workshop to develop these systems. It involved select staff from the combined companies but also several HR and finance consultants with the latest thinking. They came up with:

Management Performance Metrics: Delivery Dashboard	This innovative traffic light (green-yellow-red) dashboard tracked every web, telephone, or in-person inquiry whether it led to an order or not. Four entries per inquiry: ◇ Timing: Ahead or behind the next project milestone? ◇ Expectation: Current state of customer satisfaction? ◇ Profitability: Projected profit margin once complete? ◇ Obstacles: Systemic issues hindering completion?
Management Reporting & Review: Employee Ownership	The dashboard was posted on the intranet and each location and updated daily. The coordination council met every Monday to review progress in a meeting open to all. These meetings became the focal point for Sense as people brought in observations on the work and landscape.
HR Individual Performance Reward and Recognition	Baseline salaries set just under industry average but with performance bonus of up to 100% of base salary, based on each employee's contributions to the network as measured by the dashboard. Replaced the' eclectic patchwork of tradition, legacy, and rules of thumb.
HR Information & Transactions: Outsource Transactional HR	HR service provider took over payroll, benefits, employee data, and documenting performance and discipline cases. Replaced a hodge-podge of part-time and full-time staff. Existing personnel staff moved over to ensure continuity. Each company maintained its own service level contract but with agreed standards. Wood HR manager managed the contracts and maintained the other key HR systems.

Employees began taking strong personal interest and ownership in each of their orders. As the Monday morning reviews were opened up, they used the forum to explore what they could do better. Tying compensation to the dashboard and estimation accuracy succeeded beyond anyone's wildest hopes. Dashboard entries became almost obsessively honest, so the Monday morning reviews began to see and address the real challenges facing the business.

Roles/Structure: Marketing and Sales

The engagement network led by Dawn's marketing guru held a prototyping mini-workshop. Impressed by the Monitoring smart-home pilot, they decided to set up a mall kiosk with live feeds from the pilot home. They rotated Marketing, Sales, IT, and Monitoring staff to welcome and entertain visitors. Their friendly attitudes, concrete evidence of smart-home benefits, and the immediacy of signing up right in the mall led to more business than Comfort could handle. Consultations with the three business units led to a rethink of capacity and staffing. The coordination council reallocated two of Wood's maintenance teams to ramp up work on smart home technologies and service the new customers.

This is an excellent example of Flexible experimentation. They tried new things, learned from the results, and course corrected in real time. In a good example of prioritization, they wisely deferred building a product development group until later.

Comfort 30-Day Iterations

The work of the five workstreams brought increasing coherency to the efforts of the three companies as they implemented the prototype in the first 30-day sprint. The coordination council monitored the pulse of how things were going and either addressed issues in real time or captured them for later resolution.

30-Day Check

At the 30-day mark, the original workshop participants reconvened to review the results of the first 30-day sprint and address tensions and issues not resolved through individual, workstream or management action. The workstreams summarized progress followed by the now-familiar World Café rounds focused on: What's going well? What tensions have emerged? What needs to be adjusted? Then in plenary the participants defined the major issues and assigned accountabilities. The biggest success was the seamless leadership emerging and effectively using the Monday meetings.

The biggest shortfall was in Temperature Solutions. The mishmash of Joe's installation and maintenance teams, the ones from Wood, and the new project coordinators had not gelled. One customer solutions team had even erupted into shouting matches. Workshop participants concluded that Temperature Solutions was missing the Flexible leadership coordination role. Joe admitted how difficult he found it and proposed that Shawn take it on. This arrangement turned out to be a brilliant networked solution. It not only brought much-needed discipline to Joe's employees but also tightened coordination with the scheduling and logistics staff in the central functions.

The organization map on the next page shows how this networked enterprise shaped up during this first 30-day sprint.

It has several key features:

◇ The three lines of business were supported by the central functions.

◇ Leadership roles (shaded circles), including the project coordinators, coordinate and resource. Office assistants (open circles) were challenged to solve some customer requests on their own.

◇ Customer solutions teams, led by project coordinators, were staffed for each customer order with only the capabilities needed.

◇ Every employee had an original 'home base' company of original employment but was available for any of the three business units.

◇ The concept of 'craft master' was extended to the coordination and IT disciplines and labeled as a capability to reflect this.

◇ The new Monitoring Solutions housed dramatically strengthened IT capabilities, led by Wood's IT whiz until a leader was recruited.

◇ Shawn led Temperature Solutions and Dawn led Energy Solutions.

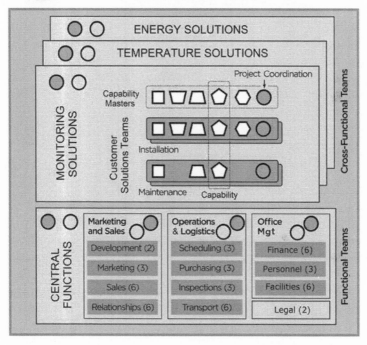

In a great nod to the Flexible culture, the coordination council had taken on the roles of week-to-week issue management and strategic resourcing. While open to all, participants were typically the shaded circle leadership roles.

60-Day Check

The 60-day meeting followed the same format as the 30-day. There were many more accomplishments to celebrate and correspondingly fewer issues. The biggest issue centered on what many at the original workshop had worried about: culture clashes between the very different mentalities in the three entities.

Joe's blue-collar folks frowned on Dawn's savvy young renewable and solar crusaders. Both groups bridled at the conservative older Wood employees and their endless stories about the 'good old days.' Where these groups mixed and worked together, what emerged was the best of each, a unique blend of cutting-edge product, quality work, and customer care.

Unfortunately, this blend was spread rather unevenly across the network. An ad hoc task group with one member from each of the three cultures was asked to work with the new HR provider to develop a training and onboarding curriculum to standardize and diffuse the resulting culture.

90 Days: Celebration and Birth

Comfort at the 90-day point had defined roles and work groups and completed the legal work. They had robust legally binding service-level contracts which could relax into habitual behavior over time as trust developed. The teams had been informally operating in the new way, but they now launched formally. The date was Wood's 150th anniversary and the planned celebration was turned into Comfort's birthday. As the gathering sang an impromptu "Happy Birthday to us" it was clear they were singing from the same song sheet!

Lessons and Closure

Comfort is a story of networking. What were initially three separate companies, who could only answer requests with 'yes' or 'no,' became an integrated enterprise ready to 'see how we can do that'! Their key lessons along with our editorial comments:

(1) Flexible Leadership: They act by bringing together the right people and fully participate rather than directing. Their primary accountability is not to approve the outcomes but ensure that they are implemented.

(2) Looking Forward: Flexible leaders run their current operations even as they encourage exploring beyond what's just the current scope.

(3) Site Visits moved Comfort's leaders from an interesting concept to collectively experiencing the sights, sounds, and sensations of a new way of doing business. No amount of study could have done this.

(4) Prototyping allowed them to bring together work expertise and map out a new business model without endless meetings or approvals.

(5) Engage Employees: During the process, their staff's mindsets shifted. They began to see that in collaboratively meeting customer needs with a wider set of offerings under one integrated umbrella, they were actually filling a niche with services no one else could do as well.

(6) Networked Organizations: Each entity has unique and complementary capabilities which with strong collaboration and administrative support, can multiply the value of the whole.

Epilogue: It's still early days for Comfort, but the cultural aspects are working out. The young and eager new head of Monitoring Solutions has his teams breaking new ground. Dawn has attracted even more renewable crusaders drawn by the promise of real change. Shawn has brought order  and efficiency to Temperature Solutions. There is more to do: product development is still a fuzzy idea. Still, the elder statesmen Red and Joe have grown close and are proud of the network. Their friendship, maturity, and 'can do' attitudes have moderated and improved the rough edges of the younger still-developing leaders. Things look good as this older generation paves the way for Shawn, Dawn, and their younger colleagues.

Chapter 10: Wilderness Directive to Participative

Wilderness Petroleum Company was a medium-sized regional oil and gas producer facing low oil prices, cost-overruns, and emerging disruptive technologies. Their case study shows a highly Directive culture needing to become more Participative to accommodate these challenges. It has five sections. The first, Sense, outlines the initial situation as they struggled to create a plan to staff eight new or refurbished facilities. The second, Mobilize, describes their start with a central design team which helped them adopt the Participative group process approach. The third, Frame Conference, describes how a new operating model emerged from the creative design process. The fourth, Customize, describes how the redefined functions filled in the details. The fifth, Resolve, describes how the renewed company brought to life truly integrated operations.

Wilderness Sense

Gather Information

Wilderness's president, Luca, was losing sleep even as his company had all the makings of a major success. His accomplished and charismatic VP Projects oversaw six major construction efforts as shown in the diagram on the next page. His experienced VP Operations managed the five existing facilities (solid black symbols) and two improvement projects (italics) and was due to take over the other projects when complete. Seasoned managers led the various functional groups in providing central corporate support. Stars indicate Luca's leadership team (WLT), the solid ones are its executive committee.

Luca had been brought in just over a year ago. The two presidents before him had been fired or demoted as the projects careened out of

WILDERNESS Petroleum

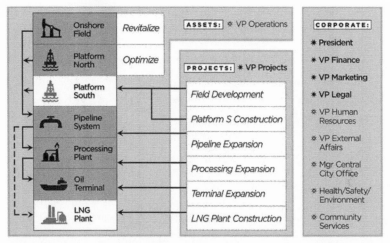

control, over budget and behind schedule. He had managed to get the projects back on track; however, his antennae were sensing information indicating that trouble was brewing. The most significant was the lack of a plan to transition to steady-state producing operations. The leadership team understood the urgency, but even with only 18 months before it needed to be in place, competing agendas and finger pointing had them hopelessly deadlocked. Now the joint ventures partners were trying to pull out and the government was threatening to revoke the production sharing agreements. Luca finally got his leadership to agree on assembling a group to discern a way forward.

Assess the Issues

Luca turned to his Human Resources VP, Theresa, to help him think through how to do this and come up with a 'plan for the plan.' She was reluctant. She was on the leadership team and saw first-hand its dysfunction. She had no magic method for getting them to a transition plan. However, she agreed to look into it. She had just read about Syngineering and began to apply some of the concepts to the situation at Wilderness.

The Wilderness workforce was highly stratified into three groupings: permanent staff, project staff, and local mostly unskilled workers. The need for central project control had produced a strict hierarchy between these groups with natural resentments and animosities. The company had a harsh performance ethic and didn't tolerate failure. As a result, project reviews were confrontations between defensive employees and judgmental executives. She saw it as a dysfunctional Directive culture.

The landscape and the culture it needed were less clear; however, Theresa was highly-involved in the business and was aware of the exploding complexity of the work due to  metering technologies and data analytics. The Wilderness hierarchy was ill-equipped to deal with this. A team called 'iOps' for integrated operations had made little progress in two years. The description of the Knowledge Work landscape matched what she intuitively felt: that more staff involvement and a Participative culture were needed.

Theresa recognized that significant behavior shifts would be required from the leadership but saw some bright spots. First, some of her colleagues were talking about an IT concept called agility that was being applied to more general work and organizational processes. Second, she had confidence that Luca and almost all of his leadership could learn, and change given the chance to see and experience collaborative working. Her training and experience as a strategic HR business partner gave her the skills to provide those experiences.

She began to see how she and a central project team could collaborate with the leadership in a Participative approach. Her greatest concern came from the harsh performance ethic that didn't tolerate failure: this could severely damage her career. However, she smiled at the sampler on her wall, "Go big or go home," and decided to take it on.

Learn Participative Agility

Theresa was ready to speak with Luca but wondered whether he would face the issues and tackle the leadership dynamics. She reviewed the Syngineering concepts, summarized her observations, and outlined the Directive and Participative approaches in Chapters 4 and 5. To her pleasant surprise he agreed completely with her assessments. Not only did he support changing the leadership behaviors, but he had also already hired a consultant to begin working on that.

Luca said that far from jeopardizing her career, leading this project could be a significant stepping stone. He had spoken with each member of his leadership team and they had unanimously agreed she was the natural choice. She formally agreed to take the lead role. They mapped out the composite approach in the sidebar, starting with a project team using the Directive approach and shifting during the Mobilize phase to Participative. They agreed that group process would be a radical new approach in overcoming individual leadership team member agendas. They also agreed that to gain management and employees' acceptance it was critical to see proof of new behaviors among leadership and more than lip service to delegating authority. Taking her into his confidence, he outlined thumbnail sketches of each team member, and together they discussed how to gain approval for this proposed project.

Theresa had an important role to play in this. By first working with the executives individually, she could 'hold up the mirror' to them collectively in meetings. This would introduce Participative practices

Wilderness Roadmap
<u>Sense</u>
◇ Gather Information
◇ Assess the Issues
◇ Learn Agility
◇ Decision to Act
Mobilize Phase
1. Charter & Plan
2. Revisit Strategy
3. Diagnosis & Criteria
◇ Decide on Culture
◇ Approve Project
◇ Announce Project
◇ Mobilize Conference
Frame Conference
I. Preparation & Intro
II. Core Work [4]
III. Operating Model [5]
IV. Deployment [6]
V. Plan & Engage
Customize Phase
◇ Deployment Detail
◇ Roles/Accountab. [7]
◇ Structure [8]
◇ Support Systems [9]
◇ Customize Conference
Resolve Phase
◇ Adjust [10]
◇ Resolve Conference
◇ Resume Sensing

while avoiding a frontal attack on the hierarchy. It provided enough psychological safety to allow leaders to discover things on their own rather than have their egos and personal agendas directly challenged. This began a powerful partnership. Luca and Theresa coordinated their behind-the-scenes and within-meeting activities to illustrate and exemplify these new collaborative Participative behaviors.

Decision to Act

Luca asked Theresa to develop a draft charter for the project and begin engaging his leaders. While a highly successful oil industry executive who was deeply passionate about Wilderness, as with most large Directive companies, he had substantial but not complete authority. Many of his VPs had enough influence to sabotage the change effort. Luca suggested that Theresa interview each one during the chartering process. This might enlist their support, solicit their ideas for the design team, and also lay the groundwork for leadership collaboration.

Wilderness Mobilize

Deliverable 1: Charter

These interviews not only provided critical chartering information, but also began to build the relationships needed for the project to succeed. Two of these conversations were especially eye-opening. The highly accomplished VP Projects leader had been the previous Wilderness president but was moved aside after massive budget and schedule slippages. He never forgave Luca for replacing him. The VP Operations had been excluded from the executive committee and saw that as a visible sign of lack of respect, especially from those on that committee.

Theresa prepared a first draft of the two charter ingredients in the tables on the next page and reviewed it at a specially called leadership team meeting. She emphasized its iterative nature. Once the design team met, they would fill in the engagement needs. It took a full day to review, deliberate, and agree. It was clear that they saw the review and the project as important priorities. There were three big sticking points:

◇ The first was 'too many deliverables.' While pleased at the roadmap logical sequence and phased approach, it seemed way over-the-top when all they really needed was the deployment or transition plan. In the end, they good-humoredly agreed that the quality of the plan would speak for itself and that they trusted Theresa.

◇ The second sticking point was the Participative approach, especially if conferences overwhelmed the already stressed project delivery. Luca suggested they revisit after the design team had a chance to fill in the first three deliverables: charter, strategy, and diagnosis.

◇ The third sticking point centered around the steering team. The VP Projects suggested the executive committee for efficiency, but Luca insisted that the culture shift would require buy-in from his entire leadership team. No one strongly objected.

Theresa ended the meeting with her commitment to convene the design team composed of each leader's candidate, have them update the project plan, and return to the WLT for review.

Wilderness Project Scope

Case for Change	As construction projects come onstream beginning in eighteen months, we need to transition to producing operations, but no plans are yet agreed. The future of the company is at stake.
Boundaries & Givens	The organization and all of its components are in scope, but no activities can impede the construction projects. Organization structure must remain functional at the senior level.
Goals and Objectives	The primary objective was Deliverable 6: Deployment Plan, within six months, but this required revising the operating model. Customize and Resolve to be handled by the high-level operating units over the twelve months after that.

Wilderness Involvement

Approach	Complexity from emerging technologies have driven the landscape to Knowledge Work while the culture remains as highly hierarchical and Directive. The approach needs to move the organization smoothly to a Participative culture.
Resources & Staffing	The Wilderness Leadership Team (WLT) steers and guides. A design team of operating unit representatives makes recommendations and plans engagement and conferences.,
Engagement	Wait for the design team to meet and determine.

Theresa started up the design team and they carved out precious time on evenings and weekends to review and further develop the charter. A key focus was to speak honestly and develop the psychological safety to collaborate. An important indicator that this was working was the number of comments prefaced by statements like, "My VP and I don't agree on this, but ...." They mapped out engagement needs, and the three elements of plan as described in the table below. They had agreed to revisit culture change with the WLT after diagnosis but scheduled a tentative Mobilize conference for one month later, then a tentative Frame conference the month after. Customize was to be done predominantly by the VPs and their functions with a possible coordination conference late in the year, followed by implementation and close-out the next year.

Wilderness Project Plan

Engagement Needs	VP Projects was "opposed"; his transition plan was to release units as no longer needed. VP Operations was a "skeptic" who didn't believe that would work. Design team members engaged them frequently. Projects and Operations technical staff and Operations local staff were all "concerned". The functions were to cascade information via normal channels.
Risk Analysis	Most serious was if leadership conflict prevented agreement. Luca made this a high priority. While the government might pull the licenses, the project itself was the best mitigation.
Commu- nications	Information was to be cascaded via design team members, the normal VP channels, and occasional President notices.
Integrated Plan	The design team made tentative plans for the roadmap Theresa and Luca had developed but put on hold until the WLT could agree on the Participative conferences.

Deliverable 2: Strategy

The leadership team were happy with the recently revised strategy, but Theresa knew that Syngineering needed clear strategy statements, so Luca suggested the design team discuss and bring any issues to the WLT. They quickly agreed the core business ingredient except for core values; many cynically saw these values as empty rhetoric. However, the tone in the room shifted as Theresa asked for their own personal core values: the conversations became authentic with real substance and emotion. They took the three corporate 'slogans' and found wordings that they could each personally identify with and own. They came together in a way that no artificial teambuilding could have done. We see this in many organizations: words on a wall are only effective when brought to life through dialogue and application to real behaviors.

Wilderness Core Business

Core Purpose	Commercially develop, operate and market the hydrocarbon resources and associated infrastructure governed by the existing offshore and onshore licenses for the sustainable benefit of shareholders and community.
Core Values	(a) Respect: We utilize every employee's talents and interests. (b) Team 1st: Where they conflict, I place the good of our joint corporate work ahead of my own individual interests. (c) Accountability: I know what I need to do, and I do it.
Core Capabilities	Current: world class reservoir management and commercial oil & gas trading skills. Needed: advanced IT skills in remote working, handling massive data flows, and data analytics.
Core Assets	Current: onshore field, north platform, pipelines, processing plant, and oil terminal, Under construction: south platform, LNG plant, and improvements to each of the current assets.

The design team solicited thoughts from their colleagues and then compiled, discussed, and highlighted these landscape themes.

Wilderness Landscape

Technology Trends	We're not keeping up with emerging developments in real-time metering, integrated operations, and drilling. Integrated operations poised to transform the business.
Markets, Social, and Customers	Low oil prices threaten long-term contract negotiations. Environmental issues and partnership conflict over cost overruns affecting regional reputation.
Competitor Developments	Global competitors trying to use their drilling and integrated operations excellence to take over our leases.
Regulatory & Government	National oil company using cost overruns and environmental offenses to take a significant portion of a renegotiated production sharing agreement.

As the design team explored the leadership's recent work on strategy, they were increasingly impressed with how well it applied operational excellence and provided clear guidance on the operating model. Their resulting articulation, outlined in the table below, is one of the best we've seen. It fits on a single printed page, has specific aspirations and details, and yet doesn't give away competitive confidentialities. The design team tested it with office staff, operations hands, and even their own families! It was instantly understandable to everyone they asked.

Wilderness Strategy

Products & Services	Develop and produce oil and gas products from existing low-royalty oil and gas leases. Ship to regional customers who prefer long-term contracts to lock in their expenses.
Value Proposition	Use state-of-the-art drilling and reservoir management to maximize value with relentless operational excellence.
Goals & Objectives	◇ Move 3rd to 1st quartile in regional cost performance ◇ Move from 15% to 90% local staffing of all positions ◇ Move from 3rd to 1st quartile in safety performance ◇ All projects on time, under budget, and meet designs
Organizational Characteristics	◇ Production-sharing agreement gives cost advantage ◇ Technology for integrated operations missing ◇ Work processes need to improve efficiency ◇ Structure is functional but needs more coordination. ◇ People skills need cutting-edge IT and drilling. ◇ Systems must foster better cost estimation and more cross-functional collaboration and teamwork.

Deliverable 3: Diagnosis

Collect Information: The design team had substantial information from the technical process audits, conversations with colleagues, advice from the VPs, and their own observations. They validated these by interviewing a cross-section of colleagues with the Diagnosis questions in Part IV, then combined them into 31 significant related but distinct issues.

Synthesis: Theresa then had the team group these issues into broad themes with recommendations for how to address each one. They came up with six themes. Half of these six involved coordination. This is often true for Directive cultures where silos create duplicate work, gaps, or conflicting demands and the culture doesn't support informal collaboration.

This part 'science' and part 'art' activity was to get below the surface and find the root causes. The two tables that follow show how this worked for the highest priority theme. The first table lists the issues. Numbers are the percentage of interviews that mentioned this issue.

Wilderness Diagnosis: Theme 1: Poor technical group coordination

Issues	55%	Poor coordination between drilling and other technical groups
	53%	IT groups in Finance, Operations, and Projects don't talk.
	46%	Project consistently allocates facilities engineering resources to Projects field development over ongoing platform operations
	37%	Poor coordination between Projects development engineering group and Projects drilling group on drill sites and follow-up
	22%	iOps has no support from Finance IT or Projects IT and has no critical mass for establishing 'continuously metered operations'.

The next table shows this theme's root causes and proposed levers. These levers are often used by Directive cultures to get silos talking.

Wilderness Diagnosis: Theme 1: Poor technical group coordination

Root Causes	Lever	Priority
No formal mechanism or reinforcement	New technical coordination council with authority to allocate resources.	High
Non-standard poorly documented processes	Standardize and implement standard technical processes.	High
Fuzzy or conflicting group mandates	Technical coordination council revise all group mandates to clarify coordination	Medium
Technical disciplines out of place in Projects	New Technical function to provide a focused home for engineering disciplines	Medium

The remaining themes and their proposed solutions below round out the synthesis. The design team had an interesting discussion around the 'ultimate root causes' and the role of behavior. They wondered whether the current leadership team members could ever get to Participative. This conversation reinforced Theresa's initial assessment that the ultimate issue was the culture and that the proposed solutions needed to move in that direction.

Theme 2: Poor Health, Safety, and Environment (HSE) coordination
◇ Create a new HSE coordination council (high priority)
◇ Matrix reporting with a strong HSE function (medium priority)

Theme 3: Project withholds support functions from Operations
◇ Written accountabilities for all support groups (medium priority)
◇ Resourcing council, possibly same as Theme 1 (medium priority)

Theme 4: Difficult to attract qualified people to working locations. This was the focus of an existing HR-led initiative, but it was stalled.
◇ Offer more attractive and locally tailored benefits (high priority)
◇ Focus on local staff development at all levels (high priority)
◇ Company operating manuals in the local language (medium priority)

Theme 5: Validate offshore field platform staffing model. This was also underway but had not yet involved platform hourly staff.
◇ Use ideal workflows to set platform staffing model (high priority)
◇ Retro-fit this model to the existing platform (high priority)
◇ Distribute existing staff across both platforms and recruit to fill any remaining vacancies (high priority)

Theme 6: Difficulty in implementing new metering technologies. The iOps team leader described how technology could transform operations but there was little interest at Wilderness.
◇ Clarify accountabilities and resourcing for iOps (high)
◇ Explore the impacts of monitoring and educate staff (high)
◇ Create a formal iOps group with a clear mandate (medium)

The design team used the organization chart to visualize the issues:

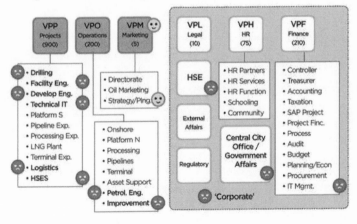

The sad or happy face emoticons on the most significant issues were a huge hit and a great speaking tool when sharing observations and insights with leadership and staff. They also highlighted the success of the Marketing function in selling future production and in setting up a small but very effective strategy and planning group.

With such a compelling case for change, the design team felt little need for a formal change readiness assessment. However, to get some sense of how ready people were to correct the issues raised in the diagnostic, each design team member talked with individuals in their functions.

Wilderness Change Readiness:

Change History	Change had been continuous but was accepted as part of project work. All employees wanted a transition plan.
Effort Priority	The need for change was compelling. Staff were eager, their leaders less so, but willing to move ahead. Local staff felt left out of the discussions but were hopeful.

To develop design criteria, the design team started with the charter, strategy, and diagnosis and came up with a list of candidates, each linked to one or more organizational components. A number of these became 'givens,' for example "meet regulatory requirements" and "avoid compromising ongoing construction." These needed to be built into any design. Several others were 'nice to have' for later, for example "implementing the dual-language commitment." They ended up with:

Wilderness Decision Criteria

Structure	◇ Minimize moving groups; focus on linking mechanisms
	◇ Corporate functions must support core work; eliminate fragmentation and competing groups.
People	◇ Locate staff as close to the work as possible
Systems	◇ Align performance management and rewards to reinforce collaborative and other Participative behaviors
Leadership	◇ Deal explicitly with conflicting motivations, especially the Project construction vs. routine Operations mentalities.

Decide on Culture

The diagnosis themes reinforced the design team's conviction that the solutions involved more coordination, collaboration, and participation.

They sensed that the changes needed were significant enough that just 'telling people' the conclusions wouldn't yield fast adoption. So far it had been a classic Directive project and just a few people had been directly involved in the charter, strategy, and diagnosis.

Before they moved to Frame, they decided to engage a broader cross-section of staff in the outcomes of Mobilize. This would give them adequate inputs, buy-in, and understanding of the implications of the project on people's daily work. The composite roadmap Theresa developed during Sense seemed the ideal vehicle. The Mobilize Conference would broaden involvement, the Frame Conference would incorporate comprehensive inputs on the organization's work, and Customize and Resolve would be handled by the functions, as given in the charter. They agreed to advocate for the composite approach and move to a Participative culture.

Theresa shared the strategy and diagnosis results with Luca in their weekly briefing. He was pleased at both but hesitated at the two issues critiquing specific leaders. Part of his job as sponsor was to address these issues and he had already put remedies in place. He asked her to delete them in the interest of unifying leadership support.

She summarized the design team's commitment to the conference model and expressed concerns about whether the leadership team would agree. Luca surprised her by disclosing that he and the Finance VP had been discussing how to orient the next leadership team meeting agenda in this direction. Once again Luca and Theresa exemplified an effective sponsor and project leader partnership. Theresa was positioning the design team to get out in front of the organization and its entrenched leadership. Luca moved behind the scenes on the same issues to develop powerful allies on his leadership team.

Leadership Approval

The design team now met with leadership to review their strategy thoughts, the diagnosis, and forcefully advocate for the conferences.

The strategy discussion turned into a pleasant and important exercise for both the leadership and design team. The design team complimented the leadership on what they thought was excellent strategy work and offered several insightful comments and suggestions that the leadership had not considered.

The diagnosis discussion was more confrontational. This is often true in Directive organizations, which tend to respond defensively to criticism, no matter how constructive. The Operations and Projects VPs in particular peppered the design team with challenging questions and objections about airing their 'dirty laundry.' The design team members from these functions responded that all this was common knowledge, but people were afraid to bring it up. Using a mixed metaphor that everyone instantly recognized, they said that not all scoreboard traffic lights can be green and perhaps it was time to clean the laundry!

Luca then brought things back to the issue of broadening involvement. He gave a blunt synopsis: Wilderness needed an effective functional organization without the silos now crippling it. He challenged the leaders around the table to carefully review the design team materials. The discussion that followed revealed that many of the design team had already lobbied their VPs. The only hold-outs were Operations and Projects. The Projects VP caved in after observing that 'his' two design team members were passionate about the conferences, but he demanded that the conferences not delay his construction work.

The Operations VP remained resistant to giving up executive control to some 'random group of engineers.' Luca reminded him that the design team had been set up because of these sorts of disagreements. Operations had the most to lose if it did not succeed. The conference would be far from random, instead their 'best and brightest.' He promised that no conference recommendations would be binding until there was leadership team approval. The Operations VP reluctantly agreed to consider the proposal.

After an extended break to cool things off, the VP Finance stepped in. He had used large staff conferences in his last assignment, and they had accelerated renewal of a fading joint venture. He offered to sponsor the Mobilize conference as an experiment. Staff would review the charter, strategy, and diagnosis. It would be a learning opportunity for leadership and staff and thus a pilot for the Participative culture. Several others offered support and, in this highly Directive culture, Luca's endorsement brought grudging agreement.

Announce and Engage

The next day was a public holiday. The Finance VP, a career oil industry executive nearing retirement, traditionally hosted a staff gathering of expatriates and their spouses with some locals to honor the day. After a few

rounds, Theresa was surrounded by staff and spouses and peppered with angry queries like, "What are you and that secret group doing late into the night?", "Are we losing the production licenses?", "Are you sending us home?", and "What's going on?"

Just as the atmosphere threatened to turn ugly, the Finance VP stepped in. He gathered the design team near the refreshment table, had the leadership team stand behind them, and got everyone's attention. He crisply summarized the project and its importance and suggested that the design and leadership teams would love to hear from everyone there. The room exploded with energy as small groups began intense and animated conversations, some continuing late into the night!

The next evening, the design team discussed this event. The plan for cascading information via design team members and VPs was clearly not nearly enough. They decided to invite all staff and spouses to the informal bi-weekly social and have one of the VPs give a brief progress report and field questions.

Luca had an additional thought. That morning the offshore platform superintendent had approached him. A fiery young local staff engineer, he had come to Wilderness with the promise of improving things. As the only local staff in management, he bent Luca's ear about the design team, all expatriates from one of the joint venture partners. Luca asked Theresa to add him to the design team to give local staff a voice.

Mobilize Conference

The design team began planning this 'experiment' as the next step on the road to Participative. Each fast-paced and highly participative session would review materials, hold mixed group discussions, develop recommendations, and then watch leadership decide yes, no, or explore further. Participants would get to think about the whole business and not just their immediate part. Collaboration would emerge naturally as individuals and groups uncovered connections and common interests.

Planning Team: The relabeled design team had key roles: plan flexible processes for the conference, coach executives on their roles, develop drafts to jump-start sessions, and facilitate maximum involvement and concrete action. The VP External Affairs offered communications and logistics support and also volunteered to invite representatives from the local community and suppliers and customers.

Executive Roles: The planning team helped the executives understand and rehearse their roles in the conference. They more or less embraced these, some more enthusiastically than others. All agreed to lead and facilitate the conference and its sessions, sharing their vision of a successful producing organization, and articulate and set boundaries as needed. They also saw the need to make decisions reflecting conference deliberations, although several had reservations about doing this in the conference, especially if it required leadership teamwork and unity at a scale they were nowhere near achieving, much less demonstrating.

Attendance: A critical leadership function was to select participants. The largest local facility held around 85 people which meant about 5% of Wilderness's 1700 employees could attend. They decided on 25 core participants to attend each conference: the leadership team and subject matter experts who knew the work. They filled another 50 places with additional subject matter experts, trusted listeners who others felt comfortable confiding in, and connection nodes who brought others together. These were distributed across work groups and job levels. They set aside the remaining ten spots for customers, suppliers, and members of the local community.

Participants: The planning team sent out the conference agenda along with draft versions of the charter, strategy, and diagnosis. They asked the participants to play three roles. First was to offer expert knowledge of their segment of the company's work and collaborate with the other participants to assemble a comprehensive picture of the organization. Second was to engage in open dialogue with informed opinions about what was needed. Finally, they were asked to serve as communications nodes and disseminate the conference's results to their colleagues who had not attended.

Session I: Welcome and Introductions: Those invited convened in late August in the local school gymnasium. Luca welcomed them and crisply summarized the challenges facing Wilderness.

Session II: Charter and Project Plan: Theresa led this session. There was little discussion aside from cynical questions about how this 'plan for a plan' would get any closer to the elusive 'transition plan'. Several attendees were surprised at the conferences in the plan but accepted the reply about experimenting to broaden input. Participants seemed to be carefully watching the leaders for cues. The leaders seemed anxious.

Session III: Directions and Strategy: A local natural gas customer was well received but the small group discussions were as quiet as in session II. Many had heard third-hand of the Operations VP's opposition to the conference and no one was willing to step out and ask tough questions. Things began to shift when the topic turned to core values. The motto "Team first" in particular led to the first intense and heart-felt sharing at the conference. One brave accountant challenged the executives with, "I will if you will" which moved the Projects VP to describe his anguish over sharing his scarce understaffed resources with Operations when it jeopardized his projects. Which team first? Which was the greater good? After a lively discussion, momentum built to change it to "Wilderness first." Visible nods from each leadership team member led Luca to accept. The mood in the room lifted.

Session IV: Diagnosis: Participants agreed with the issues lists and found it validating to see their concerns systematically noted and mapped out. The root cause observations removed any skepticism that the change effort was management 'window dressing.' The biggest surprise came from a vocal minority of IT specialists who were concerned that continuous metering and data analytics did not have a more central role. The planning team promised to explore this more fully.

Decision criteria elicited a consideration no one had foreseen. Several participants bravely volunteered that there was substantial informal coordination already going on under the VPs' noses, some of it against their direct orders. They asked for forgiveness for those clandestine efforts and suggested "Use existing mechanisms and systems as much as possible" as an added decision criterion. The VPs wisely chose not to inquire further and adopted the addition.

Session V: Road Ahead: This final session out-lined the roadmap ahead and enlisted partici-pants in planning the communications cascade they would each be part of as they returned to their workplaces. The VP External Affairs led highly engaging role playing on 'elevator speeches.' Luca closed the conference with the  challenge for each participant to put the elevator speeches to good use and announced a tentative date for the Frame Conference.

Wilderness Frame Conference

Conference Preparation

Technical VP: The next week, the organization was surprised when Luca announced a new Technical VP. While a medium priority in the diagnosis, he and Theresa agreed that it was an inevitable outcome of the operating model, and having the VP involved in the design would provide focus for the various technical initiatives and speed things up.

Planning Team: Highly energized by the success of the conference, and the movement symbolized by the new Technical VP, the planning team focused on preparing for the Frame Conference: developing draft materials on technology, work, processes, and operating model choices.

The conference would review these materials, determine an operating model, and then map out the deployment plan. In parallel Mobilize Conference attendees were generating tremendous interest as they relayed the results of this first conference.

Leadership Team: Luca and Theresa meanwhile were dealing with a divided leadership team. The VP Projects and VP Operations were still upset about not being consulted on the Technical VP and concerned that his appearance would undercut their positions. The VP Operations was increasingly agitated over the idea of letting the Frame Conference participants select an  operating model. He accused 'his' design team members (two that he had nominated plus the platform superintendent Luca added) of betraying him and ignoring his wishes. Something had to be done.

Sponsor Management: The Technical VP showed up the next week. He spent several days closeted with Luca, Theresa, VP Projects and VP Operations, the engineering specialty heads, and the design team. He made no public announcements and changed no reporting relationships. Stories began to circulate that whenever a coordination issue surfaced, somehow the Technical VP showed up, brought together the staff involved, up to and including the VPs and relentlessly kept people talking until the issue was resolved. His understated authority exemplified the humble, powerful, and agile great leader in Lao-Tzu's quote in Chapter 1.

The leadership consultant was encouraging Luca to be more transparent, so when the Operations VP asked his chances at the VP position in the new Operations function, Luca told him bluntly that his behaviors had eliminated him as a candidate and that he would be reassigned at the close of the project. In several long talks, Luca asked him what he wanted to leave behind as his Wilderness legacy, and what he wanted to change that might help him in his next assignment. The Operations VP asked Theresa to meet with him and his design team members to hear each other out and find common ground. Afterwards he grudgingly agreed to participate in the conference.

We have detailed the behind-the-scenes jockeying for control here because it is often glossed over yet it is essential to address for you to achieve agility. We don't believe in beating down resistance, rather in listening carefully, acting on the wisdom behind it, and building relationships and support. The point was not to get full leadership alignment, but rather to get them into the conference where their own staff could guide them on the technology, the operating model, and most importantly on the deployment plan.

Executive Roles: The planning and leadership teams carved up roles in the conference. Luca would kick off and sponsor. The Technical VP volunteered to carry the torch for technology and help the planning team design those sessions. Other VPs volunteered to lead different sessions.  The Operations and Projects VP's agreed to work with the planning team and find constructive ways to share their concerns.

Attendees: The 85 invitees included the 25 holdovers from the first conference plus 50 from across work groups and job levels. These included entire working teams from producing operations and engineering. Ten slots for externals included consultants who were experts in integrated operations, LNG plants, and government environmental regulations. As before, the VP and design team member from each function ensured the participants included their key people.

Participants: Each received agendas, several articles on metering and integrated operations technologies, and articles on organizing work groups. They were encouraged to discuss with their colleagues and bring to the conference comments and feedback.

Session: Welcome and Introductions: Luca's welcome promised a very different conference from the first: they would work hard together and create the new Wilderness operating model. He sat down and the Technical VP introduced the next session.

Session: Core Work

Technology Vision: An industry expert spoke about integrated operations across the globe. He listed a series of technology advances:

automated and continuously recording downhole and pipeline meters; remote videos, powerful handheld devices; sophisticated airborne and seaborne drones, instantaneous networked communications; advanced data collection and analytic algorithms. While nothing was conceptually new, the show itself was striking. Instead of a speech with fuzzy PowerPoint slides, this was a series of video snippets featuring simulated field locations and even a few people they recognized.

What had been a nebulous dream just a few years before had become a real possibility: integrated operations. Real-time connections could bring platform workers and office engineers into what seemed almost like the same room, looking at the same data and video-feeds. Many fewer  personnel remained at the remote sites. Dangerous work was eliminated, reduced, or done in safer ways. Experts roamed from one room to another and were literally part of several remote operations. This was not a one-sided sales pitch and included an honest appraisal of major sticking points: cost-benefit-value considerations, retro-fitting old equipment, and how to foster collaboration.

Mixed groups at tables were asked: if this were your company, what would you do? There were no further instructions, just "you've seen what others are doing; what are we going to do?" The experience of the iOps team members was notable. After months in obscurity, they were sought out, eagerly listened to, and respected. As participants were rotated between tables, posters and drawings and simulated news reports painted a picture of what Wilderness might look like.

Technology Realization: After a break, attendees were grouped at tables by function; many were intact work teams. These groups were asked to review the results from the last session and brainstorm how to make it work. They were asked to put on a 'future hat' and imagine working in this new world. Where did they see handoffs and breakdowns - not all of them but the few key ones? What could be done to resolve or address these? What were the logical consequences of this on Wilderness?

They then rotated in what we call the World Café method: one member of each group stayed and facilitated feedback. The requirements of this new world were staggering: handling and interpreting mass quantities of complex data, new work processes, cross-functional staff co-located and collaborating, and accelerated decision-making. One immediate opportunity would be the ability to use data to make immediate changes instead of waiting for laborious analyses.

Then there were secondary impacts. People would need more technical skills. Fewer staff at remote facilities affected transportation and logistics, work shift planning, and even compensation. Recruiting, training, and assigning staff would need to change. IT systems would need massive upgrades to get the right data to the right people at the right time to enable the right decisions. Was a siloed functional organization, a seeming 'given,' still the best operating model? A very practical issue was how to counter this culture's fantasy that one smart engineer with enough data feeds could operate all of Wilderness.

Workflows: One table of engineers were not satisfied with their text notes on these requirements and began doodling how the technologies actually fit into the flow of work. They came up with this diagram:

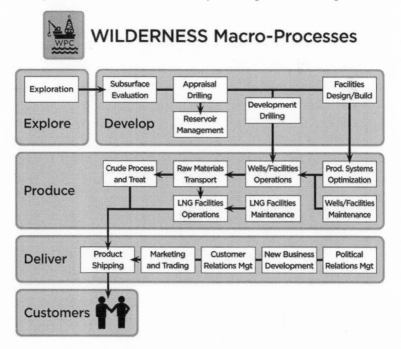

They started with the value chain: Explore to find deposits, Develop facilities to access them, Produce them, and Deliver product to customers. As the tables rotated, and other disciplines and functions added insights, the details emerged. While somewhat complicated, it allowed participants to place technology requirements in the flow of work and see the underlying order and simplicity. It described their entire business and positioned them perfectly for the next session.

Session: Operating Model

Organization Components: The VP Operations started this session by having the tables summarize the component requirements so far. They quickly converged on these, several straight from the decision criteria.

Leadership and Culture	◇ Manage collaboratively and follow Wilderness First ◇ Remove barriers to operational efficiency
Work and Technology	◇ Integrated operations; monitor emerging technologies ◇ Standard processes, especially drilling and optimization
People and Skills	◇ Clear roles and accountabilities for integrated operations ◇ Accelerate local staff recruiting, training, and retention
Support Systems	◇ Massive IT system upgrades for continuous data feeds ◇ Rewards and review systems reflect the new 24-7 world

Integrated operations had grown in importance from the beginning of the project as reflected in how many items mentioned it.

Structure Options: The next part of the session looked at the structure component. The VP Operations introduced it by acknowledging he had been against the conferences from the start. He had always held organization design to be the province of executives with the strategic big picture. However, he had been impressed with the quality of thinking and outputs from the previous sessions and challenged them to see what they could do with structure.

He placed them into 11 'home' tables by function: 6 for Operations, 2 for Technical, 1 for Marketing, 1 for Finance, and 1 for Corporate and HR combined. He reviewed the five common types of grouping from Deliverable 5 in Part IV and asked them to preserve the functional organization and follow the decision criteria. Participants were instructed to focus the first few rounds on high level groupings:

Technical Grouping	The only grouping that maintained critical mass was by engineering discipline. Two provided competitive advantage: subsurface reservoir management and information technology. Drilling and facilities were enabling disciplines as were projects and engineering capability management.
Marketing Grouping	Two advantage groups were oil and gas trading. Also, advantage were new business development and existing relationship management. Shipping operations was enabling.
Operations Grouping	All of this function, while critical, was enabling. Two options: geography (onshore, offshore, and LNG plant) and function (operations and maintenance). There was no clear preference.
Corporate Groupings	Each of these functions had few enough specialty staff that the only grouping that made sense at next level was functional.

High Level Coordination: Most tables spent little time on groupings and moved to how to get coordination and integrated operations to work. What emerged was cross-functional multi-disciplinary collaboration among engineers, technicians, IT professionals, and others as needed.

(1) Co-location of staff. Onshore field, pipeline, and processing plant have small highly skilled groups at field locations with larger groups in a control center connected by high-bandwidth channel. The offshore fields similar with active drilling projects. The LNG plant and oil terminal similar but everything at the same location.

(2) Expanded Chief Petroleum Engineer job, as with many producing operations, to be accountable for coordination across all of Operations and Technical, reporting jointly to the two VPs.

Operating Model Selection: As they rotated, the tables drew pictures of how it would all fit together. These drawings and the accompanying explanations coalesced into the diagram and bullet points below:

◇ Three core functions each managed their macro-process. At the next level strong disciplines like maintenance anchored coordination.

◇ The two Operations options, geography and function, were not resolved and were left for Customization. The overlapping groups in the diagram signaled a shift from the existing hierarchical super-interdependencies to interlocking cross-functional teams, including skills from Technical.

◇ Information Technology (IT) and Information Management (IM) were concentrated under the Technical VP and elevated to core discipline.

◇ Controversy surfaced at the Corporate/HR table. The suggestion of an umbrella corporate 'staff' function was resisted heavily by HR, Finance, and External Affairs. As these participants circulated to other tables, however, they were welcomed as valued functional experts. HR staff, for example, helped define capability roles in each core function, tasked with staff development and assignment and linked back to the HR 'home discipline'. The issue of a corporate grouping subsided as it became clear that for this operating model to work, titles and reporting would need to become secondary.

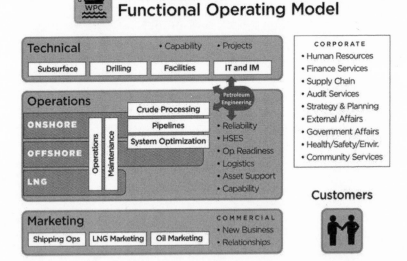

WILDERNESS Functional Operating Model

To close the session, tables evaluated the operating model against the decision criteria. The first two, cross-organizational linking and eliminate fragmentation, were clearly met. The other three, reward collaboration, locate staff close to the work, and deal explicitly with conflicting motivations, remained to be addressed in Customization.

Session: Deployment Plan

The Chief Petroleum Engineer led this critical session which ran for most of the third day. Humble and soft-spoken, he was stunned being named to his new role. but was up to the task! He summarized ongoing and new proposed initiatives. He restated the leadership given that each function handles its own Customization. He grouped attendees by function at 11 tables and asked them to draft a deployment plan. People rotated as in earlier sessions. The resulting plan is on the next page.

Each VP function is shown as a row for its own design initiative with rows below for any additional initiatives. The columns for functions ("T" stands for technical, etc.) indicate who is involved in each initiative. We don't normally recommend functions taking the lead on as many as three initiatives, as happened here, but this was a large organization, and these were mission-critical efforts.

◇ The Marketing VP announced that he and his few staff had already completed their Customize. He gave a brief presentation to help conference participants understand the process.

◇ Projects: Completing the projects continued as the highest priority, but the VP was asked to turn over immediately 'his' IT and technical groups and do everything he could to support iOps. Deployment was for them to put themselves out of business!

◇ Technical: The VP was asked to immediately take over drilling, subsurface, facilities, and all IT groups. iOps was dramatically broadened to include offshore staffing and integrated operations. It was asked to build a command center for existing Platform North as a pilot for the new Platform South. Technical was asked to take over project HSE, coordinate the entire safety effort, drawing on Corporate.

◇ Operations: Highest priority was operations readiness, developing skilled staff for taking over projects as they were completed. This needed close collaboration with Technical and the Chief Petroleum Engineer. Second priority was refurbishing the onshore field.

◇ HR was asked to defer working on their own organization and put all efforts into the Local Staff initiative. The local staff platform superintendent was detached to lead this vital initiative.

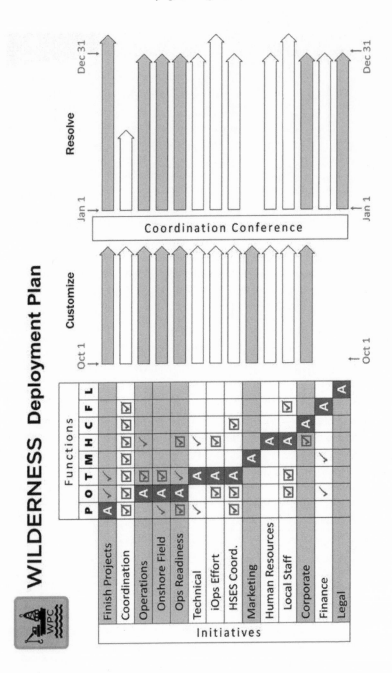

◇ Finance similarly was asked to focus all efforts on a renewed enterprise resource program implementation. At the tables, operations staff had begun to understand it could be an enabler instead of the burden they had long thought.

◇ Corporate was to focus on coordinating their fragmented functions. Because of their huge roles Finance and HR were moved out of Corporate, to be revisited later. Legal was fine either way.

For the needed intensive coordination during deployment, the planning team was refocused as a coordination team to manage engagement, support collaboration, lead issue resolution, and escalate unresolved ones to the leadership team. They were asked to convene a coordination conference at the end of the year for any remaining thorny problems.

Session: Plan and Engage

The communications team compiled outcomes throughout the conference and had a local graphics artist illustrating with sketches, including several of the ones reproduced here in the book. The External Affairs VP led a session to crystallize the key messages for all participants to take back to their colleagues.

Finally, Theresa and the coordination team met in a 'fishbowl' session with two open chairs available to those wanting to speak and contribute. Together they identified goals, next steps, and captured key coordination issues needing resolution. This set the tone for future meetings and modeled the new culture. When Luca drew the conference to a close, the energy was evident.

Wilderness Customize

Roles, Accountabilities, and Structure

The Functions got to work filling in details, mapping out what was needed, identifying roles and accountabilities, and establishing work groups at the levels required. The diagram on the next page is a summary the coordination council developed to show the composite. Numbers in parentheses are agreed benchmarked staffing levels.

The business groups mirror the operating model with a few exceptions:

◇ A core of regulatory folks was pulled from the core work functions into corporate to better leverage their agency relationships.

◇ HR and Finance were established as separate functions, each with their key support disciplines.

◇ Marketing kept their strategy and planning function and Technical set up an intermediate-term planning group, to be coordinated.

◇ Subsurface was relabeled Development to reflect its functionality and the name of the macro-process.

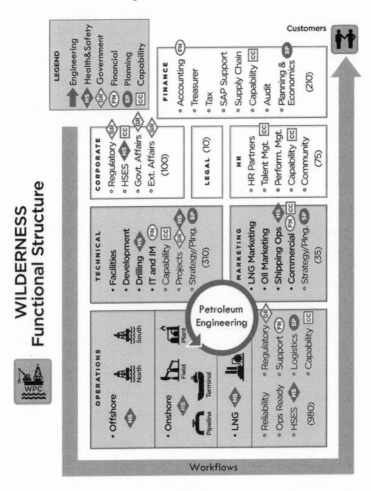

Six coordination councils were set up as shown: Government Relations (GR), Financial (FN), Health & Safety (HS), Strategy & Planning (SP), Capability & Skill Development (CC), and Petroleum Engineering.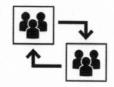

Integrated Operations

This is a story in itself. The VP Operations had stalked out of the Frame Conference angry and disappointed, particularly at the 'promotion' of his underling Chief Petroleum Engineer. He soon after retired, but what might have been a major setback under other circumstances accelerated Customize. The offshore platform superintendent, who had been leading the local staff initiative, was named manager for the new offshore operations grouping and designated as interim Operations VP while Luca searched for a qualified successor.

The effect across Wilderness was immediate and electrifying! The Technical VP and interim Operations VP called a meeting of about 50 of the most respected offshore operations staff, engineers, IT and IM experts, along with a few pipeline, processing, logistics, planning, marketing, finance, and HR staff. Theresa observed that if she were starting her own company, this would be her dream roster!

The VPs' challenge to the meeting was simple: build an integrated operations command center. Not visualize, or analyze, or assess feasibility, or plan, actually build it! The IT folks unveiled a huge flat screen connected to the command module on the platform offshore. Surprised participants on both sides of the link introduced themselves.

The Chief Petroleum Engineer introduced the process. The numerous sensors downhole, around the platform, within the pipelines, and at the processing plant were displayed in real time on a number of dedicated laptops around the room. The facilitators divided the participants into various groups based on the work they did but gave precious few additional instructions beyond "just make it work!" They got to it.

As they worked together over the next few days, some were little involved and drifted away. Some not invited were pulled in. With the

Technical, Operations, and Chief Petroleum Engineer behind it, it was priority 1. Powerful lessons surfaced:

◇ Natural Interactions: The links were crude to start, with numerous 'dropped calls' and interference, but every so often things would clear up and the office could almost imagine the platform outside the window. Then things would cut out. High-quality real-time video with good audio was essential, perhaps fiber-optic cabling or similar channels were needed for lifelike interactions between sites.

◇ Working Times: The platform worked around-the-clock while office staff headed home in the early evening. The second morning the group decided that working hours should reflect the work. It was timely as several subsea wells were in a critical phase. The engineers divided up the work to monitor the asset 24/7 over the next week, dramatically shortening cycle time. They decided that all three command centers would be in one location so that each discipline had someone at the center continuously covering all three centers.

◇ Efficiency: With all engineering and operations disciplines present, in several cases problems were solved almost instantaneously by calling across the room without a meeting or trip to the platform. A slight shift in camera angle revealed one problem! Two surveillance engineers noticed a trend in data they had been monitoring back in their own offices. They diagnosed what was causing the anomaly and fixed it before the issue escalated and threatened production.

◇ Data Systems: The scattered laptops were symbolic of the dispersed nature of data systems. There were various standards for data overlays but little enforcement. Many engineers had their pet Excel apps. The Technical disciplines made this an urgent priority.

◇ Collaboration: Participants soon no longer noticed who worked for whom! Clearly the Technical and interim Operations VPs had set that tone, but conversations revolved around who had the right skills and how to get them involved.

At their 'final' review the VPs declared the pilot a success and ended it. However, the groups refused to vacate the rooms! During the pilot they had gradually moved their offices over. Most of the new IT and IM group ended up nearby and redoubled efforts on communications links and capabilities to capture, transmit, store, process, display, and analyze the data. The logistics people brought in some drones they were evaluating for pipeline inspections and some remote undersea vehicles for platform maintenance. Continuous monitoring of wells, reservoirs, flow rates, pipelines, and sea state continued uninterrupted. Theresa and her staff documented new work arrangements and accountabilities.

An unexpected byproduct of the pilot was a sudden uptick in job applicants. The buzz had spread throughout the region. Skilled workers were taking notice. This dovetailed nicely with the local staff recruiting initiative, and the command center provided an ideal training ground. Rooms nearby were commandeered. The VPs and Chief Petroleum Engineer bowed to reality and announced that the command center was operational and the basis of the other two command centers.

Support Systems

Enterprise Resource Planning (ERP): One immediate realization from the command center was the need for an integrated work process, planning, and projects package. A project to install one was underway but limited to the financial modules. The finance staff sitting at the center saw how other modules could provide the command center needs. Without explicit authority, they joined the ERP team, arranged for these modules to be activated, and helped the center implement.

Local Staffing: The platform superintendent convinced Theresa to staff HR with local hires. They put word out and as HR staff completed their assignments, qualified locals moved in. Within a month they doubled local HR staff from 15 to 30 out of 75. These new HR staff convened 'mini-conferences' to showcase the command center, technical training, and staff development and solicit feedback. They found that pay was a minor issue but health benefits in these remote locations were huge.

Road Safety: As health and safety staff struggled to organize, road safety worsened, and there were several fatalities within a week. The command center safety representative got his colleagues to experiment with remote monitoring of company vehicle instruments back at the center. The key was to rotate those monitoring the data among the drivers. Driving habits changed as they saw the bigger picture beyond what they experienced  behind the wheel. This was a turning point and road safety began to inch up to first-quartile territory.

Performance Bonuses: To counter the old culture of masking issues with 'all-green' dashboards, the interim Operations VP got a group of hourly staff to look into bonuses based on aggressive production targets. As production improved and bonuses kicked in, it not only boosted morale, but drove work groups to focus on the reds and yellows, knowing they would be measured on results, not appearances.

Coordination 'Conference

The Theresa-led coordination council met regularly as Customization began but then less and less as the councils became operational. The petroleum engineering council in particular took on coordination and became the first stop when unresolved issues were escalated. The surprise promotion of one of its members to a leadership role signaled the shift from hierarchical Directive to facilitative Participative.

The conference at the end of the year to close out Customization turned into a joint meeting of the petroleum engineering council and the Wilderness leadership team. Although all of the Mobilize and Frame conference participants were invited to attend, they were asked to raise their issues with the relevant council instead. More than a few attended the joint meeting, but as spectators.

The executives had faced some of their long-standing turf issues and slowly begun functioning more as a unified steering team. There was just one big issue at the joint meeting. The Projects VP complained of inadequate services from groups he had 'donated' to Operations, Technical, or Corporate. The petroleum engineering council agreed. Much of the conflict was a lack of qualified staff. Even with the recent hiring, Wilderness was short of the designated numbers. Budget overruns had led to a scarcity mentality that left jobs vacant. Using the benchmarked Customize numbers, Theresa and her staff worked closely with the VPs to accelerate the staffing process.

Wilderness Resolve

New Accountabilities, Operating Model, and Issues

Wilderness had a history of 'go live' events to start up new facilities but decided to have work groups and functions move into the new operating model at their own pace. Marketing, Legal, Technical, HR, and Corporate were already functioning that way. Operations had separate Go Live events for each new or upgraded facility and were hoping to have their new VP in time for the formal opening of the custom-built command center. Finance was fully occupied with the new integrated ERP adjustments and delayed other changes until done.

Lessons and Closure

A new VP Operations arrived in time for a mini-conference to capture lessons. Here are their key findings with our editorial comments.

Collaboration: Leaders had to get out of the way and let the collective knowledge and wisdom of their staff guide a complex organization as it embraced even more complexity. Group process in conferences gave proof that broader input was worth the effort. The Directive leaders were surprised and delighted with the outcomes.

Leadership: Becoming more Participative was an iterative process with leadership and design teams getting to trust one another and then pushing their boundaries of comfort with the staff. Luca played a key role in legitimizing the project but sought out like-minded allies among his leadership and their lieutenants. This coalition and the Luca and Theresa partnership were key ingredients in the project's success.

Technology was a key ingredient but sounds more preordained than it actually was. Integrated operations, like many advances, had a tipping point. Even five years earlier, the command center that emerged through this project would have foundered on inadequate data transmission technology. By the time of the pilot, it was almost industry standard, but still novel in a remote location lacking infrastructure.

Structure: Collaboration in the Participatory culture shifts decision-making from purely vertical to being informed by horizontal input, and ultimately to shared leadership. For the vertical to trust and delegate, they must reserve the right to modify decisions which threaten the goals of the organization. In the end, the functional structure wasn't changed but the new collaborative culture was symbolized by the interlocking coordinating councils.

Involvement: The design team found local staffing and iOps stagnant but revitalized them with the right people involved. Visual workflows helped everyone see how the business actually operated end-to-end.

Epilogue

After several of the big projects had come onstream, the Chief Petroleum Engineer hosted a lookback and follow-up. All production targets were being met. The Projects VP had left. The new local HR VP had made HR 100% local. Total local staffing was nearing 80%. Most remarkable was that the petroleum engineering council was now playing the pivotal integration role in day-to-day operations while the leadership team concentrated on strategy and resourcing issues.

Luca had moved on. His successor was a 'local guy' who had made his career elsewhere and then had returned. While less polished than Luca he was as visionary and much more extroverted. He spent intensive sessions talking, then listening, and understanding. He loved sitting in the new command centers just watching the action around the revitalized Wilderness.

Part IV: The Deliverables

Many details for these ten deliverables may be familiar, but some reinforce specific features of Syngineering. Core Work emphasizes the greatly increased role of technology today. Operating Model builds landscape and culture explicitly into the process. Structure and Roles & Accountabilities illustrate the emerging ascendance of clear and rigorous accountabilities over traditional hierarchies. We first used these deliverables with Directive cultures and easily extended them to the conferences in Participative cultures. We didn't explicitly use them when we began work in Flexible and Adaptive cultures but found that we were incorporating many of the ingredients or their elements.

Deliverable, Ingredient, and Element Index

The boxes show the five agility stages first introduced in Chapter 1. The ten deliverables are those first introduced in Chapter 2. Diamonds list each deliverable's ingredients followed by their key elements.

Sense Learning | Information | Issue Assessment | Decision to Act

Mobilize

Deliverable 1: Charter
◇ **Scope:** Case for Change | Boundaries & Givens | Goals & Objectives
◇ **Involvement:** Approach | Resources & Staffing | Engagement Needs
◇ **Plan:** Risk Analysis | Communications | Integrated Plan

Deliverable 2: Strategy
◇ **Core Business:** Purpose | Values | Capabilities | Assets
◇ **Landscape:** Technology | Markets | Competitors |Regulatory
◇ **Strategy:** Products/Services | Value | Objectives | Characteristics

Deliverable 3: Diagnosis
◇ **Information:** Design Process | Questions per Component
◇ **Synthesis:** Issues | Themes | Levers | Root Causes | Priorities
◇ **Readiness:** Change History | Effort Priority | Organization Factors
◇ **Criteria:** Components | Strategic Factors| Implementation Factors

Frame

Deliverable 4: Core Work
◇ **Key Technologies:** Product/Service | Operational | Customer Focus
◇ **Value Chain:** Outputs | Advantage Work | Enabling | Hand-Offs
◇ **Workflows:** Process Descriptions | Capabilities & Functions | Flows

Deliverable 5: Operating Model
◇ **Organization Components:** Leadership | Work | People | Systems
◇ **Structure Options:** Advantage Work | Other Work | Coordination
◇ **Option Selection:** Prioritized Criteria | Comparison and Selection

Deliverable 6: Deployment Plan
◇ **Initiatives:** List of Changes | Grouped into Initiatives | Prioritized
◇ **Change Impacts:** Stakeholders List | Stakeholder Impacts
◇ **Deploy Method:** Procedure | Groups Involved | Engagement
◇ **Accountabilities:** Lead Roles | Other Groups | Coordination

Customize

Deliverable 7: Roles and Accountabilities
◇ **Technology:** Key Requirements | Supporting Technologies
◇ **Process Details:** Tasks/Activities | Required Skills | Flow Details
◇ **Roles Needed:** Grouped Tasks | Accountabilities | Role Efficiencies
◇ **Skills & Numbers:** List of Roles | Job Benchmarking | Final Numbers

Deliverable 8: Structure
◇ **Unit Staffing:** Unit Mandates | Roles into Units | Sizing | Evaluation
◇ **Final Grouping:** Organization Map | Grouping Evaluation
◇ **Coordination:** Critical Interfaces | Coordination Type | Solutions

Deliverable 9: Supporting Systems
◇ **Management:** Metrics | Reviews | Decisions | Strategic Planning
◇ **Financial:** Accounting | Budgeting | Investments | Treasury
◇ **HR/People:** Performance | Information | Talent | Development

Resolve

Deliverable 10: Adjust
◇ **New Accountabilities:** New Role Understanding | New Skills
◇ **New Operating Model:** Planning | Go Live | Follow Through
◇ **Emerging Issues:** Issue Identification | Issue Assignment
◇ **Effort Closure:** Lessons Learned | Celebration | Resume Sensing

The terms 'deliverable,' 'ingredient,' and 'element' are the core of the Directive and Participative approach 'recipes' in Chapters 4 and 5. The materials here in Part IV are also helpful in the Flexible and Adaptive approaches in Chapters 6 and 7, but are used more selectively and often in different sequences.

Key Terms Reference List

This convenient reference list of the concepts in Chapter 1, 2, and 3 helps put the deliverables, ingredients, and elements in context.

Types of Agility: (1) strategic or business market agility (2) internal enterprise or organizational agility (3) customer product/service agility.

Landscapes and their associated ➡ **Corporate Cultures]**
◇ Mass Production [stable and simple] ➡ Directive
◇ Knowledge Work [stable and complex] ➡ Participative
◇ Mass Customization [volatile and simple] ➡ Flexible
◇ Co-Configuration [volatile and complex] ➡ Adaptive

Organization Design Approaches:
◇ Directive projects develop recommendations for executive approval
◇ Participative conferences share decisions: leaders and employees
◇ Flexible cultures develop and implement organizational prototypes
◇ Adaptive cultures assign accountable parties to develop solutions

Stages of the Agility Cycle:
◇ Sense: gather information, identify issues, determine whether to act
◇ Mobilize: charter the effort, refine the strategy, then diagnose needs
◇ Involve: broad range of employees input, design and implement
◇ Frame: decide roles, working relationships, and support systems.
◇ Resolve: adjusts the designs, completes the cycle, return to Sense

Organization Components:
◇ Strategy: operational excellence, product leadership, customer focus
◇ Leadership sets strategy **and** allocates resources accordingly
◇ Work Types: advantage, enabling, essential, non-essential
◇ Work Hierarchy: value chain, macro-process, process, activity, and task
◇ People: skill capabilities grouped into specialties then into functions
◇ Structure: roles and accountabilities, reporting lines, coordination
◇ Supporting systems: management, financial, and human resources

Common Functions
◇ Product/Service Development,
◇ Customer Services, ◇ Operations,
◇ Management, ◇ Marketing/Sales,
◇ Procurement, ◇ Human Resources,
◇ Technology, ◇ Process Management

Deliverable 1: Charter

Every organization has some way to define change efforts consistent with its culture. A single page with just a few speaking points helps communicate and focus the effort.

Charter Ingredients
◇ Scope
◇ Involvement
◇ Plan

Scope

These elements define and bound the effort. The discussions that go into them can begin to create collaboration and shared leadership.

Case for Change	What's the opportunity: better future, fix shortfalls? What's the urgency? Benefits worth the cost? Are there alternatives?
Boundaries and Givens	What's in scope: business units, functions, or product lines? What's out of scope? Are there non-negotiable givens?
Goals and Objectives	Objectives: what changes, what are the desired outcomes? Are there measurable goals tied to the expected value?

Case for Change

This is a crisp statement to enlist initial support and action. It includes 'why change,' 'when it's needed,' and 'what's involved.' The accountable person, typically you or the change lead, talks with sponsors and key stakeholders and reviews any existing materials. They may do some research to better understand the industry, organizational objectives, governance structure, financial health, and so on. What is happening? What's needed? Is there is a genuinely felt need? Does it support the strategy? Capture all this for validation. Start with the end in mind. What will the project seek to achieve and how? Are there known barriers or risks? How will you measure success? What are the cost implications? Is the project worth the cost?

Boundaries and Givens

Know your givens. In Directive and Participative cultures these may be 'sacred cows,' so completely out-of-bounds that they can't even be talked about. These are often personal or political agreements that must be maintained but not made visible. When speaking with your sponsor, it important to ask what's in and out of bounds, what's negotiable and non-negotiable related to the change. In Flexible and Adaptive cultures, the givens are more transparent, thus more easily identified. Regardless of culture, you need to know these upfront as possible design criteria.

In the Wilderness case in Chapter 10, the sponsors made it clear that there would be no significant changes in leadership or first-level structure. The design team were initially dismayed but this ended up saving them a lot of time, and it didn't hinder at all the design of a robust organization.

Goals and Objectives

Know upfront what you are trying to achieve. Why are you doing this effort? What value will it bring when it is complete: save money or time, reduce resourcing needs, improve cycle time, increase profits, reduce dependencies, and so on? Try to quantify as much as possible to give the effort staff a goal to work towards. Break it up into smaller goals or additional measures if it is an audacious goal that will take a significant amount of time and effort to achieve or if different groups are responsible for different areas of it, but make sure everyone can see the bigger picture and how their work will fit into this.

Involvement

In Syngineering, change management is not a separate item but instead integral to the method. These elements involve the right people.

Syngineering Approach	Culture: does it fit the landscape? If not, will it need to change? Which of the four approaches are best suited?
Resources & Staffing	Who steers & legitimizes? Are the right skills involved in the project? Who leads? How to enlist others as needed?
Engagement Needs	Who are the stakeholders? What's their influence? What are their attitudes and concerns? Why and how to engage?

Syngineering Approach

The conversation to have here is explained in the Chapter 3 section Start with Sensing. Initial assessments of performance, strategy, the culture, and landscape help determine whether you need to change the culture to better match. Your change approach should be one of the four in Chapters 4, 5, 6, or 7, or a mix depending on the desired culture.

Resources and Staffing

Staffing typically involves the accountable sponsors, a lead change role, and often a group of change staff. While the sponsors are likely already set, you need to make sure that they are major players who have both the authority and willingness to keep the effort moving in tough times.

Regardless of culture, most change efforts have a lead role. It is important to define the accountabilities: is it project manager, change team lead, planning team lead, facilitator, or a combination? What is the right authority level? Desired characteristics: expertise, project or facilitation skills, sponsor comfort, development, availability, and so on?

To resource the change team, the challenge is to choose a small nimble group that represent the major stakeholders, have the needed expertise and perspective, and can bridge from the current to the needed culture. Their responsibilities vary depending on culture but include providing the expertise to design and/or plan, engaging staff, coaching, collecting feedback, addressing concerns, and escalating issues when needed.

There are a number of other common roles on change teams. IT and technology issues may require a skilled IT professional. A project administrator may be critical for budgeting and tracking, logistics, administrative tasks, room bookings, and travel. A communications lead can facilitate its development and delivery. Occasionally, you might need an organization design expert.

The nature of this formal or informal team and its composition will look different for each culture. Team members should be as diverse as the organization and represent the different work style preferences. There is no one perfect team member, but there can be perfect teams. We often use a number of the concepts in Chapter 1 to improve a change team's effectiveness and create the psychological safety that enables this team to role model agility.

Engagement Needs

Stakeholders are groups or individuals impacted by or able to impact the effort. Getting to know them is an important activity to be revisited frequently throughout the effort. Each time you engage with them you will surface additional information. How this is captured depends on the culture, but Directive and Participative cultures often track dates and results of engagement. Not every stakeholder group identified merits the same amount of attention.

Mapping by attitude and influence can help identify where to focus engagement. Influence is the impact of each stakeholder group on the success of the project, including their influence on others. Attitude at the outset falls on a spectrum from very negative to very positive. This mapping is typically done by change staff in collaboration with a broad range of employees, customers, suppliers, leaders, and sometimes even labor unions and government or industry officials. The diagram on the next page is an example. When used, the circles and diamonds are labeled with the names of individuals or groups.

Start in the upper right, the most influential early adopters. They are likely already voicing commitment to the effort and hopefully showing ownership in leading and advancing the effort. These are your sponsors. Show them with different symbols (diamonds here) and engage them in an honest dialogue around their placement and how to use their positions to engage the others, especially the 'wait and see' majority.

Work down the right-hand side of the map. Those a bit less positive may show passive alignment or skepticism. This 'wait and see' majority requires rigorous engagement, not only to improve attitude, but also to identify stakeholders and to work with others once onboard.

For those in the lower right who actively oppose, yet must be onboard, find out what's behind the attitudes: their fears, concerns, or other known issues. The best insights sometimes come from asking directly. Rather than ignoring or brushing aside legitimate concerns, pay attention, incorporate their views, involve them in resolving problems, and even invite them to join the effort. This can result in surprising shifts as word will rapidly spread through informal communication and trust networks. Use these networks: they know which of the opposers are immovable cynics and will respect you for not being held hostage by them! Look for these opportunities and mine them.

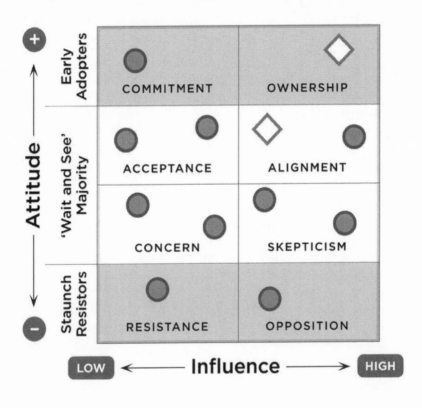

Not everyone needs to be positive; sometimes neutral is adequate if they are quiet. Some cynics you may never convince, so don't waste effort. When they try derailing things, mobilize your advocates.

Finally, look at the left-hand side of the map. Do you need to engage some or all of them? You can't please everyone, but you can listen and look for places to enlist them to engage challenges. Giving people air time and accountability to fix their concerns and responding to their questions can show that you are listening to them and that you respect their input and involvement.

Plan

Most change efforts require some sense of timing and prioritization, who is accountable for what, anticipated risks and their mitigation, and communications. This is an iterative process to be updated as the work unfolds.

Risk Analysis	What could derail the effort? How seriously and how likely? How to monitor and mitigate the higher priority risks?
Commu-nications	What do each stakeholder group need to hear? When and how often? How best to handle: meetings, messages, etc.?
Integrated Plan	Depends on culture: Do groups need plans and schedules? Are groups resourced? Coordinated? An integrated whole?

Risk Analysis

Risks are potential eventualities that could derail the effort and need a mitigation plan. This is an iterative process: as you know more about the changes, you can update these plans. For each potential risk you estimate its likelihood and the impact if it does occur. If you have a company risk management framework, use it! Adaptive organizations often incorporate this into daily work, but there may be a risk register for coordination purposes. Format is not important as long as you identify, assess, manage, and monitor any serious risks.

The diagram below is an example of a risk analysis we did with a health safety and environmental agency client. High likelihood and impact risks placed in the upper right need remediation. Some may be very unlikely but fatal to the effort. Some have lower impact but the cumulative impacts of so many are similarly fatal. After prioritizing, have the team decide how to manage at least the critical few. Involve parties outside of the change team as needed to analyze the risks and determine how to mitigate, monitor or manage them. The middle band may need remediation or just close monitoring to see if the likelihood increases. The risks placed in the lower left need no action.

As the effort progresses, update the risk analysis. Teams often want to skip this step or conversely want to go into too much detail.

Risk Assessment Matrix

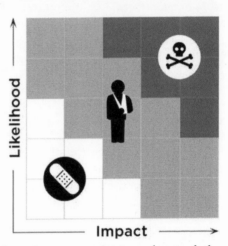

Try to avoid both extremes and use the opportunity to surface underlying fears and concerns. We have seen a number of events put client projects in jeopardy: unexpected top leadership changes, deteriorating or poor economic conditions, having the change team's recommendations rejected, and significant change in the company's strategic context. Could your project survive these?

Communications

In the uncertainty of change, most people naturally desire information and resist change if this need is not met. A steady stream of communication appropriate to the time and place can be developed by actively sensing in to what is being asked and responding. Even a "we don't know yet" response can help to decrease rumors and speculation. Otherwise, people may fill-in-the-blanks with possibly the wrong answers!

The type of communication will depend on the attitudes sought. Study the diagram below and compare this with the Engagement Needs for key stakeholders shown previously. To begin, you may want to provide awareness from most employees. This typically comes from one-way channels: announcements, mass e-mails, blogs, other social media, and newsletters. Answer questions like "Why is this change needed?",

"Why now?", "What does success look like?", and "What's in it for me?" You then need to move most people over to understanding what the change will involve. Videos, webinars, presentations and more detailed materials help to personalize this information and answer questions such as "What will be different for me?" and "What will change in my everyday work?"

Later on, you need a significant portion of the 'wait and see' majority to end up at least in acceptance. Face-to-face contact is crucial to get them to arrive here. Team meetings, coffee chats, social events, and lunches are all opportunities for people to hear directly from those involved in the change. Expect confusion and resistance; it's a sign that people are listening. Speak straight, listen generously, and be willing to address challenging questions. Ultimately, most staff need to move into action, which will reduce their desire for more information as they participate in Frame and in Customize.

Types of Communication

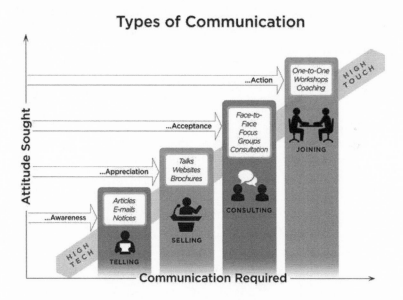

Communications supplement engagement; they provide content and direction, help people to stay connected, and show stakeholders that you are still interested in hearing from them. Which key groups need communications? Why? What messages are appropriate? When? Who will prepare and deliver them? Make sure that they have the knowledge and skills to do this!

Integrated Plan

Planning starts with the roadmap from the chosen approach, as shown in Chapters 4, 5, 6, or 7. The mode and detail of planning (spreadsheet, T-Map, Kanban board, or others) will be dictated by the culture of the enterprise and by the needs of the specific alignment effort. A key thing to keep in mind as you become more agile is to focus on providing more detail for the near-term to be able to get the work done and less detail for the later planning effort so that you can more easily adjust as you go based on the experience and feedback you receive in doing the work.

All of these need to be knit together into an integrated whole: the roadmap for the chosen approach, engagement needs based on the stakeholder analysis, risk mitigation and monitoring activities, and communications planning. Do work groups have plans and schedules commensurate to the culture? Are they coordinated? Are the plans resourced adequately?

More on Chartering

The Wilderness case study in Chapter 10 is a great example of the traditional formal Directive project chartering process. Stratos in Chapter 8 shows the iterative chartering of a Directive culture needing to be more Adaptive. Chartering in Comfort Home Services in Chapter 9 was informal and implicit and managed to get just the right people involved.

Deliverable 2: Strategy

Strategy is a tailored guide to how you intend to succeed in your marketplace: the products and services you provide, the way you distribute them, who are your customers, and your value proposition for them.

> **Strategy Ingredients**
> ◇ Core Business
> ◇ Landscape
> ◇ Revised Strategy

Core Business

This is where strategy begins. These elements are the underlying basis for your business: your core purpose, values, capabilities, and assets.

	Where We Are	What We Aspire
Core Purpose Why we exist	What we actually produce, for whom?	Our aspired products, services, customers
Core Values What we believe	What people infer from observing us	Which would support our core purpose?
Core Capabilities What we can do	What we currently possess and can use	Our purpose requires, possibly missing now
Core Assets What we own	Which we currently can access and use	Our purpose requires, possibly missing now

Core Purpose

What is your organization's reason for existence? What products and services do you produce, for what markets and customers? Start with what you do today. What documents describe this? Involve a cross-section of employees to be as complete as you can.

Now turn to the realm of aspiration. How good could things be? What products, services, and markets could take you there? It is extremely helpful to perform the next activity, landscape review, in parallel, especially the analysis of others in your industry. What are your competitors and partners doing that you need to be aware of, compensate for, and possibly emulate? This should be very iterative as change staff and sponsor engagements with all staff provide input.

Note different perspectives and particularly discrepancies, but don't yet try to resolve differences, just harvest different viewpoints. Resolving differences too early squashes the necessary creativity to discover innovative approaches and limits intuitive thinking and feeling.

Core Values

What are the few important behaviors and ethical values the organization holds most dear? These are the ones you hold onto even if and when they create operational difficulties. What people are rewarded for typically reveal values. What do your customers and others outside infer from your behaviors? Are these values shared across the organization?

How well do these current values and behaviors support your aspired core business? Do some need to be changed or replaced? Some companies founded on the value of 'individual merit' struggle to balance that against today's need for collaboration and community. Values often relate how employees regard and treat each other and how the enterprise sees its shareholders and its role in the community.

Core Capabilities

What capabilities do you have that others cannot match, and which provide a competitive advantage? These can be employees with expert knowledge or specific skills, documented intellectual property, innovative hardware or software technologies, and so on. These are the lifeblood of your business. Which ones do you have today? Are they providing a competitive advantage? Are they nurtured and maintained?

Now turn to the aspired future. Which current capabilities support your aspired core business: Are some of these missing and do they need to be acquired? Are some current ones unnecessary? This can be a painful conversation. What may have once been vital professions may have faded in importance as collaboration, networking, and integration have become so much more important than specific content expertise.

Core Assets

These are the important non-human assets you need for your strategy. They can be unique strategic loca- tions or facilities, access to raw materials, or advantageous contracts. Together with core capabilities, they should give you a clear competitive edge. What are these? Which actually support your core purpose? Are they nurtured and maintained? Do you have access to any and all the raw materials your strategy requires?

Landscape

This ingredient focuses on the environment around the organization. It helps not only to evaluate strategy but also to identify what  alterations might be needed in the organization's components. The elements here are well covered in the Continuous Sensing section in Chapter 1.

Technology Trends	How is technology changing business? Novel goods or services? New markets? What's just now emerging?
Markets, Social, and Customers	What are your customer's demographics and economic situations? Your reputation? How are these trending?
Competitor Developments	Who are your competitors? What supports their success? What you can learn? Are there better ways to work?
Regulatory & Government	Environmental, health, or safety issues? Integrity, social responsibility or other trends? Regulatory changes?

Revised Strategy

Effective strategies are agile: current and responsive to the marketplace. They provide the basis for prioritizing and allocating resources, deciding where to operate, and maximizing long-term value.

Products & Services	What are our products and services? What are their markets and customers? What sets us apart from others?
Value Proposition	Why do customers prefer us? Products? Distribution channels? Cost? Relationships? Our competitive edge?
Goals & Objectives	Revenue or profit goals? Process or intermediate goals or objectives? Specific change or growth aspirations?
Organizational Characteristics	Are strategic goals reflected in your leadership, core work, people, structure, and systems components?

An organization's strategy may be well-defined and understood, but if not, it is important to articulate it. This needs to be in place early in the effort; you must align the organization around it. Review the materials in the section on Business Strategy in Chapter 2. As the change staff and leaders discuss strategy, you may begin seeing differences between what is said and what is done. Be curious and capture these observations. These discrepancies may indicate that misalignment and inefficiency are present. In the absence of shared strategy, even well-intended individuals may do things that make no sense to others.

Products and Services

Start from the core purpose but refine and add specificity. Which of your core competencies, assets, purposes, and values give you an advantage over your competitors? What sets you apart? Could any of these open up any new opportunities or minimize any threats for you? Why do you lose business? This may involve minor tweaking around products and markets or a radical rethink.

Value Proposition

It often helps to think about broad generic strategy types. We have been especially influenced by the ideas of Michael Porter as well as Michael Treacy and Fred Wiersema in understanding strategies that can be implemented to create competitive advantage.

Cost Leadership (Porter) or Operational Excellence (Tracy and Wiersema) strategies seek to produce standard products, often commodities, at lower cost than the competition. The cost margin translates directly into profits.

Differentiation or Product Differentiation strategies seek to offer products and/or services that customers prefer over those of their competitors. This preference justifies higher prices, which translate into profits.

Porter's Market Segmentation and Tracey and Wiersema's Customer Intimacy are a number of related strategies focused on specific markets and even individual customers. Deep understanding of these markets or customers enables satisfying their needs in ways that competitors cannot.

What is your strategy? Why do customers prefer you? What value do you deliver that others don't? Have you kept up with technology? Do you use data analytics to target potential customers? Do you need to make changes in the specific details of your strategy?

Goals and Objectives

Business objectives are the intermediate to longer-term strategic goals, which provide the basis for shaping future design decisions, rewards, and alignment and coordination activities. They are milestones on the way to achieving the strategy.
These are typically phrased in terms of outcomes from lines of business and support functions that would result in achieving your core business in the next quarter, or year, or three to five years in the context of your business and industry. These should include financial and concrete output measures. Often called key performance indicators or KPIs, these intermediate process goals or change aspirations provide some leading indication for how things are trending. They provide information and insights while there's still time to respond.

The longer-term strategic and shorter-term tactical objectives should fit together, complement each other, be realistic and attainable, and be clear to the staff involved. As they cascade down to group and individual performance management targets and goals, they align these with the organization's strategy.

Examples of strategic goals and objectives are:

◇ Globalizing an aspect of your business within a specific timeframe

◇ Becoming more customer-centric within a certain time period

◇ Becoming more innovative to get ahead of the competition within a specific timeframe.

Organizational Characteristics

Your chosen strategy and business objectives dictate a number of organizational characteristics, which operationalize the strategy. These typically involve one or more of the organization's components: leadership, work, people, structure, and systems. You want only those critical few that are key to delivering your strategy, not a long laundry list. In the section on Strategy in Chapter 2 we introduced generic strategies and highlighted how they influence the Participative culture in the Knowledge Work landscape. Below are suggestions for how each of the generic strategies shapes an organization's components.

Cost Leadership or Operational Excellence involves price differentials over competitors gained from operating efficiencies: McDonald's, GEICO, and Dell exhibit some or all of these characteristics. Core assets should provide cost advantages; core values focus on efficiency. Work typically focuses on standard processes with strong controls, which ruthlessly drive excess costs out of the system. Improvements are rapidly replicated across the enterprise. Technology shapes the work processes and makes them more efficient. These can be proprietary process innovations or automation. Structure: emphasizes the accountabilities and coordination needed to control consistency in the processes and their outcomes. People: must have the skill sets needed. Core capabilities include cutting-edge technical expertise in the processes, constantly seeking improvement. Systems: are designed to track and maintain the process controls, reward efficiency and consistency, and stay on top of expenses.

Product Leadership characteristics: Here the premium is on developing and maintaining these products: Google and Harvard have some or all of these characteristics. Core assets should support innovation; core values should foster creativity. People must have core capabilities and expertise in developing these products. Technology: is often either the product itself or a key enabler used by the skilled People. Work processes focus on effectively innovating, researching, and developing the distinctive products and then effectively bringing them to market. Structure often segregates the high-performance work groups needed for product development from marketing and sales to help customers understand and appreciate the differentiated products. Systems need to systematically reward and foster innovation; financial systems need to track product performance for timely decisions.

Customer Segmentation characteristics: Here the emphasis is on providing exactly what each unique customer or market segment demands. Whiting-Turner and Wolfgang Puck are less well known than the examples above. Core assets should enable delighting the customer and should be a core value. Structure often involves having specific customer facing groups; these 'front room' groups often have corresponding 'back room' groups that design and deliver the tailored solutions. People must have core capabilities centered around understanding customer's needs and adapting what may be industry-standard solutions to satisfy specific customers' requirements. Systems, technology, and work processes: all must be designed to coordinate activities seamlessly across the front-end customer groups and the back-room development and delivery groups that take 'off-the-shelf' technology and applications and fashion the needed solutions.

More on Strategy

The Stratos case study in Chapter IV is an example of an organization grappling with purpose and building a new strategy. Comfort Home Services in Chapter 9, from the start, held continuous dialogues around the strategy of the new combined entity. Wilderness in Chapter 10 was a rare organization crystal clear on their strategy; this greatly facilitated the project's work.

Deliverable 3: Diagnosis

This deliverable evaluates the current state against what is needed by the strategy. The four ingredients gather information, interpret and synthesize it, assess change readiness, and determine decision criteria.

Diagnose Ingredients
◇ Information
◇ Synthesis
◇ Change Readiness
◇ Decision Criteria

Collect Information

These elements look component by component at what the strategy requires. Design thinking sees any shortfalls as issues needing solution.

Design the Process	Pick the right people to solicit for information Decide the vehicle best suited to this culture
Awareness of Strategy	Can staff articulate the core business and strategy? Is it consistently understood across the organization? How well is it used in making operation decisions?
Culture and Behaviors	How do employees behave, with each other and customers? What behaviors get rewarded with pay or promotion? What are the deeply held community mindsets and beliefs?
Leadership & Governance	Are leaders clear on their accountabilities and authorities? Are their actions and behaviors consistent with core values? Do they have the business and facilitation skills needed?
Work and Technology	Does technology enable innovation and market disruption? Do your work processes deliver the needed core work? Are interfaces and hand-offs identified and managed?
People and Competences	Do roles and their accountabilities cover all work tasks? Are these coordinated by functional skill groups? Are employee skills and numbers adequate to do the work?
Structure and Coordination	Do work groups have the skills for their accountabilities? Are reporting relationships clear and support the strategy? Are cross-organization issues effectively coordinated?
Supporting Systems	Supervisory and management systems support strategy? Human resource and people systems support strategy? Financial metrics and reporting systems support strategy?

Design the Process

The questions above focus on just a few critical dimensions for each organization component. The starting point will be the Organizational Characteristics from the strategy deliverable. The key is to ask the right people, those with expertise in the work. This includes all aspects of the core work as well as support disciplines HR, Finance, Legal, and IT. In most cases simply asking these questions begins improvement. As people realize where they are currently, they will already start thinking about what needs improvement and how.

How you gather diagnostic information will help the organization to focus on the areas that most need attention and to make meaning out of its complexity. How you proceed depends heavily on culture. Directive project teams should involve a representative spectrum of employees. Participative conferences will tap into participants and their colleagues. Flexible and Adaptive cultures typically don't ask these questions; rather the key issues emerge naturally from sensing tensions. In every culture the ability to see patterns, manage tensions, and to focus on solutions rather than problem solving will support agility.

The six components are interrelated parts of a single system so issues may show up in multiple components. Don't fret about this; you will sort out the root causes in synthesis. It is important to be curious, rather than critical, of what you see as the diagnosis unfolds. You want an awareness of what can improve, not a litany of problems and culprits.

Awareness of Strategy

While you may have agreed the strategy, you still need to diagnose how well this is understood across the organization. In fact, if there is substantial work to be done on strategy, these questions can provide useful input into that work. Across the enterprise, when you ask people to  articulate the strategy, how consistent are the answers? If there is an identified strategy, how close do the answers come to it? How do the answers vary across groups and departments? Is there a systematic pattern?

Diagnose Culture and Behaviors

Here you move beyond the four cultures and assess what is actually happening. This gets people thinking about the entire organization as a system. Misalignments from the components almost always show up in culture. We can't directly change the culture, but diagnosing it can often point to root causes in one of the components. Changing the components does change the culture.

Behaviors are the most visible aspect of culture. What behaviors do we observe in everyday work? Are they consistent with our core values? Do people work together collaboratively as a community on behalf of the entire enterprise? Do we act safely and sustainably?

Less visible are cultural norms about advancement and success. What are the unwritten rules about getting ahead around here? What do individual, group, and leadership performance management systems reward: what's best for the individual or the whole?

Even more deeply hidden are mindsets, the collection of beliefs and thoughts that predetermine people's responses to events. Groups develop collective identities anchored in common mindsets. What are your organization's stories? Heroic customer service? Brilliant breakthroughs in research? These can be positive but not necessarily. The Stratos case study surfaced stories of bureaucrats playing the 'corporate game' to survive waves of change initiatives.

Diagnose Leadership and Governance

Every organization has a governance structure, how power and authority flow from owners to those doing the work. How clear is this flow? Are authorities for decisions distributed to the level that has the best information? Are authorities clearly spelled out and effective?

Every organization has leadership roles. These may be executives in a hierarchy, ad hoc roles assigned via accountabilities, or anything in between. Observe the behaviors of those in these roles. Do actions and results support the strategy? Are they consistent with the core values?

Do those in leadership roles have the skills they need to fulfill their accountabilities, gauged not against some corporate ideal but rather on what's actually needed by role? Some may require deep business skills; some may need effective negotiation and interpersonal skills; and others may need coaching and facilitation skills.

Diagnose Work and Technology

Technology is the purposeful application of information and automation in delivering goods and services. It includes software, applications, information and knowledge systems, and infrastructure. Technology breakthroughs can totally disrupt markets and industries. Do you scan constantly for useful new technologies, use or adapt them to strengthen your competitive position, and seamlessly integrate them into your processes, systems, and roles? Do you seek automation opportunities to increase quality, volume, efficiencies and/or morale? How effectively is information and knowledge transferred across individuals and groups?

Work refers to all activities involved in delivering your products and services. Is your value chain clear end-to-end across functions, suppliers, and customers? Do you understand your core activities that offer value for the customer, and provide your competitive advantage? Are these tied to your core capabilities? What do customers say about timeliness, cost or expense, quality, and responsiveness? Do you effectively manage the key processes and do people know and follow them consistently? Do support processes reinforce the core work?

Have you identified all key process interfaces between work groups and the hand-offs associated with them? Do all parties at each interface agree on the hand-off requirements? Are the key interfaces actively managed? Are there clear escalation procedures when conflicts arise?

Diagnose People and Competencies

Are individuals clear on their roles and accountabilities and how they contribute to the organization as a whole? This includes not only the core work experts but also those in the supporting functions and leadership roles.

Do you group roles into skillsets or groups of closely associated skills and these in turn into high level functions? Common functions that show up in most organizations are product and service development, procurement, operations, marketing and sales, customer services, management and governance, human resources, and technology and process management. Do you manage the skill groups and functions to develop and deploy the skills needed by the business?

Do you have the right number of people with the right skills to do your current and future work? This includes technical skills, process skills, business skills, interpersonal and collaborative working skills, and the capabilities to change as circumstances require. Are these employees and their skills in the right locations? Do you have adequate diversity in how people's thinking styles help see all facets of issues, so you make good decisions?

Diagnose Structure and Coordination

Are roles assembled into work groups that enable effective and efficient delivery of work? Are their purpose and accountabilities clear and under-  stood? Do all groups have the people, skills, or other resources to deliver on these?

Can you show relationships between groups and levels? A traditional organization chart may work but leaves out substantive details. Are reporting relationships between groups and individuals clearly delineated? Do they support the work? Be mindful that structure looks different for each culture. In Directive this is often just the organization chart. Participative extends this to a matrix or workflows involving business units and functions. Flexible and Agile may only have workflows or just accountabilities.

Finally, how do work groups coordinate their activities across reporting lines? How well are these cross-reporting integrating mechanisms identified? Are all the critical interfaces between teams, departments, and functions included? How effective are they? Are these coordination mechanisms and their associated networks connected into our customers and suppliers?

Diagnose Supporting Systems

Systems are the last component to be set but can be powerful in fostering the needed actions and behaviors.

Supervisory and management systems keep activities focused. Do your metrics capture what is needed? Do you review and hold people and groups accountable? Do you use authorities to make good decisions at the right levels? Do you regularly review and correct strategy?

Human resource systems align people with strategic requirements. Does your performance management hold people accountable? Is the right information available for staffing decisions? Do you manage talent to meet strategic needs? Do you effectively develop people's skills?

Financial and reporting systems support effective decisions. Do your accounting practices meet fiduciary accountabilities? Does budgeting resource the strategic priorities? Are investments objectively analyzed and carefully tracked? Can you survive cash flow contingencies?

Synthesis

This combs the information for patterns and themes that allow you to determine root causes and assess their priorities. We have found this one of the most difficult aspects of organizational design, especially for those new to the work. We have found these elements helpful.

Issues	Compile a list of the significant issues from the information
Themes	Group these into themes of similar or associated issues
Levers	Determine levers or changes that might correct the issues
Root Causes	Identify the root causes; many may cause multiple issues.
Priorities	Prioritize the levers that best address the root causes

Issues listing can be as simple as paper index cards or sticky notes or as complex as sortable spreadsheets. What you choose should be familiar to the organization and ease the sifting and sorting into themes, levers, and root causes. It may help to group them by component.

Themes: These may have emerged during the diagnosis or may need an intense review of the compiled issues. There are no limits on number, but more than ten can get unwieldy. These typically involve one of the three questions for one of the six organization components.

Levers: What specific component changes might correct the issues in each theme? This is a lever to pull and likely one of the three questions for one of the components. Each theme may have two or more levers.

Root Causes: Consider each lever. If fully implemented, would it correct the theme? If so, it's probably connected to a root cause. If not, it's likely just a palliative for a symptom. A frequent example is where individuals aren't held accountable. A proposed lever might be to redesign the performance management system. However, the root cause is often a culture of conflict avoidance and any new system will be just as ignored as the old one! It's a symptom. Naming root causes is an iterative art so keep revising as you work the themes.

Priorities: Finally assess how important each lever is for correcting the root causes. We often use a simple high (H), medium (M), and low (L) scale. While not science, it can surface the wisdom of the group.

Change Readiness

How ready is your organization to take on more change? These elements help determine prior experience, the importance of this change, and various other factors.

Change History	How many significant changes have occurred recently? What have you learned? Are people weary of change?
Effort Priority	Is the case for change broadly understood and agreed? Do leaders and staff agree that this initiative is a priority?
Organizational Factors	Do those impacted have change experience and resilience skills? What might support or hinder the change effort?

Change History: What significant changes has the organization experienced recently? What happened? Positive or negative? If successful, what key factors can be emulated? If failure, what can you learn? How many organizational realignment initiatives have occurred? How often? Are people weary of change? Asking for it?

Effort Priority: How widely understood and agreed is the business case for change? Are the symptoms or pain points and underlying reasons understood? How many initiatives are in progress right now? Is this one seen as a primary one or subsidiary? Is it really a priority? It is important to hear this directly from your sponsors, customers, and employees.

Organizational Factors: To what extent will stakeholders' day-to-day work be affected by the likely outcomes? What do you know about their willingness to change? Will the skills in these stakeholder groups be enough? Are they resilient and able to maintain their equilibrium? Will there be significant resistance? Are there other cultural or component aspects that support or hinder the effort?

Decision Criteria

Good decision criteria will help you make quantitative or qualitative judgments between design options. These two elements provide insights into picking effective ones.

Component Requirements	Leadership roles, technology and work requirements, people skills, reporting and coordination, and systems
Strategic Considerations	Product, customer, market, and competitor issues; supply chain issues; regulatory and/or compliance issues

Component Requirements: Start with the charter. There may be givens or scope boundaries. Add in any levers that have shown up during diagnosis, those related to root causes. You may combine some of these if they cover essentially the same ground.

Strategic Considerations: The decision criteria need to align with the strategy and be agreed by those accountable for resourcing decisions. Look at the organizational characteristics from strategy, especially those involving the components as these may provide decision criteria.

Decision criteria will be used to assess various design options through the rest of the effort. They should be the topic of a wide-ranging discussion. Many ideas won't be criteria. "All changes should be fit for purpose" is too fuzzy and ambiguous. "Improve the morale score on staff surveys" is specific enough, but you're better off looking at its root causes. There are often givens that must be observed no matter what, "Meet all safety and regulatory rules" is a good example. You will be unlikely to consider changes that don't fully satisfy this, so it won't be useful in deciding between change options. It's a given, not a decision criterion. These discussions almost always converge on the five to eight criteria that facilitate decision making. Good examples are "Reduce new product time-to-market" and "Improve collaboration among work groups."

More on Diagnosis

The Stratos case study in Chapter 8 traced many of its presenting issues to a culture that no longer fit its landscape. The diagnosis was a powerful tool to bring that clarity. Wilderness Petroleum in Chapter 10 surfaced the need for strong coordination and a more Participative culture instead of major organization chart changes. Comfort Home in Chapter 9 reverse-engineered the Diagnosis questions to design their new organization!

Deliverable 4: Core Work

The core work of an organization includes the formal and informal processes and procedures that turn inputs into customer products and services. The ingredients in the sidebar enable you to assemble these.

Core Work Ingredients
◇ Key Technologies
◇ Value Chain
◇ Workflows

Key Technologies

Building agile organizations starts with the technologies and work tasks that offer strategic competitive advantage. These define its core work.

Product/Service Innovations	What inventions, integrations, or knowledge can yield something no one else does that the market wants?
Operational Technologies	What technologies would enhance your customer's experience, most often integrations or knowledge?
Customer Focus Technologies	What integrations or automations can speed up outputs, improve efficiency, and cut costs below competitors?

Key technologies are those that can provide a competitive advantage so this needs to be the first stop in determining core work. In Deliverable 7: Roles and Accountabilities we will look at supporting technologies, but here the focus is on the few key ones. They generally provide the edge that supports one of the three generic strategies. The three elements help you explore these.

Product and Service Innovations

These are inventions or knowledge no one else has. They can be inventions like new automotive engines, or integrations like pilotless drones, or the knowledge in new and innovative software packages. The advantage is having what the market wants that no one else has. Examples: software applications, pharmaceuticals, reaction catalysts, patented equipment or machinery, the formulas for Coca-Cola or Kentucky Fried Chicken.

Operational Technologies

These can cut costs, speed up output, or improve efficiency. They can be inventions like manufacturing equipment or innovative software solutions like artificial intelligence, machine learning, and automated spreadsheets. Team-based tools like SharePoint, Team, Slack, and River help to manage the overwhelming magnitude of incoming information with a common location that enables team management. Automated activities can bring unprecedented speed, efficiency, and agility, all yielding operational advantages. A great example is bar coding for merchandise check-out. It was already being used for shipping so required no new inventions, yet revolutionized retail and inventory control.

Customer Focus Technologies

These enhance customers' experience. They are most often integrations like social media marketing or knowledge like details of what specific customers prefer or need. The advantage is in knowing things about existing or potential customers that no one else does. Data mining and data analytics enable this customization using an ever-growing number of customer data points. A good example is the emerging importance of personalized medications, interventions specifically tailored to individuals' DNA and body chemistry.

Value Chain

Next is to determine where value is added within your organization's work. These elements may be straightforward if things have remained relatively stable, or dramatically different if disruptive technologies have emerged.

Customer Outputs	What products and services and also customers and markets do your strategy target? Does technology change anything?
Advantage Work	What are the 3 to 5 high-level macro processes? How does each add value? Which provide competitive advantage?
Enabling Work	Which of the other macro-processes are critical enablers for the Advantage work? How does each add value?
Hand-Offs and Inputs	What inputs are needed: expertise, capital and expense, raw materials, technologies? What are the intermediate handoffs?

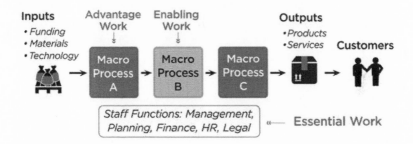

Customer Outputs

Agility shifts the focus from traditional management goals to objectives and key results (OKRs) centered on delivering products and services that are of value to the customer. Start with Deliverable 2: Strategy. Did the Deliverable 3: Diagnosis discussion change anything? What about the key technologies in the previous ingredient? The products and services that result anchors the end of your value chain, above.

Advantage Work

Now segment the work to gather these products and services into a few (three to five) 'macro' or primary work processes. Processes fall into four general categories. Advantage work has the activities that create a sustainable competitive advantage per your strategy. For example, Nike differentiates itself through its strategic marketing work (sending non-advantage work such as manufacturing overseas), while Apple excels at product design. Advantage activities directly contribute to the customer value proposition and have a high impact on company financials. Value comes from effective performance that exceeds that of peer organizations at acceptable costs. These work processes are always performed and managed in-house in order to protect the vital intellectual property involved. Be explicit where your competitive advantage originates: products or services, how they're delivered, their price, or how you work together with your customers.

Enabling Work

Enabling work provides value for the customer by leveraging or supporting advantage work. Both Apple and Nike must manufacture products at least as well as their competition, but they may not need to be significantly better. Enabling work is a balancing act: if done too well, it cuts into profits; if done below industry standards, the shoddy work cuts into sales and revenues.

There are two additional categories of work. Essential work must get done but doesn't add value visible to the customer. Non-essential work is work that has lost its value, but is still done out of inertia. Both of these are outlined more fully in Deliverable 7: Roles & Accountabilities.

Hand-Offs and Inputs

What inputs do these macro-processes need: investment capital and expense, raw materials, technology hardware, software, infrastructure, or knowledge? Keep track of the hand-offs from one macro-process to another. What information or outputs flow from one to another?

Value Chain Examples

On the next page are several simplified value chain examples.

Healthcare: Here diagnosis and treatment are advantage work. Intake and follow-up are enabling. This is true for many healthcare outfits, although advantage sometimes sits with location or marketing.

Consumer Products: This company lives and dies on their R&D and marketing, much like Intel. The other processes are important enablers. Other consumer companies may compete on low-cost manufacturing.

Service Providers: This is representative of companies that provide services to consumers or other businesses. Advantage work is often in higher quality or more reliable delivery, but it can also be in developing services no one else can offer. Some enterprises offer the same services as everyone else with average delivery, but they excel at advertising.

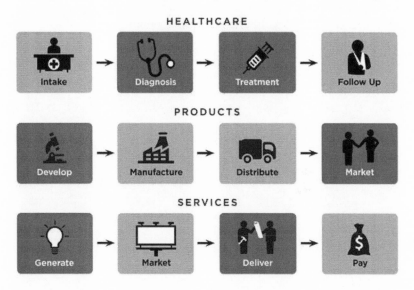

Workflows

Change teams often find it useful to visualize core work in the desired state by using workflows or process maps. These elements might help:

Process Descriptions	High-level summaries of the macro-processes. Define the 3-5 processes for each. High-level summaries for these.
Capabilities & Functions	Determine the capability groups important for each macro-process and process. Group into functions.
Flows between Processes	For each macro-process and process where not obvious. Describe and identify any timing considerations.

Process Descriptions

At this point you don't need detailed process maps, just understand the key aspects of the important processes to determine what changes may be necessary. Knowledgeable employees can together provide overviews of current work and adjust to address any significant issues from the diagnosis. If the diagnosis yielded no major issues with work, some or all of this mapping may be unnecessary. The audience is your change staff, sponsors, and affected employees, not professional process engineers, so keep things simple. The important items of information are high-level process and macro descriptions, which capabilities and functions perform the work, and the hand-offs involved.

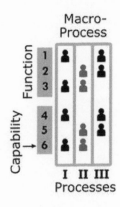

For each of your macro-processes, describe in a few sentences its start, inputs, involved groups or individuals, end, outputs, and recipients. Now identify three to five processes, which together make up this macro-process. Briefly describe their start, inputs, accountable parties, end, outputs, and recipients. This can be high level; any details that are fuzzy can wait for Customize. Show the macro-processes and their constituent processes, perhaps as columns as in the diagram below. In some way indicate which are advantage and which enabling. In the diagram, black icons denote advantage work, gray enabling.

Capabilities and Functions

This element focuses on 'what skills do the work,' the individual capabilities or skill sets that enable the processes to be accomplished. They almost always require some level of training or education, often extensive. In the Comfort case study in Chapter 9, building and maintaining stone and brick structures is done by skilled tradespeople who work with all types of brick, stone, and their mortars and binding agents. Their collection of knowledge and skills is called the masonry capability and requires extensive training and apprenticing.

We will explore this more in Deliverable 7: Roles & Accountabilities, but for now just identify the capabilities needed to accomplish these processes. Include all of the core capabilities from Deliverable 2: Strategy and any new capabilities from the technology discussion. On the process

and macro-process diagram show these capabilities in some way, perhaps in rows as in the diagram. Show which capabilities are involved with which processes. This can be as simple as a check mark or symbol or it can be an actual description of the work performed.

Combine your capabilities into a few high-level functions. A function is a collection of related capabilities. In the Comfort case, the skilled craft capabilities like masonry, electrical, and plumbing, were combined with the logistics capabilities like scheduling and transportation, and the project coordination capabilities into an operations function.

Flows between Processes

Now focus on the flow of inputs and outputs from one activity or process to the next. Start with the hand-offs from the macro-processes. Indicate which of these are sequential and dependent and which are independent and can be done in parallel. These descriptions can often wait for Customize if needed. Provide enough detail to begin making choices around the operating model.

To see how this shows up in practice, you might want to study the Comfort Home workflow map from Chapter 9. The value of this mapping shouldn't be underestimated. It provides a single graphic of what the organization is all about and helps everyone involved see their relationship to the whole. It's an important lead-in to discussing Deliverable 5: Operating Model.

More on Core Work

Comfort Home in Chapter 9 is a great example of how process mapping can identify opportunities for streamlining and removing redundancies in a networked organization. Stratos in Chapter 8 found that making the core workflows visible helped staff understand the activities they had in common and the resulting interdependencies in their work. In Wilderness Petroleum in Chapter 10 the high-level workflow map suggested how natural groupings could be translated into a reporting structure.

Deliverable 5: Operating Model

You have now explored your corporate culture, competitive landscape, strategy, and the resulting core work. The operating model describes at a high level how this all fits together into an integrated high-level picture of the organization.

Oper. Mod. Ingredients
◇ Org. Components
◇ Structure Options
◇ Option Selection

Organization Components

The operating model describes the organization components at high level. There are four elements here, which build on the prior deliverables. Strategy was set in Deliverable 2. Structure is the next two ingredients.

Leadership	How are leadership accountabilities distributed or shared? What are the expected styles, behaviors, and skill sets?
Work and Technology	How is innovation, operational, new product, or customer, built into the work and incorporated by employees?
People	Are new roles and new accountabilities, capabilities, skill sets needed? Different ways of collaborating and behaving?
Systems	Designed for control, coordination, or transparency? What key systems are needed to reinforce the desired culture?

Leadership

Start with the characteristics from the agile version of the aspired culture, Chapters 4, 5, 6, or 7. How is leadership shared, among the identified leaders, and with working teams and their members? How is strategy decided? Who allocates resources and how do they do this? What skills and behaviors do they need to have to function in this agile culture: group process, collaboration, and design thinking?

If the strategy has changed to an appreciable extent, does it require any changes in leadership? Some operational excellence leaders struggle to support the creativity required for product leadership. Has diagnosis identified any corrections? Do the core work and technology findings indicate concerns about current leadership? Use these inputs to express a high-level view of this component.

Work and Technology

The work you just did for Deliverable 4: Core Work is the basis for this. Are there any major technology or advantage work process changes? Have you incorporated any issues identified in the charter or emerging from the diagnosis? Finally review the agile version of your aspired culture in Chapters 4 through 7. Does it match what you have so far? Any corrections?

People

This includes skills, competences, numbers, and behaviors. Start with the characteristics from the agile version of the aspired culture, Chapters 4 through 7. What skills and behaviors are needed: group process, collaboration, and design thinking? What came out of the diagnosis deliverable? The work and technology deliverable? Is skills training needed? Are any functional capabilities missing? Are specific roles and accountabilities dictated by the work or technologies, especially advantage work? Do these need to be shared between individuals and groups? If the strategy has changed, does it require any changes in people? Use all of this input to articulate a high-level paragraph.

Systems

Start with the characteristics from the agile version of the aspired culture in Chapters 4 through 7. What sorts of culture reinforcements are indicated? Are the management, financial, and human resources systems more for control (Directive), or coordination (Participative), or transparency (Flexible), or connectivity (Adaptive)? Do changes in strategy, or the diagnosis, or the core work and technology discussion indicate any changes in the systems? Take an especially hard look at any culture characteristics that need to be reinforced through performance metrics or recognition and rewards criteria.

Structure Options

The final organization component, structure, facilitates collaboration and clear accountabilities by grouping individuals into work units and defining the relationships between units. The elements are:

Advantage Grouping	What units provide your competitive edge? How can you best group these to minimize barriers and deliver?
Other Work Grouping	What units enable the advantage work? How can they best support it, even if sub-optimizing themselves?
High level Coordination	What handoffs around advantage work need to be coordinated? This can be procedures, roles, or councils.

Traditionally organization design has revolved around changing structure. This is no longer true as organizations have been recognized as complex systems. The components in the previous ingredient may have already addressed many of your issues. This ingredient will look at structure to correct those remaining. There is no perfect structure and there will often be two or three robust alternatives. The elements that follow will help you identify them.

Advantage Work Grouping

Structure should enable the core advantage work. Start with the macro-processes involved. At the working level how are products or services delivered? For product leadership these are product development teams. In healthcare, these might be the integrated care teams. There are only a few ways to

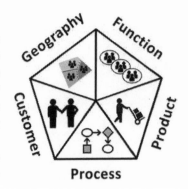

group these units, and the five dimensions in the diagram summarize the most common. Most organizations combine two or more of these at different levels in their reporting structures. Review the groupings below and pick one of the work level units that satisfies the strategy, the other four components, and the decision criteria. What groupings at the next level or two above this work best? See the three case studies in Chapters 8, 9, and 10 for good examples. If possible, look at one or two additional groupings that seem to satisfy the strategy, the other components and decision criteria.

Functional Grouping: This is the simplest and most basic form of business structure. Employees are grouped by professional capability into functions and typically move up along their functional lines. The

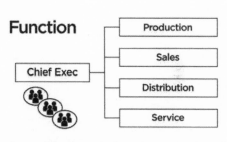

example in the diagram shows four of the generic functions mentioned in the macro-process discussion in the core work deliverable.

This grouping avoids duplication of effort since a single group performs a particular function regardless of geographical area, customer, or product line; a single face to vendors can generate buying leverage. It is well suited to operational excellence strategies with undifferentiated products or markets. The functional expertise, centralized control, and common standards help lower expenses and provide more consistent transfer of ideas and knowledge.

Functional groupings work best in the stable Mass Production and Knowledge Work landscapes which can tolerate slower response times and the longer product development life cycles. They are common in small to medium-sized organizations with a few well-developed products or services, for example legal firms with tax, contract, and criminal services.

However, functional designs may magnify barriers between functions working on the same product line or customer segment and may make interface coordination overwhelming. They may lead to conflicting performance measures, which discourage collaboration and may offer only narrow career paths. Where a functional grouping is preferred, these disadvantages must be mitigated with other design features.

Geographic Grouping: This grouping creates Line Businesses based on geographic regions, districts, or territories. Each unit has full control of all of its business activities and its own accountable leader. All functions are duplicated within each unit. We call a line business the collection of all processes and activities that produce specific products and services for specific customers or markets.

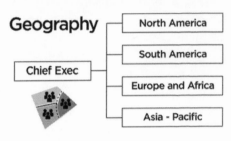

Geographic groupings minimize travel and distribution costs and thus work well with Cost Leadership strategies when different regions can take advantage of regional preferences and cost variations, low value-to-transport cost ratio, service delivery on-site, and closeness to customer for delivery. They can also benefit Customer Focus and Product Leadership strategies where market segments are geographic, and companies can benefit from a recognized local presence. This structure is often found in retail industries where many small stores spread across a wide geography: fast food, coffee chains, clothing, gasoline stations, dry cleaners, and so on. Because responsibilities are often delegated down to local units, it can foster customer loyalty and provide good training grounds for staff development.

However, these designs often duplicate functional activities and even allow the development of separate and incompatible systems. It can be difficult to service customers who cross geographies and also to maintain functional coordination and best practices. Reputation can vary from location to location. However, where a geographic grouping is preferred, these disadvantages can be mitigated with design features.

Product Grouping: This grouping creates Line Businesses around specific products or product lines. Each unit has full control of all of its business activities and its own accountable leader. All functions are duplicated within each unit. Its decentralized responsibilities can allow each business to pursue its own strategy and then organize as needed around its own value chain. This can dramatically reduce

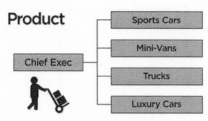

the time needed for product development. This makes it well suited to Product Differentiation strategies and can even provide multiple products for separate customers. The graphic shows an integrated vehicle manufacturer targeting four separate markets with its sports car, truck, mini-van, and luxury car divisions.

Product groupings can be inefficient if product lines 'reinvent the wheel,' duplicate or compete for resources, and lose economies of scale. It can be hard to maintain consistency across product lines and transfer best practices. Where product groupings are needed, these issues must be mitigated.

Customer Grouping: This grouping creates Line Businesses around specific customers or customer segments. Each unit has full control of its business activities and its own accountable leader. All functions are duplicated within each unit. The office supply firm shown below has divisions focused on retail stores, commercial wholesale distribution, small business contracts, and large corporate customer outsourcing.

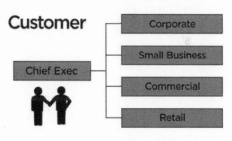

The ability to cultivate superior knowledge about specific customers or market segments makes this grouping well suited for Customer Segmentation strategies with clearly defined customer or market segments, each with its own specific and different problems or needs. They can also support Product Leadership strategies if products are focused on specific customers or markets.

This grouping has many of the same disadvantages as geographic and product groupings: duplicated activities, incompatible systems, and difficult coordination across line businesses. It can also cause unhealthy business unit competition if corporate loses touch with the businesses. Where this grouping is needed, these issues must be mitigated.

Process Grouping: This design maintains the strengths and discipline of functional groupings while addressing some of their disadvantages. The focus shifts from functional tasks to the end-to-end business processes and thus emphasizes process-level outputs instead of just departmental efficiency. It targets actual customer needs instead of just functional goals.

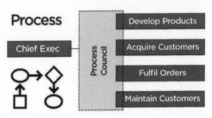

A reflection of the new shared governance is a move from siloed leadership teams to process councils.

By taking an end-to-end perspective on processes and using quantitative measures, this grouping can shorten cycle times and improve product quality. This works well with Cost Leadership or Operational Excellence strategies. It is often the choice for functional organizations trying to improve coordination and responsiveness. Because it tends to be highly customer focused it can benefit Customer Focus strategies. Since it strengthens the cross-functional or horizontal dimension, it fits the Participative culture much better than the functional groupings. Since it can be responsive and flexible to change, it can also support Flexible and Agile cultures.

This can be a difficult grouping where core processes are not well defined, and where systems don't support process integration. Moving to a process configuration require substantial effort understanding how work gets done, but it can reap dramatic benefits in streamlined flows.

Other Work Groupings

Enabling Work: Now consider the segments of the value chain involving work that enables the advantage work. At the working level, what are their outputs and how do they get delivered? This may be a manufacturing plant, an online ordering center, or a raw materials procurement center, each providing key outputs for the advantage work. Create groupings of enabling work units around the advantage ones in the previous ingredient, which make sense to deliver on your strategy.

Mixed Groupings: You may notice that you need a mix of different groupings. Local retail stores might be grouped by geography with their manufacturing plants grouped by product, or both might be by product, depending on strategy. Or a plant and several retail outlets may be grouped into one geographic unit. This will define your overall structure shape and is highly iterative and interactive. For large organizations you may need to repeat several times.

Outsourcing: Increasingly businesses focus on their core advantage and enabling work and look for opportunities to turn over essential work to others. Your strategy may have already indicated such opportunities, but if not, take the time to do so now. Are there portions or entire segments of your value chain that are essential or possibly even enabling work that could be  separated out and entrusted to others? While often called 'outsourcing,' this is better considered partnering or networking your enterprise with another. You will look into this again in Deliverable 7: Roles and Accountabilities.

Restricted Choices: These are hard concepts to generalize but for any specific organization, the convergence of chosen strategy, business landscape, corporate culture, and specific products and services almost always results in very restricted choices for grouping at each level. What seems at first glance as an impossible array of possibilities in reality rapidly collapses down to a few logical choices. Each of the case studies illustrates an example of how this works in practice.

In your work, the specific details of your business dictate what makes sense. Resist the temptation to carve out specific groupings of work units just yet. Some first-level functions may not even need to have the second-level groupings until Customize. Delaying these decisions until then broadens engagement, gets the right knowledgeable staff involved in the decisions, and can help to build ownership and commitment.

High-Level Coordination

Every organization will have several realistic structure options. Each one often involves a mix of types of grouping. Some have a grouping at the second level that compensates for shortfalls in the first level, for example a geographic grouping within a larger functional organization to help address local legal, regulatory and market needs. Some retain several central functions to support a first-level grouping, which would sub-optimize the functions if distributed over geographies or product lines.

No matter how well the above groupings fit the strategy, there will always be shortfalls unless coordination is provided to complement the groupings. A company providing home services may choose to group by geography to maximize service delivery but manage standards and careers through councils or functions that reach across the 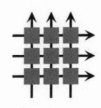 geographies. We will spend much more time on coordination in Deliverable 8: Structure, but for now review that material and specify at least the high-level coordinating mechanisms as part of the operating model.

Option Selection

You now have what you need to choose an operating model: strategy, several structure options, and descriptions of the other components. There are two elements in this ingredient: you first prioritize the decision criteria, then use them to compare operating models and select one.

Prioritized Criteria

Important factors in comparing the candidates will be the decision criteria from Deliverable 3. It is helpful to identify whether some criteria are more important than others. It is best to have this discussion separately before comparing the candidates. Some engineering cultures actually assign a weighting factor from 1 to 5 or 10. More frequently each criterion is assigned a qualitative rating of high, medium, or low. Some criteria may not be useful at all, if they are true for all options.

Comparison and Selection

Build operating model candidates around each structure option using the descriptions in the 'organization component' ingredient. Fully explore the problems or issues each grouping introduces. Can you adjust the other components to compensate? It is often helpful to research organizations that use that grouping option to understand how they resolve some of these tensions. Include enough detail to facilitate distinguishing the candidates, but reserve detailed design work to Customization.

You might find the table below helpful. The column labeled 'All' contains the component features that are present for each of the candidates. The columns for each candidate are then features that distinguish one option from another.

Operating Model Candidates

	All	1	2	3
Leadership: Are accountabilities distributed or shared? What are the expected styles, behaviors, and skill sets?				
Work and Technology: How are product, customer, and operational innovations incorporated into the work?				
People: What roles, accountabilities, capabilities, and skill sets are needed? Different ways to collaborate and behave?				
Systems: For control, coordination, or transparency? What key systems are needed to reinforce the desired culture?				
Structure: How are the advantage work units grouped? How are the other work units grouped to support them? What high level coordination mechanisms are needed?				

Sometimes the 'best' operating model is clear. In several hundred change projects, we have yet to work with a client who didn't already at this point have a good idea what was needed. It may even emerge on the back of a paper napkin over dinner, but invariably contains insights from bright people very close to the situation. The art of Syngineering is looking for this emergence and testing it with structured techniques like the decision matrix below to compare different alternatives.

Option comparison is now a matter of examining how well each fits the decision criteria. Use the prioritized criteria from the previous element, possibly some numerical rating but more typically just high, medium, or low. While these may lend themselves to some sort of a numerical summary, the focus is not the numbers; the  value is in the conversation. There are often intense discussions about priorities as sponsors wrestle with a best-fitting candidate that doesn't match their 'napkin' answer. Each of the case studies in Chapters 8, 9, and 10 illustrates such conversations.

Operating Model Selection

	Priority	Option 1	Option 2	Option 3
Decision criteria A	H, M, or L			
Decision criteria B	H, M, or L			
Decision criteria C	H, M, or L			
Decision criteria D	H, M, or L			
Decision criteria E	H, M, or L			
… etc.				

More on Operating Models

Just about every published case study in the past few years has featured examples of how operating models are changing. This is especially true of those organizations embracing digital technologies and data analytics. Within this book, the Wilderness case study in Chapter 10 is a great example of a new operating model focused more on cross-functional coordination than changing reporting lines. The Stratos case in Chapter 8 is highly iterative: the chosen operating model involved product-focused work groups but during Customize it became clear that these needed robust customer-focused front-room functionality to work. The Comfort case in Chapter 9 shows how prototyping can build an operating model where none existed before.

Deliverable 6: Deployment

This prioritizes the activities to move from the current state to the desired future. The changes identified in Deliverables 1 to 5 are often too many and interrelated to be done simultaneously in an uncoordinated manner. This deliverable connects and plans them.

> **Deployment Ingredients**
> ◇ Initiatives
> ◇ Change Impacts
> ◇ Deployment Method
> ◇ Accountabilities

Initiatives

The first step is to identify and prioritize discrete initiatives, then decide which to undertake so that no part of the organization takes on more work than it is able to handle. This ingredient's elements are the columns:

List of Changes				Grouped into Initiatives	Prioritized Initiatives
1	What	Who	How	Size	Initiative A: how to take these changes and weld them into an effort that will resolve the issues.	How important? Now or later? Interdependencies? Resourcing factors?
2	What	Who	How	Size		
3	What	Who	How	Size		
4	What	Who	How	Size		
5	What	Who	How	Size	Initiative B	Priority
6	What	Who	How	Size		
7	What	Who	How	Size		
... etc.				... etc.	... etc.

List of Changes

Start with changes that came out of the strategy, markets, customer base, relationships, and distribution channel discussions. Include activities already underway, even if they seem like minor tweaking. Then look at technology, core work, and structure from the operating model: What are the key changes to move to the desired future?

Identify what's changing, who is impacted, how, and the size of the impact.

Now look at the other components from the operating model. You may not yet know the exact nature of the changes but simply that change is needed. To trigger your thinking, look through the charter / scope / case for change, the strategy / revised strategy / organizational characteristics, the diagnosis and identified shortfalls, and the complete list of decision criteria, and any givens that came out of that process. Finally, are there any other changes that aren't already included?

Be as specific as possible. For example, 'data entry must become more accurate and efficient' is too high level for this list. It's not detailed enough to decide who needs to do what in deployment. Consider whether 'define the role of data entry in the field offices' and 'develop a procedure for evaluating and maintaining data accuracy' might be more helpful. The final comprehensive list may range from a few up to 30 or more items depending on the size and extent of the changes.

Grouped into Initiatives

Now group the changes into ones that are most interdependent and/or involve the same groups. Implementing a new technology or changing a major function may involve changes in each organization component and touch most of the lines of business, yet it is still a single initiative and should be planned and managed as such. Changing the focus of a specific line of business may involve every central function and may well benefit from coordination as a single initiative with leadership from the line of business. There are numerous ways to make these groupings. There is no 'best way' but, when the affinities are not clear-cut, it can be useful to create a table that indicates which organizational ingredients are involved in which changes, like the one above. Fully describe what is involved in each initiative.

Prioritized Initiatives

The case for change and especially the decision criteria will provide guidance. Move your way down the list of initiatives and organize them by urgency and by importance. Which initiatives need to be prioritized to be done first? Which are also important but can be scheduled for later action? Which are seemingly of pressing urgency but need to be done only if other important changes depend on them? What other considerations are relevant beyond urgency and importance, such as the capacity, capabilities, and resources available? Be ruthless in prioritizing and in sequencing the initiatives and then decide which ones to undertake so that no part of the organization takes on more than it is willing and able to handle.

Change Impacts

To plan deployment, you need to know which groups will be affected. The elements of this ingredient, the columns below, help do that.

Stakeholder List			Stakeholder Impacts	
Group	Influence	Attitude	Extent Impacted	Deployment Considerations
I				
II				
III				
... etc.			... etc.	

Stakeholder List

Revisit the list of stakeholders you developed in charter / involvement / engagement needs. A lot has happened since then, so update it now. Are these still the important stakeholders? Are there additions? Do they have the same level of influence heading into Customize as they did initially? Have their concerns or attitudes changed?

Stakeholder Impacts

Start with your stakeholders that have the highest influence and take each initiative in turn. Your stakeholder groups may include some or all of the various line businesses and functions. To what extent will this initiative impact this stakeholder? This can be as simple as H-high, M-medium, and L-low with a few-word descriptor

of what's impacted. Or it can be a quantitative analysis like: under this new plan the marketing function needs 20 additional staff and an increase in budget by $15 million. Consider each of the individual changes grouped into this initiative. Work your way through each stakeholder. Do the impacts suggest any ideas that could make the deployment more effective?

Deployment Method

The columns below are the elements for deploying the new operating model. The rows show how each of the four cultures tends to do this. Your initial approach was based in the current culture, typically Directive. In Customize, you continue introducing aspects of the desired culture.

	Procedure	Groups Involved	Local Engagement
Directive	Executives cascade down through functions and business units	Business units and functions lead Customize with central guidance	Local group engagement builds understanding and provides feedback
Participative	Functions and business units customize via mini-conferences	Business units and functions convene their own mini-conferences	Mini-conference participants extend outcomes into all work groups
Flexible	Operationalize prototype	Executives lead own work units	Customize and diffuse further
Adaptive	Diffuse from change circle	Change networks involved as needed.	Ad hoc groups Customize

Procedure

Consider the various issues that have surfaced in the analysis. What implications do they have for deployment? Brainstorm what you might do to mitigate or reduce any risks and address the issues. Update the Stakeholder Analysis from Deliverable 1 Charter. How can you use groups with high influence and positive attitudes to further ease the deployment? Each culture has preferred ways of doing this, as shown in the table above. Consider how to handle this for your own organization.

Groups Involved

In Customize, work groups will be detailing and customizing the operating model. There may be reporting structure changes; staff movements, reductions or additions; asset reallocations; management systems changes; and cultural or behavioral changes. All work groups will need to evaluate their own roles and structure. Functional experts will lead the work on systems and coordinate across the enterprise due to the interdependencies of the different systems and risk of any one function perfecting their own systems but sub-optimizing the whole. Each culture has a different way of involving its business units, functions, and their executives. The table above has thoughts for each of the four common cultures.

Local Engagement

Ultimately every individual will get involved in the changes through their local work groups. This element describes how you will involve these groups. The table above has suggestions appropriate for each of the common cultures.

Accountabilities

This assigns who will lead, work on, and coordinate the initiatives during Customize. The important elements to consider as you plan this:

◇ Lead Roles: For each initiative, noted by **LEAD** in the example below
◇ Other Group Roles: Involvement is **HIGH**, Some, or x (none at all)
◇ Coordination: How the initiatives are connected to the whole

	Line Businesses				Functions			
	1	2	3	… etc.	I	II	III	… etc.
Initiative A	**LEAD**	Some	x	… etc.	**HIGH**	**HIGH**	**HIGH**	… etc.
Initiative B	x	**LEAD**	Some	… etc.	**HIGH**	Some	x	… etc.
Initiative C	HIGH	HIGH	HIGH	… etc.	**LEAD**	Some	x	… etc.
… etc.	… etc.	… etc.	… etc.	… etc.	… etc.	… etc.	… etc.	… etc.

Lead Roles

As you listed the changes and grouped them into initiatives, you probably made some tentative judgements about which groups to involve in each initiative. Which will take the lead accountability for each initiative?

In many cases this is obvious. Major functional changes normally sit within that function, but complex initiatives with many moving parts may need to be subdivided, with different groups taking the lead for each one. However, don't be too quick to make these assignments; make sure the required leadership, mindsets, and capacity are present. Filling out a table as above will quickly surface groups with too much on their plate. Their involvement in some initiatives may need to be deferred.

Their accountabilities include laying plans for the work. They do a critical path review of the work to-date. What are the key points of the proposed framework within their initiative? Which are the most controversial and/or which are likely to encounter resistance? What actions must be taken, by whom and by when? They then need to determine work streams, steps and required deliverables, dependencies, and overall timeline to get work done.

Roles of Other Groups

For initiatives led by one of the functions, the line businesses need to be involved for critical expertise and feedback. They may all be heavily involved, but typically one or two are involved heavily and represent the others, which are either involved to some extent, or not at all. This involvement should share the load across the business.

Similarly, for initiatives led by one of the line businesses, one or more of the functions need to be involved for expertise and feedback. This should also be arranged to share the load equitably.

Coordination

During Customize the focus shifts to detailed design across numerous work groups. This almost always requires some way to connect and coordinate the effort, especially the initiatives working on supporting systems and operating processes that span multiple business units. This strongly depends on culture and landscape, but it typically involves not only coordination, but governance: those accountable for coordination frequently also play the role of holding others to their accountabilities, timely escalation of issues, and effective enterprise-wide decision making.

More on Deployment

The Comfort Home case in Chapter 9 shows how Deployment works in a networked organization and the importance of accountabilities. The Stratos case in Chapter 8 used the development of an integrated plan for deployment as a vital part of moving to the Adaptive culture. The Wilderness Petroleum case in Chapter 10 actually focused primarily on the deployment plan from the beginning. The sponsors grudgingly accepted that articulating the operating model was a critical first step.

Deliverable 7: Roles and Accountabilities

This deliverable starts the detailed design work that operationalizes the operating model and actually builds agility into its components. By working at both individual and group levels, this quickly surfaces any issues around what is feasible and realistic and permits corrections to be introduced in an iterative way.

Role Ingredients
◇ Technology
◇ Process Details
◇ Roles Needed
◇ Skills & Numbers

Technology

Technologies alone deliver no value. It's only the combination of a clear strategy, the right technology, lean processes, appropriate skills, and high-quality data systems that together create value. Any weak link in this chain yields poor-value delivery. These are the key elements:

Key Requirements	Are these still aligned with the strategy and new operating model? Are there any modifications needed?
Supporting Technologies	What technologies are needed to support the advantage work? Are emerging technologies actively managed?

Key Requirements

You have already in Deliverable 4: Core Work identified the possibly disruptive technologies, which might dramatically replace one way of doing work with a new and vastly better way. A good example is the emergence of Uber transportation, which disruptively changed the face of taxi services. Here you involve a wider segment of staff. They should validate these technologies before getting into the detailed design. Have your conclusions held up during the operating model and deployment discussions?

Supporting Technologies

Now you identify what technologies are needed to support or enable these key technologies. For Uber's this is GPS navigation and its web-based request, response, and payment systems. Make sure these supporting technologies are fully incorporated into the appropriate work processes and management, financial, and people systems.

Do you have groups constantly scanning for useful new technologies? Are strategic and resourcing decisions made in light of emerging technologies? Are emerging innovations quickly integrated into all systems? Have you incorporated all possible automation opportunities to increase quality, volume, efficiencies and/or morale?

Identify any technology risks, especially compliance with all regulatory requirements. Some innovative data mining runs afoul of right-to-privacy laws. See that the design can assess and address cybersecurity issues. Most large enterprises have been hacked, but still dimly perceive their risks and consequences. Analyze whether your company could survive technology failures. A software malfunction from a single misplaced digit can cost a company huge customer upset and damages.

Process Details

This deepens the Deliverable 4: Core Work descriptions and positions you to determine how many people you need and with what skills.

Tasks and Activities	Identify the individual work tasks, group them into activities, for all of the advantage, enabling, and essential processes.
Required Skills	Identify the capabilities needed for each task and activity. Aggregate capabilities into specialties and then functions.
Flow Details	Link the tasks, activities, processes, and macro-processes into integrated work flows. Add further description for clarity.

Describing work is not a mysterious black box, but an integral part of agility. These three elements are interdependent so must be done in parallel as it is near impossible to describe tasks without capabilities.

Tasks and Activities

Tasks are the basic unit of work. Some are simple, but most involve some level of skill. A number of tasks strung together form an activity. Two or more activities make up a process. You now need to identify individual work tasks and activities for all of your processes.

We characterize tasks using the well-known RACI framework but apply it to the tasks rather than the employees, emphasizing that the work needs to be understood independent of who performs it:

◇ R (responsible) tasks involve work that delivers business results

◇ A (authorize) tasks assign work, resource it, and ensure it delivers

◇ C (consultative) tasks provide input to those doing the work

◇ I (informative) tasks inform others about progress and results

The graphic on the next page from the Comfort case in Chapter 9 shows how this can work in practice. It highlights the 'assess' activity, part of the 'prepare' process, which sits within the 'deliver' macro-process. These are shown as nested columns. The tasks are shown as cells or boxes. The initial one authorizes (A) the work. The responsible tasks (R) evaluate the feasibility of an order and identify what's needed to fulfill it. The consulted tasks (C) provide order clarification, customer preferences, and logistics advice.

Required Skills

In Deliverable 4: Core Work you listed the functions and capabilities involved in your advantage and enabling work. Here you validate and update those lists and extend them to all the work that the organization does. There are several important terms we need to carefully define.

As a reminder, capabilities are the knowledge and skills required to perform certain tasks. Roles are filled by agents, which perform related tasks using the needed capabilities. A role can be filled by a person, such as a rotating equipment technician, or a combination of hardware and software, like an automated manufacturing assembly line. A specialty is a collection of closely related capabilities and a function is a set of related specialties.

To bring this to life, let's explore the rows in the diagram below from the Comfort case. Skilled crafts persons who have the knowledge of brick, stone, mortars, and binding agents and who have the skills to use this knowledge to build brick and stone structures possess the masonry capability. Masonry is combined with electrical, plumbing, carpentry, and equipment into the skilled crafts specialty, shown in the diagram. Capabilities from the IT and skilled crafts specialties perform the responsible work (R) of evaluating feasibility and deciding what's needed to fulfill the order.

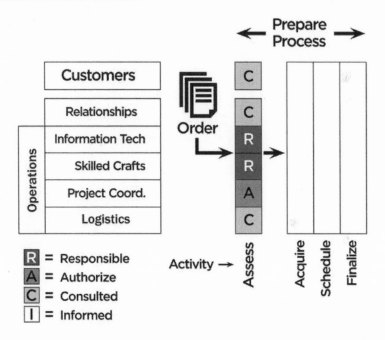

The project coordination capabilities for heating systems, solar energy systems, and integrated electronic control systems together form the project coordination specialty. The capability for whichever system is involved in the order authorizes (A) and oversees this assess activity. Capabilities from the logistics specialty are consulted (C) for schedule, purchasing, shipping, and inspections considerations.

After listing the capabilities needed for each task and activity, identify their few high-level specialties and/or functions. At Comfort, the individual capabilities form the specialties of logistics, project coordination, skilled crafts, IT, and customer relationship management (relationships in the diagram). Customer relationship management is part of the marketing and sales function; the other specialties here together form the operations function.

Flow Details

Now link the tasks and capabilities into integrated workflows by identifying important interfaces and hand-offs. Continue the dialogue with the employees actually doing the work. To be agile, processes shouldn't be weighed down by multi-level committees and difficult sign-off procedures. Balance strategic intent against the specific needs of the local organizations. At Comfort in the diagram above, the input into the access activity is an order, to install a boiler, repair a solar panel, overhaul a security system, or something similar. The intermediate products for hand-off to the acquire activity are a 'go-ahead' approval and a list of resources needed.

Roles Needed

This ingredient groups the tasks into roles, lists the accountabilities for each, and looks for opportunities for improved efficiency, such as automation.

Grouped Tasks	Group similar tasks performed by the same capability into roles. Do this for all tasks across the organization.
Account-abilities	What does each role need to complete its tasks: specific responsibilities, authorities, outputs, and relationships?
Role Efficiencies	Possibly outsource roles not doing advantage work. Remove non-essential work. Identify automation or technology roles.

Grouped Tasks

As noted in the 'required skills' element, roles involve the capabilities that perform similar related tasks. A role can handle tasks within just one activity, across an entire process, or span all the organization's work. It can be all or part of a person's job, or include many jobs, or be handled by hardware and/or software technology.

Accountabilities

Accountabilities are simply what needs to happen for this role to complete its tasks, and it entails three core requisites: the required knowledge and skills, any associated tools and technology, and adequate authority. It can be as simple as 'complete task 1,' 'complete task 2,' and so on, but more often it includes specific responsibilities, authorities, key outputs, and important relationships. They can include any details needed to fully describe the required capabilities and skills. They often include communications and liaison needs, telecommuting or virtual working considerations, and geographic, timing, or other constraints.

Focus on negotiating boundaries between roles. Find the areas where accountabilities overlap, where there are gaps, and where a clean hand-off is critical. Consider assigning RACI descriptions to clarify who does what with whom. The choices of roles and accountabilities often need to be incorporated into other components: roles filled by equipment and software often impose requirements on supporting systems. Carry this forward into Deliverable 9: Systems. Most HR staff are quite experienced in developing role and accountability descriptions: involve them closely but be cautious with existing job descriptions.

Role Efficiencies

Outsourcing involves farming out selected work to maintain a focus on your strategic core work. Not every business culture permits this, but if yours does, look for work that is not advantage or enabling. This will be essential work, which does not add value visible to the customer and does not differentiate a business from its competitors but is required by the landscape. Common examples include product distribution, human resources recruiting and payroll, accounting, property management, and even 'compliance' with governmental regulations. This must be considered carefully because if not done well, it can have a significant negative impact on the bottom line. There are national and global organizations that specialize in these areas and can provide capabilities beyond what a specific organization may want to invest given resources needed for advantage and enabling work.

Non-Essential Work is work that has lost its value but is still done out of inertia. If you were starting the business today, would you need it? If not, it's non-essential. In most cases, your process mapping should have identified and eliminated all such work, but if not, do that now!

Technology Efficiencies: Most roles today involve technology, but in some cases the roles may be the technology itself. Automated assembly-line robots have a role independent of their handlers. Equipment may be doing the advantage work with handlers doing enabling work. Increasingly, software applications perform critical security roles. Include all such roles and their accountabilities.

Skills and Numbers

This ingredient has three elements, shown as columns in the table below: list of roles, job benchmarking, and final numbers.

			List of Roles			Benchmark	Final Numbers		
		Name of Role	Capabilities	Tasks Performed	Account-abilities	Numbers	Numbers & Qualifiers	Location	Numbers	Comments
Function I	Specialty A	1								
		2								
	Specialty B	3								
		4								
... etc.						... etc.	... etc.			

List of Roles

You now have all the information you need to compile a full list of all roles. Your HR function almost certainly already has templates for this, populated with current employees. This can be your starting point, but make sure that the list is modified for the desired future, not a rehash of the current state. This includes any requirements from the technology ingredient, including roles filled by equipment or software, and any requirements from the process details ingredient.

Have the groups working and carefully catalog a complete set of roles. One project we supported shows how this can go wrong. Six months after their new organization's 'go live,' power in the main plant went out. A little study uncovered the reason. The clerk who paid the electric bills was let go after her job was eliminated by an unaware design team bent on minimizing costs. The outgoing clerk had no incentive to mention the oversight and was likely amused by the blackout.

Use some template like the table above to list the roles, capabilities, specialties, functions, tasks, and accountabilities. Seek to understand which roles are the same across different processes and work groups but be open to distinctions. In Comfort Home, the role of mason was almost identical for both gas boiler and solar panel installation; however, the role of equipment specialist was quite different because of the radically different equipment types.

Let work groups collaborate and emerge with their own assessments. Have them estimate how much of each role is needed. For people this can take the form of hours per week or the more traditional FTE (full-time equivalent employees). For technology roles you may use price, rental fees, or maintenance, whichever captures true annual costs.

Job Benchmarking

The estimates above are 'bottoms-up' from those doing the work. They must be tested against a 'tops-down' view of how similar organizations do things. This is job benchmarking. It provides objective information to counter the unconscious biases of those close to the work. It can also stimulate looking at alternative ways of working. The difficulties are twofold. Organizations often resist sharing this type of information, especially with competitors. Even where this can be arranged, however, it can be hard to define jobs accurately enough for useful comparison. Both external and internal sources have strong reasons to 'shade' data to suit other agendas. Take care not to expand this into a major project; initial conclusions are often 'good enough!'

Externally: Use partners and competitors to show how comparative organizations operate and extrapolate conclusions based on the desired state. Most often these are available as gross ratios for best practice for support functions. Ratios for HR and finance range from 1.0 to 2.0 per 100 employees depending on type of business. Core work staffing is quite a bit more challenging unless work practices can be compared as well. The best approach is often to look at organizations that are similar in some way in terms of processes and work practices.

Internally: For a division within a larger company, looking across the same company can also be useful, especially since work practices can be compared much better. However, functions across the same company may have consistent biases that won't be uncovered this way.

Reconcile: To compare your bottom-up staffing model against the benchmark results, take into account various possible differences in types of work, its complexity, and location. Work in Arctic mountains may not translate well to tropical plantations. Length of workday, number of working days per month, vacation or leave entitlements, and any seasonal variables can be specific to an organization, country, or society and need to be factored in and noted in the table.

Final Numbers

Taking into account the benchmark comparisons, adjust your staffing. Many factors may need to be built into the final model including expected volumes of work, time and frequency per activity and task, seasonality, facilities, utilization, and culture. Carefully consider the physical location of each role if it's of consequence. Make sure there are appropriate groups looking into the leadership roles involved in the governance processes and the technology roles in the core work processes. These are generally best handled centrally.

Once adjusted, compare the resulting numbers to your current staffing. If you need to dramatically augment or reduce staff, immediately build this into the deployment plans. You may have already foreseen this eventuality, but if not, there may be substantial work to be done: severance, reassignment, retraining, and recruiting can each require large lead times.

The comments column can include thoughts on the 'incumbents' in the roles, 'candidates' with higher skills but currently in other roles, and any other considerations like legal requirements or special skills. In a 10,000-employee organization, building this spreadsheet can seem a daunting task, but agility involves aligning the work to the strategy, and the rows in this spreadsheet represent the people who actually do this work!

More on Roles and Accountabilities

The Comfort Home case study in Chapter 9 illustrates the fundamental concepts in this deliverable. Process mapping was essential in understanding how the different organizations fit together. The Stratos case in Chapter 9 shows how understanding the process requirements allows the individual work groups to identify the needed roles and estimate numbers. In the Wilderness Petroleum case in Chapter 10, a relatively simple technology change (real-time metering and integrated operations) dramatically affected staffing and work dynamics.

Deliverable 8: Structure

Structure details the relationships between work groups. For years reporting structure was the dominant component used to address organization design. While still important, in different ways for each of the four cultures it

provides the coordination of resources needed to deliver the strategy.

Unit Staffing

This ingredient groups roles into the units actually doing the work. The four elements are constructed in parallel, often with multiple iterations.

Unit Mandates	Work unit mandates: purpose of unit, work performed, outputs delivered, and any other important responsibilities.
Roles into Units	Populate each work unit with roles, including capabilities and skills, work performed, accountabilities, and numbers.
Unit Sizing	Determine the optimum size of each work unit considering mandates, task interdependencies, and spans of control.
Unit Evaluation	Appropriate membership, the needed authorities, realistic workloads, challenging jobs, and ability to meet mandates.

Unit Mandates

These are the purpose, scope of work, technologies, responsibilities, product and service linkages, and authorities for each work unit. Start this process with the operating model's high-level units. Then from the process detail in the previous deliverable, extract out who does the front-line work. The shape and mandates of these front-line units are often clear. Work from the bottom up and top down to outline units at all levels. This will be iterative, but often falls into place.

At each level, start with the units performing advantage work. Identify their mandates, especially those that link together to provide the products and service outcomes. Make sure these include any new technologies, whether they rest with advantage groups, or a technology function, or an IT operations function. It is vital to determine clearly who is accountable for delivering business value from the work and technology that provide your competitive edge.

Move to the units doing enabling work. Often, they service or manage the critical technologies. Their mandates must enable the advantage work. Finally move to units doing essential work. These are often governance, legal, procurement, human resources, and finance. Some work in these areas can be simplified and automated to reduce bureaucracy. It is important to recognize when seemingly essential work is actually something more. One of our clients found that their tax department was actually providing a competitive advantage through novel interpretations of the tax code.

You should end up with the overall shape of your organization at all levels top to bottom, including all outsourced units. It is difficult to articulate exactly how to do this, but the convergence of a specific organization, its strategy, landscape, culture, and products and services almost always results in restricted choices for grouping at each level.

The Comfort Home case in Chapter 9 provides a simple example. Their operating model had three levels. The highest level were the three operating units focused on solar, gas heating, and smart-home systems, all supported by a central administration. The front-line units were advantage work installation teams and enabling work maintenance teams, all managed by the middle level operations function. The central administration functions of marketing and sales, operations and logistics, and office management had teams of specialists handling enabling work like scheduling and purchasing, as well as essential work like facilities management.

Roles into Units

Now distribute all the roles from the previous deliverable into all the work units. This will be messy and iterative as you refine mandates to fit the groupings of roles. Start with natural groupings in the front-line advantage work units based on your strategy, operating model, and desired culture. Combine into full-time or part-time jobs. At Comfort the various capabilities of the skilled crafts and IT specialties populated the installation and maintenance teams. Most jobs filled roles on a single team, but some filled part-time roles for a number of different teams. There are just a few generic groupings for teams.

Populate Units with Roles

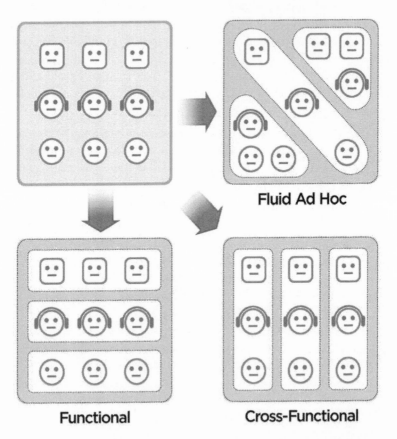

Fluid Ad Hoc

Functional

Cross-Functional

Functional Grouping: This groups people with similar capabilities for professional growth, group identity, and mutual support when needed (e.g., helping out during crunch periods or vacation coverage). The boundaries need to facilitate accountability and decision making within and between units. While useful with any culture or strategy, these can be especially helpful where standard, prescriptive, and/or compliant functional processes and accountabilities are needed: operational excellence strategies in Directive or Participative cultures in particular.

Cross-Functional or Process Grouping: Assembling people with different capabilities encourages day-to-day collaboration and cross-functional skill development. This is the core of agility as work avoids silos. Where possible, use natural breaks in work processes to reduce the need for hand-offs. It requires clear inputs and outputs across boundaries to facilitate timely measurement and feedback on performance. It is often useful to build in some slack in the value chain to allow for identifying and addressing issues to improve flow and quality by implementing lessons learned and innovation improvements. 'Cross-functional' teams can mix functions, specialties, or even capabilities. This design shows up in all strategies and cultures. The three case studies have different examples of this.

Ad Hoc Groupings: Flexible and especially Adaptive cultures build first level work units only as needed to meet customer and/or business needs. Unit mandates and membership are handled in real time at the lowest possible level in these cultures. Often these are temporary, and task focused, but some are more permanent. Those called 'quasi-functional' have mostly functional team members but also a few specialists. The call center of one of our clients was a good example. The 20 or so telephone order-taking associates worked on the same team with two IT applications specialists who provided the technical expertise to keep the systems running.

Unit Sizing

As Flexible and Adaptive cultures have emerged, emphasis on unit size has shifted from how well a supervisor can control them to how to mix capabilities for self-management and optimum effectiveness. The generalization from research and experience is that teams function best with five to seven members, but this depends on team maturity, nature of the work, and interdependencies of the roles. Teams can function effectively with three to nine members, and we have designed high performing teams with up to 24 members.

Smaller teams in general are more likely to be interconnected and cohesive while larger teams tend to operate more like a network, which can work well if intentionally designed and maintained. These larger teams can be effective in configurations that are more routine and standardized and are also useful for ad hoc efforts like strategic planning input, design, coordination, collaboration, consistency, and project communication.

That said, span of control, the number of employees that a leader can directly supervise, still merits at least some consideration in all of the landscapes except Adaptive. Routine repetitive front-line work may allow

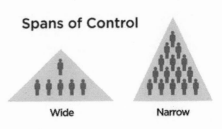

Spans of Control

Wide   Narrow

up to 20 or more. In organizations with a strong vertical focus, large spans of control are also common at senior executive levels where subordinates are fully capable leaders heading their strategic business units. Spans of control are typically smallest in mid-level management where the complex variable work might restrict it to as few as six.

Most Flexible, Adaptive, and some Participative cultures favor wide spans of control and 'flat' structures with fewer levels. These create more innovative risk-taking customer responsiveness but provide less control and require that leaders move away from 'micro-managing.' Too few levels in wide organizations, however, may not provide sufficient oversight. Directive cultures prefer more narrow spans of control and more levels, creating a 'tall' structure. This may well be necessary but can be an expensive way to control employee behavior and tends to be less flexible and slower to respond to innovation and change.

Unit Evaluation

First look at the jobs created and ask the employees most knowledgeable: Are workloads from the combined roles reasonable? Does each job have business relevance, clear processes, and flexibility to adapt to changing business requirements? Can everyone in each unit clearly relate their work to accomplishment of the work unit's accountabilities? Do job challenges stimulate learning, professional growth, and motivation? Distribute tasks so there are no 'good versus bad' jobs. Undesirable yet essential roles can be shared equitably among different jobs. Consider quality of work life for employees.

Every culture has roles that coordinate work. Formal supervisors do this in Directive, and shared leadership roles handle it for Participative and Flexible. In Adaptive, these accountabilities can be assigned to anyone. The coordination questions must always be addressed: Are spans of control realistic? Is decision-making clear? Are interfaces with suppliers, other teams, departments, and functions effective? Does the unit have the right skill sets to provide the capabilities to deliver on its mandate? If there are not enough people with key skills to be assigned to every team, can they easily be accessed by the work units when they need them? Finally, does each unit's mandate still fit?

Coordination

Mechanisms of various kinds coordinate and share information across groups. This ingredient's three elements form the columns in the table:

Critical Interfaces	Type of Coordination	Coordination Solution
Critical Interface 1		
Critical Interface 2		
Critical Interface 3		
… etc.		

These mechanisms can provide guidance and direction. They are even more important in Participative and Flexible cultures as horizontal coordination becomes as important as the vertical hierarchy.

Critical Interfaces

Identify the critical interfaces not addressed adequately in the structure evaluation above. These could be within or between critical processes or organizations that must work collaboratively. Look especially at important external interfaces. List which groups are involved, the exact nature of the coordination issue, and some sense of how often and with what intensity the coordination needs to occur.

Type of Coordination

The graphic below shows a wide range of coordinating mechanisms:

Coordinating Mechanisms

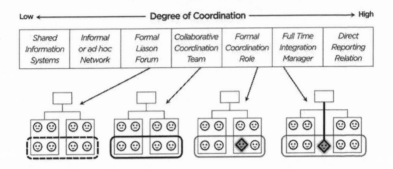

- ◇ Shared Information Systems: When the degree of coordination is low, people don't even need to talk to each other, just have access to the same information, which is updated accordingly.
- ◇ Informal or Ad Hoc Networks: If slightly more coordination is required, people can get together informally when required. In Directive and Participative cultures, people tend to do this just to make things work. In Flexible cultures it can be a cornerstone of the design. Agile cultures respond to tensions in just this way.
- ◇ Formal Liaison Forum: When even more coordination is required, identified employees meet regularly to resolve coordination issues.
- ◇ Collaborative Coordination Team: Still more coordination may require an actual coordination team with key members from different work groups sharing responsibility.
- ◇ Formal Coordination Role: Even more coordination may require that this team actually have one person identified among team members accountable to ensure that coordination is effective across the team.

◇ Full-Time Integration Manager: Even more coordination can require an integration manager who has this formal role and is a direct report to the next level leader. This role is typically at the same level as the leaders of the teams needing coordination.

◇Direct Reporting Relation: If coordination of these tasks becomes the most important issue in the organization, all those employees needing coordination can become a separate work unit reporting in to the integration manager.

Coordination Solutions

Use the suggestions above to think through the interface issues and identify effective solutions. Other mechanisms we have seen include informal matrix relationships, often shown as 'dotted lines'. We have also seen formal communities of practice or shared accountabilities. The right accountabilities can be a very effective coordinating mechanism. Pick just the critical few and avoid overloading the organization with too much complexity.

Be careful when during implementation you hear that "we've just created new silos" or "we still don't know what is going on in other parts of the organization" or "our internal communication is poor" or similar. These may indicate that your coordination mechanisms need more work.

The coordination solutions plus final grouping are your organization structure. We recommend that you do these two activities in parallel.

Final Grouping

This ingredient has the final description of the relationships between all work units, then analyzes and validates that it can deliver the strategy.

Organization Map	This helps everyone involved visualize the various units at all levels in the organization and how they fit together.
Grouping Evaluation	Test the components for effective delivery. Be ready to revisit key assumptions and iterate design decisions.

Organization Map

It is often extremely useful to represent the structure graphically. These are often called organization maps, or in some Adaptive cultures, relationship maps. These can be as simple as the cartoon diagram at right. It shows a generic small five-level company with operations and a separate headquarters. Level 1 are the individual employees, level 2 are working unit leads and specialists, level 3 are the major functions and operating unit leads and advisors, level 4 are corporate advisors, and level 5 is the CEO. Round faces are individual staff, robotic arms represent automated assembly lines, Diamonds are roles with that have accountabilities for leadership.

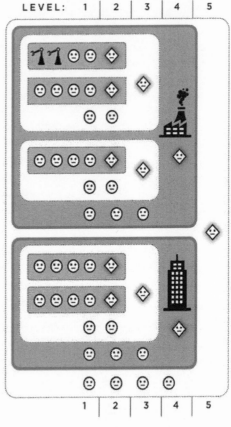

The result is less a true organization chart and more literally a map, typically accompanied by the unit's mandates. The important messages are not who reports to whom, but what is expected for each work unit. It can be linked to individual accountabilities. Use what fits your culture and don't overdo it. Directive and some Participative and Flexible cultures may need to see traditional charts, but can still benefit from some sort of graphical representation. Adaptive cultures dispense with the levels and simply focus on relationships between units.

Grouping Evaluation

To test the groupings, consider the questions below. If you surface issues, you may need to revisit the key assumptions and iterate.

◇ Strategy: Do the core capabilities deliver the desired products and services to all market segments in all geographies through the identified distribution channels? Is it clear how unit or groups of unit capabilities flow together to deliver each strategic priority?

◇ Leadership: Are leadership roles and accountabilities clear, whether concentrated or distributed? Do they have the needed authorities? Is decision-making spelled out? Are there appropriate metrics?

◇ Work: Does the grouping enable effective delivery of the advantage work? Does enabling work support it? Is essential work optimized and separated from the other two?

◇ People: Does the grouping fit the available people, or can they be trained or recruited? Are the required skills and behaviors for all work identified and protected?

◇ Structure: Are there significant roles for every individual work unit? These can be vertical layers, horizontal coordination mechanisms, or integrative networks. Are hand-offs between units and interfaces with customers identified, effectively addressed?

◇ Systems: These are designed in the next deliverable, so here you can test the requirements. Do these recognize the needs of the culture, whether control, efficiency, transparency, coordination, or some combination? Will they drive the desired behaviors?

More on Organizational Structure

The Comfort Home case study in Chapter 9 shows how to develop the rigorous accountabilities required in a networked organization, especially with legally autonomous entities. In the Stratos case study in Chapter 8 the roles that grew out of the process and workflow mapping led to departments that naturally incorporated all of the front-line work groups. Wilderness Petroleum in Chapter 10 solved cross-functional coordination issues without changing reporting lines with a mixture of coordination mechanisms and technology enabled solutions.

Deliverable 9: Systems

Management, finance, and HR systems are each vital in aligning around the strategy, reinforcing the desired culture, and channeling the organization's energy. When they are done well, they can unleash tremendous synergy.

Systems Ingredients
◇ Management
◇ Financial
◇ HR and People

Previous deliverables provide design requirements for these systems. The highest priority ones are already built into deployment initiatives, but others may need some tweaking. You have these four choices:

◇ Improve the systems already in place but needing improvement. This is the most frequent action. Enterprise-wide SAP-type systems that haven't fully realized their benefits are common targets.

◇ Build again from scratch, systems that had key ingredients missing or were fatally flawed. This might be collaboratively designing recognition and reward programs that reinforce the desired or new core values.

◇ Dismantle systems that are so misaligned that they actively undercut the business and symbolize what's wrong with the current systems. For some companies this is 'forced ranking' of all employees.

◇ Systems too difficult to change or serving vital purposes must be tolerated. One performance management system we worked on was hindering team-based collaboration. It emerged that a tightly held corporate value focused on individual 'merit.' The client kept the system but built in items for collaboration and teamwork and accepted any resulting misalignment. Be careful that you're not actually dealing with a root cause of poor performance, since not addressing this can sabotage the entire change effort.

Management Systems

These critical systems focus the organization on delivery. Often owned by senior executives or functions, networks, or work units with the needed capabilities, they are closely connected to the financial systems.

Performance Metrics	What critical information and insights are needed to meet business objectives and make important strategic decisions?
Reporting & Review	Is information available when needed? Do you hold people accountable for business performance? Are risks mitigated?
Decision Making	Are decisions timely, effective, and at the right levels? Is there diverse input and involvement? How do we escalate?
Strategic Planning	Are you continuously sensing? Can you reassess and reallocate resources in response to changed circumstances?

Performance Metrics System

Effective management starts with information. Business objectives for financials, customers, stakeholders, and employees need to be quantified and associated with leading indicators. The relevant metrics need to be distributed across the organization, tracked, and acted upon locally. Much of this is built into Sense. Institutionalize these and any meant to sustain the change process, perhaps monitoring workloads, tracking the business impacts of the changes, and assessing how well the systems are reinforcing the changes.

Be careful not to unintentionally reinforce things you do not want. One of our clients linked executive bonuses to employee survey results. Some of their management teams ended up spending more energy on cosmetics to raise survey scores than on addressing underlying issues.

If done right, you can gain substantial value from integrating all work processes, financials, and management reporting into a single seamless beginning-to-end process. However, many attempts at this have failed. When owned by Finance or HR, core work applications often suffer. When owned by IT, user interfaces and operability can be suboptimal. When owned by core work functions, support functions can be poorly tied in and unable to harvest the infor-  mation they need. Carefully consider the implications as you select and implement such systems.

Reporting and Reviews

Measures are only effective if reviewed and used at the right places at the right times. Make sure your management reporting systems give you the accurate information when you need them. This includes legal, regulatory, and external compliance information. Build in regular business performance reviews to probe and analyze any issues, hold each other accountable for delivering results, and take corrective action when indicated. Risk management practices should prioritize key operating threats.

Decision-Making

Management reviews are only effective if the information is used to make decisions at levels with the needed authority but avoiding unnecessary delay. Strategic and operational priorities need to be built in. Diverse inputs and viewpoints should be respected, valued, and effectively used in decisions. There should be clear guidelines for when groups cannot reach agreement.

Strategic Planning

The above three systems focus on analyzing and correcting near-term issues. Strategic planning looks further out. In Adaptive cultures, every individual and unit have some accountability for it and building similar practices into the other three cultures increases their agility. You have already involved staff from strategic analysis and planning at the beginning of the change process when you began to Sense. How is this working? Can you accelerate the review cycles to near real-time? Can your leaders take action to change strategy or reallocate resources quickly and effectively in response?

Financial Systems

The finance function manages the financial health of the organization. To do this they use the tools and methods in the following four elements.

Accounting	Are these systems accurate, efficient, and transparent?
Budgeting	Is the process clear to all, understood, and efficient?
Investments	Is the process timely, effective, and updated as needed?
Treasury	Is cash-flow managed to retain value and minimize risks?

Accounting System

Are all financial transactions accurately recorded and
tracked? Are they transparent to the extent expected in
your culture? Is the cost and burden of this minimized
to the lowest level? Is the process transparent and controlled effectively? Is the right amount and quality of

information captured and clear? Is it easily accessible when and where
needed? Are the proper financial controls, regulatory compliance, and
audits in place? This will of course look different in each corporate culture.

Budgeting System

Are the budgeting processes clear and understood? Is there widespread
confidence or skepticism? Do you balance bottoms-up roll-ups against
top-down management 'adjustments'? Is the effort required justified by
the results? Is there too much detail? Perhaps not enough?

Investment and Tracking System

Does the investment process yield timely and effective decisions? Are the investment criteria updated as
needed to address changing economic conditions?
Are individual investments and the whole portfolio
tracked and course-corrected as needed?

Treasury and Cash-Flow System

Do you manage cash-flow with prudent protocols that preserve value?
Does the level of transparency provide the needed information and
match your culture? Are you aware of and willing to accept any risks
associated with your approach?

HR/People Systems

These systems provide skilled staff and align them with strategic business goals. There are typically these elements:

Individual Performance	Do performance systems align individual, work unit, and enterprise goals? Are people and units held accountable?
Information & Transactions	Is employee data accurate and useful? Are HR transactions handled effectively? Could you outsource?
Talent Management	Does hiring provide the needed skills? Do your careers accommodate different ages, work habits and lifestyles?
Skill Development	Do you foster knowledge and skills development? Do you value org. design, change, and inclusiveness efforts?

Many of these systems heavily impact behaviors and thus influence the resulting culture. They are some of the most important ways to build in agility. Ideally, they are revised with the users and lines of business collaboratively, so they reinforce the business strategy and make sense to the employees. Staff assigned HR or people accountabilities can be powerful partners in this work if they understand organization development and human dynamics.

Individual Performance

The foundation of agile systems is to make visible, reward, and emphasize collaborative efforts and shared leadership over individual performance. The questions to begin that discussion include: How well do your performance systems align individual goals and priorities with those of work units and the entire enterprise? How effectively are people and work units held accountable? Do you reconcile what they produce against their promises? Is this objective and fact-based? Is it managed in a positive and learning atmosphere? Do people receive financial compensation and non-monetary recognition for delivering results and learning with experimentation? How much accountability do employees have for helping to developing the skills of their teammates?

Information and Transactions

Do you have accurate and useful employee data? How well do you manage remuneration and compensation, financial and non-financial benefits, and recognition and reward programs? Could you outsource or partner to cut expenses and possibly improve effectiveness?

Talent Management

Do your hiring procedures maintain the skills you need? Do you consider different types of skills in hiring and seek a good fit between candidates and your culture? Does your workforce planning fit your culture and involve work units? Do you have recognized careers with the requisite assignment and development paths? Do employ-
ees have access to career progression opportunities and advice? Do your people strategies address a wide variety of ages, work habits and lifestyles, and enable quick changes when needed?

Skills Development

How well do you manage the development and application of business and management knowledge and skills and exemplifying values with words and actions? To what extent do you actively nurture staff involvement, learning, and development? Mentoring and knowledge management? Organization development, design, and change? Employee communications, diversity and inclusiveness? How much accountability do employees have for their own and teammates' skills?

More on Supporting Systems

Stratos in Chapter 8 provides excellent examples of changes in decision-making, compensation, and reward systems to broaden involvement and reinforce the new Adaptive culture. The Comfort case study in Chapter 9 highlights how simple and visible performance metrics can knit together formerly independent entities. Wilderness in Chapter 10 shows how systems changes can enhance attractiveness to local staff.

Deliverable 10: Adjust

Adjust institutionalizes the new design. People learn the new roles, turn on the new operating model, address any issues, close the effort, and resume sensing. In Adaptive cultures these actions are integral to the change processes built into everyday work.

Adjust Ingredients
◇ New Accountabilities
◇ New Operating Model
◇ Emerging Issues
◇ Effort Close

New Accountabilities

Everyone whose job changes needs to learn their new accountabilities, gain the skills they need, and be ready to step into their new roles.

New Role Understanding	Do all employees understand their new accountabilities and what's changing from their old assignments?
New Role Skills	Have all employees gained the needed skills via formal or hands-on training? Have they kept up their current jobs?

New Role Understanding

What was developed in Customize now must be transferred to those who will be doing the work moving forward: what's changing and what's not. Revised training and development programs may meet the need, but it depends on culture:

◇ In large Directive projects this is often formal training and can be a substantial undertaking: scheduling and logistics, coaching, and ensuring everything is ready for the new operating model. The change staff can handle this or they may enlist other groups. The challenge is to keep staff focused on current work even as they learn their new jobs.

◇ In Participative cultures, this likely takes place in a conference. The challenge is similar to Directive: keep the business stable during the transition, even as conference distractions make it more difficult.

◇ In Flexible cultures, this often involves informal discussions. It requires less coordination, but the challenge is to ensure that the accountabilities discussed are accurate and consistent.

◇ Adaptive cultures most often handle this in routine circle meetings.

New Role Skills

Knowledge and understanding are necessary, but not enough. Staff must have the skills to perform their new roles. Simulation workshops or limited pilots may help, but often the first few hours or days of using the new operating model are explicitly seen as testbeds to develop these skills, especially those involving new technologies. The organization may  need to run both operating models in parallel for some time.

An example was a telecommunications company that installed a new IT system to support cross-selling in stores. Revenues stayed flat until sales staff learned new skills: how to record accurate customer data in the new system and use it to provide a better customer experience.

New Operating Model

Once the new role accountabilities are learned, the new operating model can be turned on. This requires planning, thoughtful delivery, and deliberate and intentional follow-through.

Operating Model Planning	Is every unit ready to shift, either all at once or across individual units? Are dates scheduled?
Operating Model Go Live	Is the shift underway? Is there a mechanism for coordinating during it? Is it working?
Operating Model Follow Through	Have you followed up with all functions and operating units? Are the right issues surfacing?

Operating Model Planning

Your deployment plan indicates how you will begin using the new operating model: all at once across the enterprise or a portion at a time. Many of our clients use the term 'go live' for turning a new organization on. The term comes from software systems where the move to a new system is carefully planned. This element ensures that each organization component is ready. Every culture is different, but here are some key considerations.

◇ Leadership: Everyone in these roles, especially those new, know and are skilled at their accountabilities and expected behaviors. People know who to contact with resourcing and strategy issues.

◇ Work/Technology: New technologies are seamlessly incorporated. New hardware, software, databases, interfaces, and security protocols are tested, effective, complete, and inter-operable. All workflow and process changes are documented and rehearsed.

◇ People: Every employee, whether doing core work or in supporting roles, understands their roles and accountabilities and how they fit into the whole. They have had opportunity to practice new skills.

◇ Structure: Everyone understands how roles are grouped, the unit mandates, and the mechanisms for coordination between units.

◇ Systems: Changes in formal policies and procedures support agile behaviors, especially performance appraisal, compensation, and promotion. As you turn on the new operating model you will be testing whether these systems work as intended.

After verifying readiness, set a 'go-live' date, whether you call it that or not, for each part of the organization during a time that minimizes the business risk. Review and reaffirm the changes and goals with key stakeholders. Set the expectation that not everything will go perfectly but that the organization will be fully functional.

Operating Model Go Live

Now throw the switch and initiate the new operating model. Those in leadership or coordination roles should be present and visible, whether for a day, shorter, or longer. They should role model the new behaviors, especially as unexpected issues surface and things get tense. They focus especially on multiple work units' issues, holding debriefing and status sessions to head off serious problems before they deepen.

Escalation procedures should kick in when issues can't be handled at the local work unit level. This typically includes first-level support from technical or functional staff, second-level support from those with local leadership accountabilities, and third-level support from those within your organization who have organization-wide authorities to make or approve critical changes on the fly.

Operating Model Follow-Through

It is important to stay committed to the new design and keep working on the desired performance results. Adjust when needed. Be prepared to change track. Caucus with all three levels of support above. If things go really wrong, be ready to pause and revert to the old processes and systems. Identify in advance situations or points where this might happen and how to restart Customize to resolve things.

Emerging Issues

The transition will surface what is not working. If 'go live' is turning on a switch, some issues are 'short-circuits,' dangerous and urgent. Just as dangerous but harder to see are potential short circuits like loose wires.

Issue Identification	Track tensions around business performance. What are the root causes? Will solutions have unintended impacts?
Issue Assignment	Prioritize and assign accountabilities to existing or ad hoc groups, forums, or functions. Ensure they are addressed.

Issues Identification

Look for tensions affecting business performance, then review the questions in Deliverable 3: Diagnosis. Are the components working together effectively? If each is fine on their own, do they reinforce each other? Major changes in one component can cause misalignments with others: work unit boundaries may not support work processes; accountabilities for leaders may not support the desired behaviors. Capture these, perhaps in a table, with columns and rows for each component. For small changes, this may be just a few cells with minor entries. Large organization wide efforts may yield large tables with major issues. This can help sort through unintended impacts to identify root causes.

Issue Assignment

Some issues fall within the purview of a single group, function, line of business, or one of the deployment initiatives. It should be clear from their accountabilities who will resolve these and how, and this work should be undertaken without waiting for any formal or informal hand off. If there is any hesitation, it may signal the need for escalation, often a change in accountabilities or additional resources.

Some issues cross multiple units but were not assigned to any function, line of business, coordination mechanism, or deployment initiative. If important enough, they need to be addressed, either by adding to the accountabilities of an existing group or assembling a new group for this purpose. In either case, there must be a clear description similar to Deliverable 1: Charter, of who will bring together the right people to resolve the tension. Giving specific timeframes and more information on the issue(s) to be resolved are helpful.

Resolving tensions is a continuous process. Each organization should determine which issue resolution method works best for them. One we use is Holacracy's Integrative Decision-Making Process: (1) proposal presentation, (2) clarifying questions, (3) reaction round, (4) clarification and amendment, (5) objection round, and then (6) integration.

Effort Closure

By now units should be using their new mandates as the 'new normal.' These should include any assigned issues that emerged during Customize or Resolve. If so, you must graciously close out the teams or circles involved. This is true even where some have morphed from ad hoc project teams to part of the new structure. There needs to be a formal ending of one and beginning of the other. It's important now to close out the effort. There are few things less productive than staff still engaged on pursuing efforts that they and everyone else in the organization know are over. There are three elements to this:

Lessons Learned	Agile entities learn. What went well, what didn't, and what improvement opportunities can be used next time?
Celebration and Recognition	Have we celebrated success and recognized those that have contributed, considering involvement and impact?
Resumption of Sensing	Are all work units operating in the 'new normal'? Have you moved to continuous operation of the Sense stage?

Lessons Learned

Research shows that in as little as two weeks memories fade or get embellished. Before that it is important to capture and build on learnings. What went well, what didn't, and what opportunities exist to improve future projects?

Assess the effort in a way that is in line with your culture. Directive cultures may hold an after-action review with design team, sponsor, a few experts, and key stakeholders. In other cultures, it may involve selected interviews with team members, key stakeholders, and customers, and then reviewing the findings with sponsors and the change team or circle to share, discuss, and complete the activity.

◇ What Was Intended? The review should be anchored in the original project expectations, objectives, approach, and scope.

◇ What Actually Happened? How did the effort actually proceed? Who was involved: roles, skills, and relationships? What support information, technology, and budget were used? What activities, timeline, outputs, and tools were used? How well did it all work?

◇ What Were Outcomes? Results, performance measures, and values? Has the effort delivered its objectives? How well? What's left?

◇ What Was Learned? What best practices could help the next time? What made the effort successful? How could it have been more so?

Summarize your learning so that others can benefit even if they were not directly involved but may need the information at a later time.

Celebration and Recognition

It is important to recognize the progress made. Recognize those who have either made high-impact contributions or significantly supported and championed the effort. Recognition and awards could range from thank you cards, small gifts or monetary awards, workplace perks, public recognition, and promotions. This is frequently done in an event with some celebration involved: a visible activity of this nature can acknowledge a successful completion.

This is often overlooked or is an afterthought, but if done well and at the right time, it can dramatically reinforce the desired results of a change. Honor your culture. Look at company norms for similar projects or initiatives to determine acceptable rewards and recognition. You do not even have to wait until the end of the effort. Do it along the way, quickly while people still remember what was done and while the knock-on effects can help to accelerate change.

Resumption of Sensing

Move back into the sensing that you created as the effort began. No matter the culture, encourage everyone in the organization to foster their own individual awareness about how things are going. Help create the climate where people can articulate and share their conscious awarenesses, intuitions, and emotions.

More on Implementation

The Wilderness case study in Chapter 10 shows a Participative culture successfully implementing changes and handing-off to the business. Comfort Home in Chapter 9 exemplifies operationalizing the operating model prototype in a Flexible culture and how it pulls the organization together as it flows naturally into the 'new normal'. Stratos Information Solutions in Chapter 8 is a good example of how an Adaptive culture manages tensions as they made substantial revisions to their operating model during Resolve.

About the Authors

The Syngineering Website

You will find more material for your use on our website, www.syngineering.solutions, including:

Glossary of Terms: While we have tried to write in 'plain English' the field of organizational design has numerous specialized terms. We define these as they are introduced and offer a brief overview at the start of Part IV. Still, it's nice to have a glossary. To keep it current and to avoid adding pages to the book, we have placed it on the website.

References and Links: In the dedication and text, we mention only a very few of those who have provided us their wisdom, guidance, and counsel. We have devoted a section of the website to a more extensive list of references, including links to their websites with their latest thinking.

The Syngineering Solutions Journey

While we three authors, Rich, Monique, and Bill, come from different traditions and experiences, we each empathize with organizational leaders frustrated by the issues facing today's businesses. We have come to understand that organizational performance is a direct result of how well its constituent components drive and reinforce each other. Every organization is perfectly designed to get the results that it does. Those frustrated with the results must change the components.

That's what Syngineering does and why we wrote the book, to support leaders of all types and levels in effectively and sustainably making these changes. To do so, we have sat at the feet of the gurus, synthesized and integrated their various disciplines, and added several things of our own. It was a joint product with equal contributions, so we

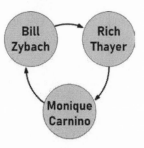

struggled with order of authors. In the end, we decided that Rich's visibility at international conferences and training programs positioned him well to be first in our authorship circle.

We have learned that it's not about the best or latest models but about what works. Most often this means listening to the wisdom already present in the organization and finding ways to make it visible. But we have learned that there are powerful blockers in these systems, which even the most sophisticated data analytics rarely address. The complete picture emerges only through the myriad relationships in day-to-day operations. Some disparage this as 'office politics' but for us it is the underlying reality of how work gets done. Understanding this rich tapestry enables our clients to see the blockers hampering their performance and to act to correct them.

We are pleased to offer you these approaches, ones that we have found to be effective. It's a roadmap, but does not include detailed driving directions. You will need to place your own organization and its challenges on the map, determine where you're headed, and chart your own course. Our hope is that having a detailed map of the terrain will make this effort much easier. All the best in your endeavors!

Rich Thayer: Managing Director

Rich Thayer for years supported global organization design efforts for Royal Dutch Shell. His specialty is helping organizations and individuals discern and satisfy their development needs. Rich uses a whole system view with data-driven analysis to get behind symptoms to underlying causes. This often involves culture and behavior changes to create the needed engagement, psychological safety, and honesty. Addressing root causes better aligns operations with strategy and yields superior performance. To sustain these results, Rich helps clients develop their own internal capabilities.

Rich's early research and technical career showed him the vital role of technology and provided tools for understanding complex landscapes. Work process re-engineering led him into organization consulting at Shell's global headquarters where he worked on major change efforts like the Sakhalin II mega-project, Gulf of Mexico producing operations, the North Caspian Operating Company, Shell's enterprise-first behaviors initiative, and several joint science symposia. In 2010 Rich joined Bill and Monique in setting up what is now Syngineering Solutions. He now lives in Baltimore, Maryland where he serves on the boards of several local non-profits and facilitates programs to teach alternatives to violence in detention and corrections institutions.

Monique Carnino: Org. Effectiveness Director

Monique Carnino has over 20 years of experience working with leadership, teams and individuals in industries as diverse as energy, finance, IT, aviation, and security to create, communicate and carry out their strategies. Monique has led multiple cross-organization strategic transformational change programs where she focused on bringing about changes in the way people work, think and behave to achieve targeted outcomes. Throughout her studies and career, she has lived in eight countries on four continents and traveled extensively to over 65 countries. She has a master's degree in Business and multiple professional certifications.

After leaving a long-time career as an Organizational Development and Change Management Consultant with Shell, she set up her own consultancy business in South Africa. Here she consulted with large organizations in other industries and government on organizational design and development, and then joined forces with Bill and Rich. After seven years in Johannesburg, Monique returned to Houston, first with Shell and then with Chevron as an external change management lead on multiple agile change programs since 2017. She is a full-time working mother who enjoys going beyond boundaries as she collaborates with others to explore, learn and grow.

Bill Zybach: Innovation Director

Bill Zybach has a long history of supporting organizational change in government and the public sector. During the Bill Clinton Administration he worked on 'reinventing government,' which led to a balanced federal budget and increased public confidence in government. He helped build state-level agencies in Washington DC to support its on-going statehood drive, and helped bring organization design principles to the government, business and not-for profits in South Africa. He has deployed agile approaches in manufacturing in France, in government in Washington DC, and in banking in the United States and in South Africa.

Bill is certified as an automotive mechanic, rodeo chute coordinator, yoga instructor, and Holacracy practitioner. He has completed 5 years of post-graduate work at the Gestalt Institute of Cleveland with certificates in organizational systems, executive coaching and group practice. Bill was on the board of the Organization Design Forum for nine years and is a member of the European Organization Design forum. He lives in and works virtually from his home on Senior Creek in Mollusk, Virginia.

CHANGEMAKERS
BOOKS

TRANSFORMATION

Recent bestsellers from Changemakers Books are:

Integration
The Power of Being Co-Active in Work and Life
Ann Betz, Karen Kimsey-House
Integration examines how we came to be polarized in our dealing
with self and other, and what we can do to move from an either/
or state to a more effective and fulfilling way of being.
Paperback: 978-1-78279-865-1 ebook: 978-1-78279-866-8

Bleating Hearts
The Hidden World of Animal Suffering
Mark Hawthorne
An investigation of how animals are exploited for
entertainment, apparel, research, military weapons, sport, art,
religion, food, and more.
Paperback: 978-1-78099-851-0 ebook: 978-1-78099-850-3

Lead Yourself First!
Indispensable Lessons in Business and in Life
Michelle Ray
Are you ready to become the leader of your own life? Apply
simple, powerful strategies to take charge of yourself, your
career, your destiny.
Paperback: 978-1-78279-703-6 ebook: 978-1-78279-702-9

Burnout to Brilliance
Strategies for Sustainable Success
Jayne Morris
Routinely running on reserves? This book helps you transform
your life from burnout to brilliance with strategies for sustainable
success.
Paperback: 978-1-78279-439-4 ebook: 978-1-78279-438-7

Goddess Calling
Inspirational Messages & Meditations of Sacred Feminine
Liberation Thealogy
Rev. Dr. Karen Tate
A book of messages and meditations using Goddess archetypes
and mythologies, aimed at educating and inspiring those with
the desire to incorporate a feminine face of God into their
spirituality.
Paperback: 978-1-78279-442-4 ebook: 978-1-78279-441-7

The Master Communicator's Handbook
Teresa Erickson, Tim Ward
Discover how to have the most communicative impact in this
guide by professional communicators with over 30 years of
experience advising leaders of global organizations.
Paperback: 978-1-78535-153-2 ebook: 978-1-78535-154-9

Meditation in the Wild
Buddhism's Origin in the Heart of Nature
Charles S. Fisher Ph.D.
A history of Raw Nature as the Buddha's first teacher, inspiring
some followers to retreat there in search of truth.
Paperback: 978-1-78099-692-9 ebook: 978-1-78099-691-2

Ripening Time
Inside Stories for Aging with Grace
Sherry Ruth Anderson
Ripening Time gives us an indispensable guidebook for growing
into the deep places of wisdom as we age.
Paperback: 978-1-78099-963-0 ebook: 978-1-78099-962-3

Striking at the Roots
A Practical Guide to Animal Activism
Mark Hawthorne
A manual for successful animal activism from an author with
first-hand experience speaking out on behalf of animals.
Paperback: 978-1-84694-091-0 ebook: 978-1-84694-653-0

Readers of ebooks can buy or view any of these bestsellers by
clicking on the live link in the title. Most titles are published
in paperback and as an ebook. Paperbacks are available in
traditional bookshops. Both print and ebook formats are available
online.

Find more titles and sign up to our readers' newsletter at
http://www.johnhuntpublishing.com/transformation
Follow us on Facebook at
https://www.facebook.com/Changemakersbooks